Beyond Contractual Morality

Julia Simon

Beyond Contractual Morality

Ethics, Law, and Literature in Eighteenth-Century France

First published 2001
by the University of Rochester Press

The University of Rochester Press is an imprint of Boydell & Brewer Inc.
668 Mount Hope Avenue, Rochester, NY 14620, USA
and of Boydell & Brewer, Ltd.
PO Box 9, Woodbridge, Suffolk IP12 3DF, UK

ISBN: 1–58046–056–9

Library of Congress Cataloging-in-Publication Data

Simon, Julia, 1961–
    Beyond contractual morality: ethics, law and literature in eighteenth-century
France / Julia Simon.
        p.   cm.
    Includes bibliographical references and index.
    ISBN 1–58046–056–9 (alk. paper)
    1. Social contract. 2. Social contract in literature. 3. Liberalism — Moral
and ethical aspects. 4. Enlightenment. I. Title.
JC336.S47   2000
320.1'.1—dc21   00–060743
                                                                 CIP

British Library Cataloguing-in-Publication Data
A catalogue record for this item is available from the British Library.

Printed in the United States of America.
This publication is printed on acid-free paper.

To Charles

Contents

Acknowledgments

THE TOPIC OF THIS BOOK—the problems associated with the attempt to reduce moral relations to contractual ones inherited from political liberalism—gained a certain urgency for me personally during my tenure process. Although I have attempted to temper my moral outrage in the following chapters, in the interests of academic objectivity and the desire to encourage dialogue, I acknowledge that traces of strong moral positions, nonetheless, may still be detectable. I hope that the reader will bear in mind the fact that personal experiences often shape academic study. For these lapses, I ask the reader's forgiveness in advance.

This book slowly took shape over a period of six years. During that time, many colleagues and friends contributed in significant ways to move the project forward. First of all, I would like to express my gratitude to my colleague, Norris Lacy, for his continued support of my work and me. By demonstrating through his actions his belief that moral relations involve personal commitments and are not reducible to legal principles and contractual formulae, he helped to renew my faith in the academic profession.

Many other colleagues also helped the ideas in this book to take shape. First, I wish to express my gratitude to Dick Terdiman, whose support and encouragement helped me through a most difficult time. As if that were not enough, I am also indebted to him for his challenging questions on central issues in the book. I would like to thank Suzanne Pucci for both the valuable feedback she provided and the invitations to present my work at professional meetings that led to lively and informative discussions. My experience of teaching in tandem with Joan Landes helped me to clarify some of my ideas concerning key issues in Rousseau. Our teaching experience together was enriching and rewarding, and for that I am grateful. I would also like to thank Monique Yaari for reading and commenting on early drafts of the manuscript. My graduate students at Penn State during the summer of 1999 challenged me to revisit early formulations of arguments. I would like to thank Henry Piper, Amelia Woehrman, and Véronique Zara for providing stimulating dialogue in that summer seminar. I am especially grateful to Jim Lawler, whose careful reading of the manuscript induced me to reformulate some central concerns. Finally, I thank the editorial staff at the University of Rochester Press for their support for the project and the time and care they contributed to the production process. I am extremely grateful to the editorial director, Timothy Madigan, and the managing editor, Louise Goldberg. I would also like to thank the copyeditor, Ann O'Hear. For her help with proofreading, I thank Rachel Shackelford. I also wish to thank LuLu Simon for her assistance with the cover design.

Finally, I owe my family a tremendous debt of gratitude for inspiring my concern with moral relations. My parents both inspired a deep sense of commitment in me and also taught me early on to examine acts of commission as well as acts of omission from an ethical point of view. I would like to thank my daughter, Sabina, for pushing me to explore questions of justice and fairness on a daily basis. In all seriousness, I acknowledge my dog and companion, Willy, who has taught me a lot about the loyalty and commitment of imperfect duties. Most of all, I would like to express my sincerest appreciation to my partner, friend, and husband, Charles, without whose love, support, encouragement, and challenges this book would not have been possible.

Chapter 2 represents a revised version of an essay that was first published as "Natural Freedom and Moral Autonomy: Emile as Parent, Teacher and Citizen," in *History of Political Thought* 16, no. 1 (Spring 1995), pp. 21–36, and is reprinted here with permission from the publisher, Imprint Academic, Exeter, U. K. The material was revised and reprinted as a chapter entitled, "Jean-Jacques Rousseau's Children," in *The Philosopher's Child: Critical Essays in the Western Tradition,* edited by Susan M. Turner and Gareth B. Matthews, Rochester: University of Rochester Press, 1998, pp. 105–120, and appears here with additions and changes with the permission of the University of Rochester Press.

Introduction

> ... [P]olitical theory is a branch of moral philosophy, which starts from the discovery, or application, of moral notions in the sphere of political relations.
>
> —Isaiah Berlin, "Two Concepts of Liberty"

IN RECENT YEARS, in the context of pluralistic democracies, liberal political theory has come under attack from all sides. Feminists, radicals, communitarians, and conservatives alike have been critical of liberalism, particularly in the area of moral life. In defense of liberalism, thinkers such as John Rawls, Jürgen Habermas, and Ronald Dworkin have reformulated classical political theory to meet the needs of contemporary pluralistic democratic societies. The debate over liberalism has revolved around several important issues, among them multiculturalism, public education, tolerance, and the rights of women and members of minority groups. The debate has also focused attention on the drawing of the boundary that separates the public and private spheres, a boundary on which liberalism depends in order to protect the private sphere from government intervention.

In light of these contemporary debates over liberalism, and informed by the problems of contemporary democratic, pluralistic culture, *Beyond Contractual Morality* reexamines the roots of current discussions in eighteenth-century texts. Enlightenment texts demonstrate the historical intertwining of political, legal, and moral problems in their extension of social contract theory into various realms of public and private life. Specifically, these texts point to an overreliance on the notion of contract to resolve ethical dilemmas.

Contracts, whether public or private, create and define relations of obligation. The French *Code Civil* defines a contract broadly as "a convention by which one or several persons obligate themselves, to one or several others, to give or to do or not to do something."[1] Contractual relations of obligation, regulated by a set of normative expectations informed by practice, functioned within the realm of commerce as far back as the Middle Ages. R. C. van Caenegem describes the slow emergence of commercial law in Europe as a set of practices that developed "from the twelfth to the fifteenth centuries" and that "was dictated essentially by the needs of practice and commercial efficacy in commodity and money markets, in trade fairs, corporations, banking operations and means of insurance and credit."[2]

Among the first significant efforts to codify commercial law in France were the *ordonnances* created in the seventeenth century under Louis XIV. The *Ordonnance sur le commerce de terre* of 1673 and the *Ordonnance sur le commerce de mer* of 1681 dealt with "partnerships and companies, negotiable instruments, maritime law, bankruptcy and the special commercial courts."[3] After the revolution in 1789, these would be incorporated into the Napoleonic *Code de commerce* and eventually into the *Code Civil*.

In the eighteenth-century French context, there is an increasing secularization and codification of private law, begun in the seventeenth century with the *ordonnances*, extending the jurisdiction of the royal courts to questions of marriage, separation, and inheritance. The development of commercial law and a certain understanding of the rights of contracting parties continues to extend jurisdiction into the area of familial relations throughout the eighteenth century.

The notion of contract as a political paradigm developed out of the growing market in which individuals freely contracted trade agreements. These contracts concluded between private citizens depended on the freedom, autonomy, equality, and reciprocity of the parties to the contracts. Without these prior conditions, it was argued, contracts could not be equitably concluded.

Building on this model of independent, free, equal, private citizens with reciprocal claims on one another, the social contract tradition created political paradigms that ensured the noninterference of the state in the concluding of private contracts. The social contract paradigm assumes that individuals bear certain natural rights and freedoms that must be protected from violation both by the state and by other citizens. Following the model of economic contracts, the social contract foundational for society was postulated as an agreement freely entered into by autonomous, independent individuals for the purpose of protecting their natural rights and freedoms. Rather than a restriction on natural rights and freedoms, the social contract and the society it creates represent a cooperative effort to ensure individual liberties.

The social contract theories of Thomas Hobbes and John Locke posit a state of nature prior to social existence that envisions the possession of private property. The transition to social life arises due to conflicts, often over property, between individuals in the state of nature. Motivated by the desire to protect their persons and their property, these individuals freely come together in an act of association to form a social bond. This act of association—the social contract—creates a sovereign who then rules with legitimate political authority. Despite their differences, the theories of Hobbes and Locke both emphasize the retention of individual freedoms within civil society as well as the protection of private property after the pact is made.

Although there are significant differences between the formulations of Hobbes, Locke, and Rousseau—the last-mentioned disagreeing on the question of property and in his formulation of a conception of community that I will examine in later chapters—concerning both the conditions in the state of nature and the terms under and through which the contract is concluded, all three share basic assumptions about the individual and about the divide between the public and private spheres that are at stake in contemporary debates. The liberal tradition that they founded, thus, called for a minimal conception of government designed not to infringe the rights of private economic man. Isaiah Berlin ably summarizes this liberal conception of "negative liberty," which ensures the freedom to conclude private contracts and protects property: "Most modern liberals, at their most consistent, want a situation in which as many individuals as possible can realize as many of their ends as possible, without assessment of the value of these ends as such, save in so far as they may frustrate the purposes of others."[4]

If social contract theory protects the rights of individual contracting parties in the economic realm, it also presupposes a divide between the public and private spheres. Protecting the rights of individual citizens to conclude private contracts presupposes a division between the public realm and/or the state and the private sphere of the family and economic contracts. Although these private contracts are enforced by the state, their creation, maintenance, and dissolution, in theory at least, depends on nonintervention by the state. That is to say, private contracts between free, equal, autonomous individuals with reciprocal rights and freedoms must be concluded independently of state intervention. Thus, liberalism erects a barrier between the state and the private sphere and limits government to a minimal role as watchdog and enforcer of private contracts.

The question of moral life in social contract theory, beyond the workings of legitimate political power, is left to the private sphere. Standing historically at the end of the Enlightenment and as a pivotal figure for the turn to Idealism and Romanticism, Immanuel Kant's formulation of the categorical imperative represents the culmination of the liberal tradition in its insistence on the privatization of questions of morality. While social contract theory created a space for political liberty and, in particular, individual freedom, Kant's philosophy turns to reason and individual acts of private moral conscience to establish a universalizable foundation for moral life.[5] Rather than reinscribe the question of morality within the broader question of community, Kant argues in favor of an abstract universal grounded in private experience.

Kant's formulation of the categorical imperative, while consistent with social contract theory insofar as individual behavior is regulated by reason and therefore remains within the realm of the private sphere, nonetheless represents a move away from the contractual forms of obligation that constitute the focus of this study. Because both social contract theory and Kantian ethics rely upon an abstract, universalizable conception of a free, independent, rational individual, they are subject to the same types of critiques, discussed below, from feminists, communitarians, postmodernists, Marxists, and civic republicans. However, beyond the similarity at the level of the conception of the individual lies a sharp distinction between ethical obligations in the social contract tradition and ethical obligations in Kant. I will discuss this difference at length in the introduction to Part 2: Private Moral Conscience and Public Obligation. For now, suffice it to say that ethical obligations are minimized within social contract theory to allow for maximum exercise of individual freedom, whereas for Kant, moral freedom necessarily entails the individual's self-prescribed adherence to a moral absolute, the categorical imperative.

Both the conception of the individual associated with social contract theory and the barrier between the state, the public sphere, and private sphere have been heavily criticized in recent years. Beginning with the concept of the individual, critics from a variety of traditions have assailed the autonomous, independent, free agent of social contract theory as both an unrealistic theoretical construct and an instrument of continued oppression. The communitarian challenge to liberalism has focused on the fact that the individual of social contract theory, or of liberalism more generally, is unattached to either family, friends, associations, or community. The identity of the individual seems to spring sui generis from the individual rather than being constructed through association with others.[6] Most importantly, this critique questions the conceptions of justice and the good life that attend social contract theory. According to communitarians, independent individuals and a political theory based on such conceptions cannot account for collectively constituted notions of the good. Rather, social contract theory limits itself to a moral good that can be achieved by the independent individual.

Feminist critiques of liberalism have also attacked the conception of the individual and the attendant split between the public and private spheres. Feminist challenges to liberalism have questioned the gender-neutral language used to describe the private individual, hinting that the exclusion of women lurks beneath the seemingly unbiased exterior. Susan Moller Okin, for example, has argued that there are many underlying assumptions about the family and private life that enable liberalism: "With women's status left ambiguous and the family assumed but not discussed, contemporary liberal theory has yet to take account of the fact that men are not mushrooms."[7] Such feminist critics maintain that both the conception of the individual and the divide between the public and private spheres depend on certain family arrangements that restrict women's roles. The seemingly independent and autonomous individual is, in reality, a male who depends on a female to run the private sphere. These feminist critiques have called for a reexamination of the supposedly nonpolitical nature of the private sphere of family relations.

From other perspectives, covering the spectrum from Marxist to civic republican to fascist, liberalism has also been criticized for its failure to provide "a single, unified view of the good life and society."[8] Following the traditional split identified by Habermas between liberalism—associated with Locke—and civic republicanism—associated with Aristotle, Rousseau, and Kant—these contemporary criticisms highlight the failure of liberalism to provide a more positive conception of political liberty tied to a strong sense of community.[9] Unlike communitarian criticisms of liberalism, this line of attack seeks to establish an overarching conception of political community that will provide a unified conception of the good life.

In defense of liberalism, some have offered a proceduralist revision. Jürgen Habermas and Seyla Benhabib, among others, stress the importance of dialogue in the political process.[10] Adapting liberalism to a communicative model, Habermas argues in favor of participatory democracy to ensure legitimate government. Noting the mutual implication of private liberty and public participation, he writes, "Law can be perserved as legitimate only if enfranchised citizens switch from the role of private legal subjects and take the perspective of participants who are engaged in the process of reaching understanding about the rules for their life in common."[11] In this way, Habermas maintains the individual freedom of private citizens under liberalism while at the same time creating a shared vision of the good life through deliberative procedure. In so doing, he seeks to bridge the gap between individual liberty and collective political engagement.

Many of the contemporary challenges to liberalism, as well as defenses of it, have been motivated by specific issues in contemporary political life. As has already been seen in my discussion of the critiques of liberalism, the feminist movement has foregrounded issues pertaining to the political character of relations assumed to be part of the private sphere and, as such, not subject to public or state regulation; such regulation is often viewed by liberalism as an instance of government interference. Questions concerning marriage contracts, unremunerated domestic labor, unfair division of labor, childcare concerns, divorce settlements, physical abuse, and the like have brought to light the need to examine our assumptions about the divide between the public and private spheres presupposed by liberalism, and the attendant policy of nonintervention.

In a similar vein, debates surrounding multiculturalism have focused attention on liberalism's inability to mediate between private, individual freedom, and public, collective conceptions of the good. In the context of education, the debate over multiculturalism has pitted the defenders of a traditional canon, purportedly representative of Western values designed to inculcate the virtues necessary for political citizenship and moral personhood, against those who have argued in favor of a more inclusive view of what constitute Great Works. Against the defenders of the canon, proponents of multiculturalism argue that works of women and people of color have been systematically excluded, creating a homogeneous "dead white male" perspective that has been imposed on the rest of the population. Proponents of multiculturalism seek to expand the canon to include underrepresented groups and thereby both allow for and create more cultural diversity. This debate, like Habermas's proceduralist revision, has focused attention on liberalism's failure to balance the needs of individuals or smaller subcultures within communities against the needs of the community as a whole. At the same time, it also highlights the homogenizing effect that the constitution of a unified conception of culture has on multicultural societies.

Other social issues have also underscored liberalism's shortcomings. The 1996 presidential campaign in the United States, and particularly the Republican Party platform, point to contemporary difficulties with the classical liberal conception of tolerance. Squabbling within the Republican Party, between antiabortion and pro-choice factions, led to contradictory planks in the party platform. The tolerance plank advocates respecting difference in matters of personal conscience:

> As we approach the beginning of a new century, the Republican Party is more dedicated than ever to strengthening the social, cultural and political ties that bind us together as a free people, the greatest force for good the world has ever seen. While the party remains steadfast in its commitment to advancing its historic principles and ideals, *we also*

recognize that members of our party have deeply held and sometimes dif-fering views on issues of personal conscience like abortion and capital punishment. We view this diversity of views as a source of strength, not as a sign of weakness, and we welcome into our ranks all Americans who may hold differing positions on these and other issues. *Recognizing that tolerance is a virtue,* we are committed to resolving our differences in a spirit of civility, hope and mutual respect.[12] [My emphasis.]

In spite of the declaration that "tolerance is a virtue," the abortion plank nonetheless called for a constitutional amendment eliminating choice:

We believe the unborn child has a fundamental right to life which cannot be infringed. We therefore affirm our support for a human life amendment to the Constitution, and we endorse legislation to make clear that the Fourteenth Amendment's protections apply to unborn children.[13]

The issue of abortion, like other issues involving the right to choice in matters of personal conscience, raises important questions for liberalism, a political doctrine born out of the desire to protect freedom of religious practice from government interference. In the contemporary debates—concerning abortion, private education, and home schooling, among other things—the tension between the need to protect individual freedom and the need to foster collective identity is readily apparent.

In examining eighteenth-century French texts in the following chapters, I have chosen to frame the discussions with problems drawn from contemporary American culture and society. This may seem an odd coupling for it traverses two barriers: the national and the temporal. Rather than compare, say, eighteenth-century French texts with eighteenth-century American ones, or eighteenth-century French understandings of moral dilemmas with contemporary French representations of sites of conflict, I have chosen to take debates from American cultural politics as frames of reference for French Englightenment theoretical formulations and discussions. I have made this choice for a number of reasons.

To begin with, I cite Michael Walzer's fascinating analysis of the case of France in *On Toleration*:

France makes for an especially useful case study because it is the classic nation-state and, at the same time, Europe's leading immigrant society; indeed, it is one of the world's leading immigrant societies. The extent of its immigration has been obscured by the extraordinary assimilative powers of the French nation—so that one imagines France

as a homogeneous society with a highly distinctive and singular culture.[14]

It is precisely France's continued and continuing attempts and ability to
impose a singular culture on a postcolonial immigrant society according
to the model of republicanism that make the French contemporary
situation a less viable choice as an example to test the issues at stake in
the following analyses. While the French context offers dilemmas like
the one examined by Walzer concerning the issue of whether religious
clothing, such as Muslim headdresses for women, should be banned
from public schools by the French government, it tends to pit republican values associated with the homogenization of culture against liberal
values of tolerance favoring individual freedom of expression.[15] What
these types of conflicts tend to obscure are the homogenizing effects of
even the more individualist versions of liberalism evident in the context
of an immigrant society like the United States. In other words, using
the French contemporary situation tends to de-emphasize some of the
negative effects of liberalism because of the tension between the values
of liberalism and the values of republicanism. Thus, in the French context, republicanism comes to represent the homogenization of culture
over and against liberalism, which then represents the preservation of
difference through individualism. Rather than underscore the homogenizing effects of republicanism, I want to highlight the tensions and
difficulties associated with the individualist brand of liberalism.

In the United States, the strong tradition of religious tolerance and
individualism deriving from America's origins as an immigrant society
founded to protect groups such as the Puritans and Quakers from religious persecution, I believe, better represents a multicultural society.
The desire to impose a unified national culture prominent in the
French context is far weaker in the American one. In fact, attempts to
impose a unified national culture through the public school system almost always excite public furor in the United States, while in France
the educational system has been the main avenue of cultural indoctrination and the main vehicle of assimilation. It is my contention that
multicultural societies of the future will more closely resemble the immigrant society of the United States, with its strong appeals to liberalism and individualism, than the more republican model of contemporary France.

This trend for the future is perhaps most evident in international society. That is to say, relations between and among nations in the international community already prefigure the kinds of relationships that I
believe will obtain between and among citizens of individual nations. It

is also this international culture, strongly founded on liberal principles of tolerance, freedom, and reciprocity, that makes the choice of examples from the American context more relevant for future discussions than examples from contemporary France.

Finally, the currents of French Enlightenment thought explored in the following chapters played a more influential role with respect to the American constitution and ongoing debates in American politics than they perhaps did with respect to the traditions of modern France.[16] While the United States clings to its original eighteenth-century constitution, framed by thinkers such as Benjamin Franklin, Thomas Jefferson, and James Madison, who were well versed in French Enlightenment philosophy, France is currently in its Fifth Republic since its eighteenth-century revolution. Moreover, while the United States, in a gesture of self-definition and self-constitution, threw off the yoke of the British monarchy and staked its future on egalitarian democracy, France repeatedly returned to various versions of monarchy during the nineteenth century before finally renouncing it in favor of a republican democracy that still bears the marks of a highly unified culture. In effect, it is my contention that the traces of eighteenth-century French liberal thought and their American reworkings are more apparent in American political configurations and debates than they are in French debates.

In light of the various debates sparked by contemporary controversies, *Beyond Contractual Morality* examines the roots of these problems in eighteenth-century texts. My specific focus is the overlap between legal and moral problems that highlights the tension between the desire to protect individual liberty and the need to create a shared conception of the good life. In the course of my analyses, I also question the drawing of the divide between the public and private spheres.

The focus of the study is the extension of contractual relations between individuals—with their attendant conceptions of obligation—from the economic sphere to the private sphere of moral relations including family and private life. Reversing the traditional relation between political and moral theory—so ably summarized in my epigraph from Isaiah Berlin—that sees political philosophy as a "branch" of moral philosophy, the world of eighteenth-century French social relations represented in the texts under analysis here allows political and legal theory to restructure moral relations. Relations of obligation in the private sphere between family members, but also between private citizens of the state, are inflected by notions of obligation conceived in contractual terms. Questions concerning the limits of moral obligations repeatedly return to negative contractual conceptions of duty to attempt to limit obligations between individuals, all the while pointing out the shortcomings of such limited conceptions.

The choice of primary texts under analysis in the following chapters requires some explanation due to the variety of authors and genres represented. First and foremost, my choice of texts has been guided by the thematic questions laid out above concerning the limits of contractual conceptions of obligation in the realm of moral and political life. The thematic focus has enabled me to arrange a cluster of texts from a number of different authors spanning the period from 1748 to 1795 and encompassing multiple genres. The choice of these texts facilitates discussion of the emergence of a critical discourse concerning the notion of contracts in moral and political life. But, inevitably, the choice of primary texts also poses a number of difficulties. While I do not pretend to resolve the difficulties raised by my analytical method and choice of objects, I would like to address some broad areas of concern.

The question of genre arises both from the readings of texts that in themselves pose serious difficulties of categorization, such as Rousseau's *Emile*, and from the comparative readings of texts with different generic status, such as Voltaire's *Traité sur la tolérance* and Charrière's *Caliste ou lettres écrites de Lausanne*. In general, the question of genre is problematic in the eighteenth century. While I do not wish to elide or ignore serious differences between types of discourse in the eighteenth century, I would like to argue that the status of fiction is such that it lends itself to the types of readings I propose. That is to say, fiction in eighteenth-century French invites a reading that considers its discourse to be on a par with the discourse of philosophical treatises. To put it succinctly, fiction of the eighteenth century asks to be taken "seriously."

Numerous critics have analyzed the problematic status of fictional discourse in Enlightenment France, chiefly with respect to discussions of the novel.[17] Critics have insisted on both the truth-value and the influence on social and moral behavior characteristic of eighteenth-century French beliefs about fiction.[18] In his widely influential study, Georges May chronicles the attacks, beginning in the 1730s, on the novelistic form as a corrupting influence on public and private morals. In response, "moral" fiction often claimed to represent moral lessons—both positive and negative—designed to edify readers.[19] What these debates demonstrate is the extent to which fiction in the period was believed to influence readers' behavior.

From the standpoint of literary theory of the period, it is also clear
that fiction, and the novel in particular, staked its value on something
other than mere entertainment. Eighteenth-century literary theory
most often cited Horace's precept, "the poet's aim is to mix the pleas-
ing and the useful,"[20] and either commended or condemned novels according to their ability to enlighten as well as entertain. Prefaces to
"moral fiction," as well as works that clearly parody the genre, such as
Laclos's *Les Liaisons dangereuses*, provide ample evidence that Horace's
precept was widely accepted by both authors and readers as an appropriate standard for judging fictional works.

As an example of eighteenth-century literary theory, Diderot's
"Eloge de Richardson" (1761) defends the novel, and Richardson's
novels in particular, against claims obviously still circulating in the
1760s about the dangers of reading them:

> A novel, up until today, has been understood to be a fabric of chi-
> merical and frivolous events, the reading of which was dangerous for
> matters of taste and morals. I would like it if another name could be
> found for the works of Richardson, works that lift the spirit and touch
> the soul, that breathe love of the good everywhere and that are also
> called novels.[21]

Diderot's high opinion of Richardson's novels is based on their ability
to move their readers, specifically to teach moral lessons through example.[22] Based on the verisimilitude Diderot finds in Richardson's works,
he argues that they draw the reader in and not only teach him/her
about virtue but inspire him/her to be virtuous:

> But what does it matter if, thanks to this author, I loved my fellow
> man more, loved my duties, if I only had pity for the wicked; if I con-
> ceived more commiseration for the unfortunate, more veneration for
> the good, more caution in the use of things at hand, more indifference
> to future things, more disdain for life, and more love of virtue.[23]

Casting himself as the ideal reader of Richardson's fiction, he asserts a
kind of model reading for moral fiction in the period.[24]

Even Rousseau's ironic "Préface de *la Nouvelle Héloïse*: ou entretien
sur les romans," (1761) in spite of the harsh warning in his first
"Préface" to the same work, "No chaste girl ever read a novel" claims a
didactic purpose for his novel.[25] In the novel-as-conduct-book tradition
of Richardson,[26] he writes:

> I like to imagine two spouses reading this collection together, drawing
> new courage from it to endure their common labors, and perhaps
> some new views to make them useful. How could they contemplate
> the picture of a happy household without wanting to imitate such a

sweet model? How could they be touched by the charms of conjugal union, even one deprived of love, without their own becoming stronger and tighter? [27]

He imagines—and the historical record seems to indicate that he was right—the morally edifying effects of his fiction in reshaping the reality even of the private sphere.[28] Likewise, *Emile* reached into the private sphere and changed family configurations in much the same way that novels such as *Pamela*, *Clarissa*, and *Julie* did.[29]

As these brief readings of Diderot and Rousseau demonstrate, attitudes toward fiction during the eighteenth century clearly diminish the distinction between literature as a discursive mode and other forms of writing. In particular, because of the influence on moral behavior ascribed to novels, reading them alongside philosophical treatises on morality and/or politics seems less problematic in the Enlightenment context than it does in the twentieth century. Literature was assumed to have an effect on readers' behavior, an effect that could be characterized as both personal and moral and also more broadly political insofar as it influenced relations between individuals beyond the private sphere of the family.

In addition, the authors themselves often wrote works that today are considered to be in distinctly different disciplines or that defy disciplinary categorization altogether. Diderot and Rousseau typify the extraordinary range the corpus of a single author might span. Thus, the divides between and among literature, philosophy, political science, and social critique are necessarily blurred. Literature's value and self-justification—in eighteenth-century metadiscourses—often lies precisely in its being morally formative. In other words, the cross-genre comparisons that figure in *Beyond Contractual Morality* are more or less consistent with eighteenth-century perceptions of discursive boundaries or the lack thereof.

Beyond the generic questions that attend the selection of texts in the following chapters, there is also the problem of historical period: The cluster of primary texts that form the center of the following study span a considerable amount of time. From Montesquieu's *De l'Esprit des lois* (1748) to Sade's *La Philosophie dans le boudoir* (1795), the period discussed traverses a time of tremendous social tension and change including the revolution itself. The rather lengthy temporal span makes the task of historical contextualization of the eighteenth-century texts difficult at best. My decision to read Enlightenment texts within a frame of reference drawn from contemporary America further compounds the "problem of history."

To begin at the end of the temporal span, I would like to argue that the Marquis de Sade, although the "last" author from the perspective of dates of publication, in many respects is a throwback to an earlier time. Although as a historical figure Sade was implicated in the revolution and his postrevolutionary life in Charenton was marked by many changes brought about by the revolution, nonetheless, for my purposes here, the world that he depicts represents a recrudescence of aristocratic modes of life from the early eighteenth century. As I shall argue, the world of Sadean libertines invokes a world of privilege and luxury that was permanently altered, if not altogether destroyed, by the revolution of 1789.

Setting Sade aside for the moment, the temporal span from Montesquieu to Charrière (1748–87) still represents a period of significant change. This roughly forty-year period preceding the revolution arguably produced enough social change to motivate the revolution. I would argue that the texts examined in the present study represent a discursive nexus in which questions are raised concerning interpersonal relations—both public and private. In the wake of the social contract theories of Hobbes and Locke, these texts both create and are the product of discussions concerning individual responsibilities in a world in flux.

As I have argued elsewhere, the second half of the eighteenth century in France represents a period in which rigid class stratifications are being blurred.[30] The emergence of a "bourgeois sensibility" that has a broad appeal across traditional class lines indicates the extent to which values are shared between and among segments of the aristocracy and the emergent bourgeoisie. More importantly for my analysis here, the appearance of a bourgeois sensibility underscores and is underscored by the fact that relations in the private sphere in particular are undergoing scrutiny. The conception of family life—including the raising and educating of children, marriage, and personal moral choices—is being redefined alongside the redefinition of the political.

Although there are differences both of historical and of class perspective that distinguish the authors under study here, they share a concern regarding moral relations between private persons. Whether from the general perspective of comparative political science that implicitly raises the question of tolerance (Montesquieu) or from the very particular perspective of an unhappy bourgeois wife in a novel who raises the question of obligation between marriage partners (Charrière), these authors are engaged in a debate about the meaning and value of personal obligations. At stake is the reconfiguration of social relations—both personal and public—either in a form consistent with a notion of negative liberty, as outlined above, or according to another conception that seeks to include a vision of community. With the exception of Sade, all the authors in the study seem to point *beyond* contractual notions of obligation to a richer, fuller conception of moral life.

Chapter 1 begins with the dilemma of public education. Using Rousseau's *Emile* and *Government of Poland*, I explore the tensions that fuel liberalism's often contradictory attitude toward education. These diametrically opposed texts highlight the liberal principles that have led to contemporary debates concerning home schooling, private-school vouchers, and multiculturalism. Specifically, these two texts represent, in the case of *Emile*, an argument in favor of thoroughly privatized education and, in the case of *The Government of Poland*, a call for collective indoctrination in the service of civic virtue. Chapter 2 continues with Rousseau's program for educational reform. A detailed analysis of *Emile* concentrates on the central conception of natural freedom in relation to the establishment of the student's moral autonomy. I argue that Emile's education leaves him with an insufficient understanding of moral relationships, one that will prevent him from becoming an effective parent, teacher, or citizen of a republic. Thus, liberalism's conception of the independent, autonomous, and free individual proves inadequate to the demands of public life within any sort of collective existence as well as to the deeper kinds of moral obligations characteristic of private life.

Chapters 3, 4, and 5 explore the tension between personal moral conscience and public, rule-governed, moral policy. Chapter 3 uses Diderot's *Conversation of a Father with His Children* to examine the use of legal definitions to solve moral problems. Focusing on the rise of professional ethics, this chapter questions the suitability of extending legal principles derived from formalized relations in the public sphere into matters concerning the private sphere. Turning to the broader question of tolerance, also stemming from the need to protect the private sphere of moral conscience, chapter 4 analyzes Montesquieu's efforts to create a balance between tolerance as a political policy and the need to protect the public interest in *The Spirit of the Laws*. The discussion of tolerance in Montesquieu resonates both with discussions of multiculturalism in relation to the problem of hate speech and with the debates concerning the "tolerance plank" of the 1996 Republican Party platform. I argue in favor of a strong conception of tolerance, but one that is necessarily limited in order for it to be a meaningful moral and political principle that protects the rights of the community. Chapter 5 again examines tolerance, but this time in relation to eighteenth-century conceptions of compassion and sympathy. Readings of Voltaire's *Treaty on Tolerance*, Rousseau's formulations of pity in the *Discourse on the Origin of Inequality* and the *Essay on the Origin of Language*, and Isabelle de Charrière's *Caliste or Letters Written from Lausanne* allow for the spectrum of moral reactions to cultural difference to be analyzed in terms of the nature of moral obligations entailed. I argue that while tolerance relies on negative conceptions of freedom and rights that can easily be translated into contractual terms, invocations of sympathy represent complex perfect duties that uneasily disrupt liberalism's contractual paradigm.

Finally, in chapters 6 and 7, I explicitly raise the issue of the divide between the public and private spheres drawn by liberal political theory. Chapter 6 examines the extreme position of the Marquis de Sade, whose liberal political philosophy, I argue, enables the careful regulation of the private sphere. A careful reading of *Philosophy in the Bedroom* reveals a truly minimalist version of liberalism with serious consequences for power relations. In light of feminist critiques of the failure of liberalism to recognize the political implications of matters pertaining to the private sphere, this analysis of Sade questions the desirability of retaining the public/private distinction. Chapter 7 questions the contractual understanding of bourgeois marriage. Readings of Rousseau's *Julie* and Charrière's *Letters of Mistriss Henley* juxtapose two different views of the obligations that marriage entails. Echoing the problems already revealed by the examination of Emile's education in chapter 2 and the discussion of notions of sympathy in chapter 5, chapter 7 returns to the difficulty of putting certain types of moral obligations into contractual terms, specifically with regard to the private sphere. Contractual understandings of interpersonal obligations tend to reinforce the fierce separation that liberalism enacts between the public and private spheres, making government intervention to improve the lives of wives and children very difficult indeed. This depoliticization of the private sphere and its consequences resonate with contemporary discussions of reforming marriage, divorce, and family law.

The conclusion of *Beyond Contractual Morality* returns to the contemporary themes, discussed in the introduction, that frame the readings of the eighteenth-century texts. Looking again to the implications for the future of liberalism, and specifically with regard to both the American and the international contexts, I argue for a revised vision of liberalism that will allow for a more fully developed, more positive conception of moral obligation that does not lose sight of the importance of individual autonomy.

Notes

[1]"[U]ne convention par laquelle une ou plusieurs personnes s'obligent, envers une ou plusieurs autres, à donner, à faire ou à ne pas faire quelque chose." Cited in Bernard Rudden, *A Source-Book on French Law: Public Law—Constitutional and Administrative Law: Private Law—Structure, Contract.*, ed. Sir Otto Kahn-Freund, Claudine Lévy, and Bernard Rudden, 3rd rev. ed. (Oxford: Oxford University Press, 1991), p. 298.

[2]R. C. van Caenegem, *An Historical Introduction to Private Law*, trans. D. E. L. Johnston (Cambridge: Cambridge University Press, 1992), p. 83.

[3]Rudden, *A Source-Book on French Law*, p. 210.

[4]Isaiah Berlin, "Two Concepts of Liberty," in Berlin, *Four Essays on Liberty* (Oxford: Oxford University Press, 1969), p. 153.

[5] See my discussion of the question of moral freedom in Rousseau, Wollstonecraft, and Kant in the Introduction to Part 2, Private Moral Conscience and Public Obligation.

[6]For a discussion of John Rawls's version of liberalism and the communitarian challenges represented by the views of Michael Sandel, Charles Taylor, and Michael Walzer, see Stephen Mulhall and Adam Swift, *Liberals and Communitarians* (Cambridge: Blackwell, 1992).

[7]Susan Moller Okin, "Humanist Liberalism," in *Liberalism and the Moral Life*, ed. Nancy L. Rosenblum (Cambridge: Harvard University Press, 1989), p. 41.

[8]Nancy L. Rosenblum, "Introduction," *Liberalism and the Moral Life*, p. 8.

[9]See Jürgen Habermas, "Postscript," *Between Facts and Norms: Contributions to a Discourse Theory of Law and Democracy*, trans. William Rehg (Cambridge Mass.: MIT Press, 1996), pp.447–62; and Berlin, "Two Concepts of Liberty."

[10]See Jürgen Habermas, *Between Facts and Norms*, and Seyla Benhabib, "Liberal Dialogue versus a Critical Theory of Discursive Legitimation," in *Liberalism and the Moral Life*, pp. 143–56.

[11]Jürgen Habermas, "Postscript," *Between Facts and Norms*, p. 461.

[12]Draft version of the Republican Party platform cited in *New York Times* (Saturday, July 13, 1996).

[13] Ibid.

[14]Michael Walzer, *On Toleration* (New Haven, Conn.: Yale University Press, 1997), pp. 37–38.

[15]See Walzer, *On Toleration*, pp. 60–71.

[16] While there clearly are intellectual traditions in France that follow Montesquieu (Comte, Durkheim) and Rousseau, both seem rather removed from current political debate, and certainly there is little talk of liberalism as a po-

litical paradigm. For a discussion of Montesquieu's legacy, see Isaiah Berlin, *Against the Current: Essays in the History of Ideas* (New York: Viking, 1955), pp. 130–61.

[17] See, among others, Malcolm Cook, *Fictional France: Social Reality in the French Novel, 1775–1800* (Oxford: Berg Publishers, 1993); Georges May, *Le Dilemme du roman au XVIIIe siècle: Etude sur les rapports du roman et de la critique, (1715–1761)* (New Haven, Conn.: Yale University Press, 1963); Vivienne Mylne, *The Eighteenth-Century French Novel: Techniques of Illusion*, 2nd ed. (Cambridge: Cambridge University Press, 1981); English Showalter, Jr. *The Evolution of the French Novel, 1641–1782* (Princeton, N. J.: Princeton University Press, 1972); William Ray, *Story and History: Narrative Authority and Social Identity in the Eighteenth-Century French and English Novel* (Cambridge, Mass.: Basil Blackwell, 1990); and Thomas DiPiero, *Dangerous Truths and Criminal Passions: The Evolution of the French Novel, 1569–1791* (Stanford, Calif.: Stanford University Press, 1992). For a fascinating discussion of the potential for political impact of eighteenth-century fiction, see Richard Terdiman, "Body and Story: Diderot Discovers Postmodernism," work in progress.

[18] See Ray, *Story and History*, pp. 1–23; Mylne, *The Eighteenth-Century French Novel*, pp. 1–19; and Showalter, *The Evolution of the French Novel*, pp. 38–66.

[19] See May, *Le Dilemme du roman*, pp. 75–138; Cook, *Fictional France France*, pp. 1–21; and Mylne, *The Eighteenth-Century French Novel*.

[20] See *Horace on the Art of Poetry*, ed. Edward Henry Blakeney (Freeport, N. Y.: Books for Libraries Press, 1970), pp. 34, 54. The Latin reads, "aut prodesse volunt aut delectare poetae."

[21] "Par un roman, on a entendu jusqu'à ce jour un tissu d'événements chimériques et frivoles, dont la lecture était dangereuse pour le goût et pour les moeurs. Je voudrais bien qu'on trouvât un autre nom pour les ouvrages de Richardson, qui élèvent l'esprit, qui touchent l'âme, qui respirent partout l'amour du bien, et qu'on appelle aussi des romans." Denis Diderot, "Eloge de Richardson," in Diderot, *Oeuvres complètes*, 25 vols., ed. Herbert Dieckmann, Jacques Proust, Jean Varloot, et al. (Paris: Hermann, 1975–), 13, p. 192.

[22] See my discussion of Charrière's novel, *Caliste ou lettres écrites de Lausanne*, in chapter 5.

[23] "Mais qu'importe, si, grâce à cet auteur, j'ai plus aimé mes semblables, plus aimé mes devoirs, si je n'ai eu pour les méchants que de la pitié; si j'ai conçu plus de commisération pour les malheureux, plus de vénération pour les bons, plus de circonspection dans l'usage des choses présentes, plus d'indifférence sur les choses futures, plus de mépris pour la vie, et plus d'amour pour la vertu." Diderot, "Eloge," in *Oeuvres complètes*, vol. 13, p. 200.

[24] The question of reader or spectator position within eighteenth-century aesthetics, and in Diderot's work in particular, is beyond the scope of my study. For discussions of these issues see, among others, Michael Fried, *Absorption and Theatricality: Painting and Beholder in the Age of Diderot* (Berkeley: University of California Press, 1980); and Jay Caplan, *Framed Narratives: Diderot's Genealogy of the Beholder* (Minneapolis: University of Minnesota Press, 1985).

[25] "Jamais fille chaste n'a lu de Romans," Jean-Jacques Rousseau, *Julie ou la nouvelle Héloise* in *Oeuvres complètes*, ed. Bernard Gagnebin and Marcel Raymond, 4 vols. (Paris: Gallimard, 1959–), vol. 2, p. 6.

[26] For a discussion of the novel as conduct book, see Nancy Armstrong, *Desire and Domestic Fiction: A Political History of the Novel* (Oxford: Oxford University Press, 1987).

[27] "J'aime à me figurer deux époux lisant ce receuil ensemble, y puisant un nouveau courage pour supporter leurs travaux communs, et peut-être de nouvelles vues pour les rendre utiles. Comment pourroient-ils contempler le tableau d'un ménage heureux, sans vouloir imiter un si doux modele? Comment s'attendriront-ils sur le charme de l'union conjugale, même privé de celui de l'amour, sans que la leur se resserre et s'affermisse?" Rousseau, *Julie* in *Oeuvres complètes*, vol. 2, p. 23.

[28] For an account of Rousseau's readers, see Robert Darnton, *The Great Cat Massacre and Other Episodes in French Cultural History* (New York: Vintage Books, 1985), pp. 215–56; and Joan B. Landes, *Women and the Public Sphere in the Age of the French Revolution* (Ithaca, N.Y.: Cornell University Press, 1988), pp. 66–89.

[29] Critics often hesitate to categorize *Emile* either as a treatise on the philosophy of education or as a novel. Clearly the work exhibits characteristics of both genres. The generic categorization is compounded by the existence of novels of education in the eighteenth century that more closely resemble Fénelon's *Télémaque* of the seventeenth century than the "lost illusions" novels of the nineteenth century.

[30] See my "Critical Introduction," in *Mass Enlightenment: Critical Studies in Rousseau and Diderot* (Albany: State University of New York Press, 1995), pp. 1–23.

Part 1:
Education

Part 1: Education

THE COMMUNITARIAN CHALLENGE TO LIBERALISM—together with the debate surrounding it—has raised many of the questions concerning the need to balance individual rights and freedoms against the needs of the community that will be of central concern in the two chapters focused on education. In spite of this fact, recent discussion has remained relatively quiet on the issue of education. It is true that the "Responsive Communitarian Platform: Rights and Responsibilities," with regard to education, states that "*We strongly urge that all educational institutions, [from kindergartens to universities], recognize and take seriously the grave responsibility to provide moral education.*"[1] And it further elaborates what is meant by moral education, arguing in favor of teaching

> values Americans share, for example, that the dignity of all persons ought to be respected, that tolerance is a virtue and discrimination abhorrent, that peaceful resolution of conflicts is superior to violence, that generally truth-telling is morally superior to lying, that democratic government is morally superior to totalitarianism and authoritarianism, that one ought to give a day's work for a day's pay, that saving for one's own and one's country's future is better than squandering one's income and relying on others to attend to one's future needs.[2]

In spite of the list quoted above, the shared moral values remain relatively vague. Furthermore, and perhaps more importantly, the ways in which these goals are to be achieved are never outlined, either with respect to a general philosophy of education or with respect to specific pedagogical practices. On the issue of education, the communitarian platform seems to argue against a "straw man" position that would oppose moral education in schools out of fear that it might devolve into religious brainwashing. This rhetorical strategy keeps the discussion of education at a general level in the communitarian platform.

On, presumably, the other side of the liberal/communitarian divide, John Rawls endorses a form of education that would foster political liberalism:

[Political liberalism] will ask that children's education include such
things as knowledge of their constitutional and civil rights so that, for
example, they know that liberty of conscience exists in their society
and that apostasy is not a legal crime, all this to insure that their continued membership when they come of age is not based simply on ignorance of their basic rights or fear of punishment for offenses that do
not exist. Moreover, their education should also prepare them to be
self-supporting; it should also encourage the political virtues so that
they want to honor the fair terms of social cooperation in their relations with the rest of society.[3]

Rather than the "straw man" argument opposed to moral education in
public schools implied in the communitarian platform, Rawls presents a
position fully consistent with, if a bit more tentative than, the communitarian position announced in the platform. Stopping short of condemning, for example, as the communitarians do, totalitarian and
authoritarian forms of government, Rawls seeks to educate future citizens concerning their legal rights and moral and civic responsibilities.
Nonetheless, his position on education seeks to inculcate the same
types of collective civic values, in more general terms, that the communitarians tend to favor.

One of the main differences separating Rawls's position from the
communitarian one is Rawls's distinction between political and comprehensive liberalism. In the matter of education, Rawls seeks to foster
political, but not comprehensive, liberalism in the interests of promoting a truly multicultural society with conflicting comprehensive belief
systems.[4] Having outlined the basic tenets of an education that would
foster political liberalism, he admits that, while not intended to inculcate liberalism as a comprehensive doctrine, it might have that effect.[5]

Communitarians do not seem to address the difficulty raised by
Rawls's distinction. Rather, the assumption of membership in multiple
communities in the communitarian position seemingly expects that
these various memberships will not interfere with the kind of moral
education proposed for schools. Familial, religious, ethnic, social, and
other types of communities will presumably provide a backdrop of
moral values that will be enhanced by the general moral education taking place in schools.

And yet, to return to both Rawls's and the communitarians' lists of
general moral values to be taught in school, it is clear that some of
them conflict with, for example, the tenets of some religions. That is to
say, as programs for public education, both might be questioned by
minority subcultures within the United States on precisely the grounds
that Rawls's distinction raises. In other words, such an education does

tend to inculcate liberalism as a comprehensive doctrine and some of its tenets are in conflict with beliefs held by minority subcultures.[6] More specifically, when it comes to the ways in which these values are to be taught, it becomes clearer that there are groups within the United States that might object to certain methods of teaching some of these general values.

For the purposes of my discussion thus far, I have more or less polarized communitarians and liberals for the sake of simplification. As a corrective to that polarization, I need to state that I concur with many communitarians that the opposition represents more of a spectrum of positions with various combinations possible.[7] Bearing this spectrum in mind, I would like to turn my discussion back to Rousseau to examine the roots of the modern conflict between individualist and collectivist political theory.

Without exaggerating, I believe it is safe to assert that contradictions in Rousseau's social and political thought lie at the heart of the modern dilemma. On the one hand, Rousseau's conception of the general will in the *Social Contract* represents a forceful articulation of the primacy of the interests of the community over the private interests of its individual members.[8] On the other hand, the *Discourse on the Origin of Inequality* and, to a great extent, *Emile* represent persuasive arguments in favor of individualism.[9] Rousseau simultaneously argues in favor of the need for the public good to override individual interests— even when those interests represent the interest of the majority—and in favor of the paramountcy of individual freedom, autonomy, and self-expression developed in isolation.

The crux of the problem lies in Rousseau's conflicting views concerning man's sociability.[10] As I have argued elsewhere, the isolation of the state of nature, man's lack of intellectual development, and a general condition of abundance make sociability a moot point for "natural man." Only the presence of pity in the state of nature signals any potential for social existence.[11] In the "Preface" to the *Discourse on the Origin of Inequality*, Rousseau makes it clear that he is not invoking the concept of sociability:

> It is from the agreement and combination that our mind is in a position to make of these two principles [the conservation of ourselves and pity], without it being necessary to introduce that of sociability, that to me it seems all the rules of natural law derive, rules that reason is then forced to reestablish on other grounds, when through successive developments reason succeeds in stifling nature itself.[12]

Rather than introducing the concept of sociability, Rousseau uses pity to create the potential for peaceful social existence without directly motivating society. As Zev Trachtenberg argues, Rousseau positions himself in relation both to Hobbes and to the natural law tradition with his account of pity in the state of nature. Arguing in favor of pity, Rousseau distances himself from Hobbes's self-interested, antagonistic individuals, yet he stops short of endorsing the position of natural sociability favored by natural law theorists. Trachtenberg, citing Rousseau, maintains that "Rousseau denied that sociability was part of humanity's natural constitution: it is 'clear from how little care Nature has taken to bring Men together through mutual needs . . . how little it prepared their Sociability, and how little of its own it has contributed to all that men have done to establish the bonds of Sociability.'"[13] Individuals in Rousseau's state of nature, and subsequently in social life, would not pose a threat to one another. Thus, contra Hobbes, Rousseau ensures the preservation of the species with his account of pity.[14] Yet, his individuals would not automatically be drawn toward one another to form a community as in the accounts of the natural law theorists. Rather, living in relative isolation from one another, Rousseau's natural men and, presumably by extension, his idealized citizens would have minimal social contact.[15]

Perhaps the most complex formulation of the problem of sociability in Rousseau is in the *Profession de foi du vicaire savoyard* in the Fourth Book of *Emile*. In the following passage, Rousseau brings together all the tensions and contradictions of his thought concerning the moral relation of the individual to the collectivity:

> if, as one might suspect, man is sociable by nature, *or at least made to become so*, he can only be sociable due to other innate feelings relative to his species; for, to consider only the question of physical need, it must certainly require dispersing men instead of bringing them together. And yet, *the impulse of conscience is born out of the moral system formed by this double relation to oneself and to one's fellow creatures.* Knowing the good is not loving the good: man does not have innate knowledge of the good, but as soon as his reason allows him to know it, his conscience brings him to love it: it is this feeling that is innate.[16] [My emphasis.]

What is most apparent in this formulation is the slippage in the double formulation "man is sociable by nature, or at least made to become so." Rousseau seems to hesitate in his pronouncement about whether or not man is "naturally" sociable. Yet, he cannot deny that the foundation for any moral system requires human interaction. Human sociability is crucial for any meaningful account of moral behavior. In

Rousseau's formulation, it is the double relation of self to self and self to other that forms the basis for moral behavior.

But Rousseau does not end with this double relation; he introduces another concept, seemingly to ease the transition to sociability. The final sentence of the passage quoted above denies any innate knowledge of the good and introduces a moral sentiment that arises from an exercise of reason. In effect, moral feelings and, ultimately, moral behavior require education. This is not altogether surprising, given the context of this formulation within *Emile*. Clearly, one way in which man could become sociable would be through education. Learning to exercise his reason through increased understanding, the tutored individual would come to respect both himself and his fellow man, and experience the "innate feeling" of the love of the good.

But this does not really resolve the tension between the individual self and the community in Rousseau: it merely shifts the burden toward education. And, as we shall see in chapters 1 and 2, there are competing models of education in Rousseau that lead to problematic conceptions of moral autonomy. It is my contention that neither the model for public education nor the well-developed model for domestic education provides a satisfactory solution to the tensions evident between the conflicting needs of the individual and the community.

And it is precisely this conflict between individual and communal interests that is so evident today in the debates concerning education that I outlined at the beginning of this introduction. Communitarians point to a lack of social cohesion and group responsibility, arguing in favor of increased moral education in schools. Echoing Rousseau's exhortation in the *Social Contract* that it might be necessary to force men to be free, Benjamin Barber even goes so far as to assert that "[i]t is the nature of pedagogical authority that it exercises some coercion in the name of liberation."[17] At the other end of the spectrum, libertarians defend the rights of individuals against interference by the state.

At the heart of this conflict lies a dilemma inherent in eighteenth-century liberalism concerning the balance between individual moral responsibility and collective responsibility. Mary Wollstonecraft, one of the most insightful critics of Rousseau's *Emile* from the standpoint of Sophie's education, points to the fact that women's education, as outlined by Rousseau, fails to provide a basis for moral development. Women educated according to Rousseau's program for Sophie would never learn to exercise their reason properly.[18] Because they would not reason, they would not be capable of true virtue, which requires knowledge of the good. Wollstonecraft's argument in favor of free, public education for women alongside men stresses the necessity of developing their individual capacities for reason in the service of private virtue. However, her argument does not stop with private virtue; she continues toward an argument for citizenship for women and, therewith, an exercise of public virtue, which would require the development of private morality:

> Public education, of every denomination, should be directed to form citizens; but if you wish to make good citizens, you must first exercise the affections of a son and a brother. This is the only way to expand the heart; *for public affections, as well as public virtues, must ever grow out of the private character, or they are merely meteors that shoot athwart a dark sky, and disappear as they are gazed at and admired.*[19] [My emphasis.]

Clearly, the exercise of private virtue within the family ("the affections of a son and a brother") leads to the exercise of public virtue toward one's fellow citizens.

But how is this to be achieved? Wollstonecraft's argument stops short of describing the type of education she envisions for her new public coeducational schools. How are the lessons in private morality designed to cultivate the independence of the individual to be coordinated and interwoven into an education that also cultivates a sense of collective communal responsibility? How does one create an educational program that instills private morality and public morality without sacrificing one to the other?

Eighteenth-century liberalism creates a paradox for education that still lives today. Ideally, as Wollstonecraft maintains, private virtue should feed public virtue. And yet, creating an educational program that will serve and produce both individuals and communities remains a challenge.

Notes

[1] "The Responsive Communitarian Platform: Rights and Responsibilities," in *The Essential Communitarian Reader*, ed. Amitai Etzioni (Lanham, Md.: Rowman and Littlefield, 1998), p. xxxix.

[2] Ibid., pp. xxix–xxx.

[3] John Rawls, *Political Liberalism* (New York: Columbia University Press, 1996), p. 199.

[4] Ibid., p. xx.

[5] Ibid., pp. 199–200.

[6] A recent legal decision concerning the Amish community in Pennsylvania highlights some of the ways in which the ideals of political liberalism may conflict with the values of a minority subculture. The case involved a fifteen-year-old Amish boy who was working in a harness factory, in violation of federal child labor statutes. The Amish successfully argued that apprenticeships form part of the educational system of their community, ensuring the continuity of their way of life. The state failed to make its case that the work in the factory represented a physical danger to the minor. The Amish are also exempt from mandatory schooling statutes, because, again, their "way of life" requires no formal education beyond the eighth grade. From the Rawlsian perspective, one might argue that apprenticeships (including child labor) and lack of formal education beyond the eighth grade not only ensure the continuity of the Amish community but also fail to provide the necessary knowledge for informed rational choice. In effect, one might argue that these children are being denied the knowledge of "liberty of conscience" and the sense of what it means to be a citizen that Rawls maintains is necessary for political liberalism.

[7] See Philip Selznick, "Foundations of Communitarian Liberalism"; Thomas A. Spragens, Jr., "The Limits of Libertarianism"; and Robert N. Bellah, "Community Properly Understood: A Defense of 'Democratic Communitarianism,'" all in *The Essential Communitarian Reader*, ed. Etzioni.

[8] See my discussion of the general will, in *Mass Enlightenment: Critical Studies in Rousseau and Diderot* (Albany: State University of New York Press, 1995), pp. 46–50. See also Marc F. Plattner, "Rousseau and the Origins of Nationalism," in *The Legacy of Rousseau*, ed. Clifford Orwin and Nathan Tarcov (Chicago, University of Chicago Press, 1997), pp. 183–99.

[9] See my discussion of the *Discourse on the Origin of Inequality*, in *Mass Enlightenment*, esp. pp. 27–39. For an excellent review of the literature concerning the individualist/collectivist debate in Rousseau scholarship, see Peter Gay's "Introduction" in Ernst Cassirer, *The Question of Jean-Jacques Rousseau*, ed. and trans. Peter Gay, 2d. edition (New Haven, Conn.: Yale University Press, 1989).

[10] For a detailed discussion of the origins of society in Rousseau, see Emile Durkheim, *Montesquieu et Rousseau: Précurseurs de la sociologie* (Paris: Marcel Rivière, 1953), pp. 128–48. Rousseau's equivocation on the question of sociability echoes tensions in the political theory of the period. In both Hobbes and Locke, the move from the state of nature to civil society is motivated, in part, by antagonism. Even in Montesquieu, who openly debates Hobbes in *De l'Esprit des lois* (Book 1, chapter 2), claiming that the state of nature is peaceful, the move to society is not unproblematic. Simone Goyard-Fabre reads Montesquieu's refutation of Hobbes as creating an unsocial sociability. See Goyard-Fabre, *Montesquieu: La nature, les lois, la liberté* (Paris: Presses Universitaires de France, 1993), p. 223. Allan Bloom contends that whereas

the social contract in Hobbes and Locke is motivated by self-interest, Rousseau does not see a "natural passion" underlying the move to social life. See Bloom, "Rousseau's Critique of Liberal Constitutionalism," in *The Legacy of Rousseau*, p. 147. Finally, Louis Althusser's reading of the *Social Contract* identifies a state of war in the last stage of the state of nature that motivates the act of association. See Althusser, *Montesquieu, Rousseau, Marx: Politics and History*, trans. Ben Brewster (London: Verso, 1982): 116–22.

[11] For an analysis of pity in nature, see Jan Marejko, *Jean-Jacques Rousseau et la dérive totalitaire* (Lausanne: Editions l'Age d'Homme, 1984), pp. 83–84. See also Roger D. Masters's analysis of pity and self-love in *The Political Philosophy of Rousseau* (Princeton, N. J.: Princeton University Press, 1968), pp. 136–46.

[12] "C'est du concours et de la combinaison que nôtre esprit est en état de faire de ces deux Principes [la conservation de nous-même et la pitié], sans qu'il soit nécessaire d'y faire entrer celui de la sociabilité, que me paroissent découler toutes les régles du droit naturel; régles que la raison est ensuite forcée de rétablir sur d'autres fondemens, quand par ses développemens successifs elle est venue à bout d'étouffer la Nature." Rousseau, *Discours sur l'origine de l'inégalité*, in *Oeuvres complètes*, ed. Bernard Gagnebin and Marcel Raymond, 5 vols. (Paris: Gallimard, 1959–), vol. 3, p. 126.

[13] Zev M. Trachtenberg, *Making Citizens: Rousseau's Political Theory of Culture* (London: Routledge, 1993), p. 85. Internal citation from *Discours sur l'origine de l'inégalité* (in *Oeuvres complètes*, vol. 3, p. 151): "on voit du moins, au peu de soin qu'a pris la Nature de rapprocher les Hommes par des besoins mutuels, et de leur faciliter l'usage de la parole, combien elle a peu préparé leur Sociabilité, et combien elle a peu mis du sien dans tout ce qu'ils ont fait, pour en établir les liens."

[14] Pity functions as a kind of self-preservation instinct for the species. Rousseau writes in the *Second Discourse*: "Il est donc bien certain que la pitié est un sentiment naturel, qui modérant dans chaque individu l'activité de l'amour de soi même, concourt à la conservation mutuelle de toute l'espéce." (*Oeuvres complètes*, vol. 3, p. 156) [It is therefore certain that pity is a natural sentiment that moderating in each individual the activity of the love of self, combines to bring about the mutual conservation of the entire species.]

[15] For a discussion of Rousseau in relation to the modern natural law theorists, see Helena Rosenblatt, *Rousseau and Geneva: From the "First Discourse" to the "Social Contract," 1749–1762* (Cambridge: Cambridge University Press, 1997), esp. pp. 88–158.

[16] "[S]i, comme on n'en peut douter, l'homme est sociable par sa nature, *ou du moins fait pour le devenir*, il ne peut l'être que par d'autre sentimens innés, rélatifs à son espéce; car à ne considérer que le besoin physique, il doit certainement disperser les hommes, au lieu de les rapprocher. *Or c'est du sistême moral formé par ce double rapport à soi-même et à ses semblables que naît*

l'impulsion de la conscience. Connoitre le bien, ce n'est pas l'aimer, l'homme n'en a pas la connoissance innée, mais sitôt que sa raison le lui fait connoitre, sa conscience le porte à l'aimer: c'est ce sentiment qui est inné." Rousseau, *Emile* in *Oeuvres complètes,* vol. 4, p. 600. [My emphasis.]

[17] Benjamin R. Barber, "Mandate for Liberty: Requiring Education-Based Community Service," in *The Essential Communitarian Reader,* p. 239. Barber's strong position is reminiscent of Rousseau's call in Book 1, chapter 7 of the *Social Contract* for the general will to coerce people to be free.

[18] I argue in chapter 2 that Rousseau also fails to provide a foundation for Emile's moral autonomy in his overly privatized domestic education. For an excellent discussion of Wollstonecraft's conception of moral autonomy, see Catriona Mackenzie, "Reason and Sensibility: The Ideal of Women's Self-Governance in the Writings of Mary Wollstonecraft," *Hypatia* 84 (fall 1993), pp. 180–201.

[19] Mary Wollstonecraft, *A Vindication of the Rights of Woman* (London: Penguin, 1992), p. 279.

1: The Dilemma of Public Education: Individual Rights and Civic Responsibilities

THERE ARE SEVERAL DEEP CONFLICTS running through Rousseau's work, but none is more important for liberalism than the conflict between individual rights and freedom and the needs of the state. Often dubbed the "individualist" versus "collectivist" debate in Rousseau scholarship, it both reflects and creates serious contradictions inhering in the liberal tradition.[1] With regard to the question of education, the conflict is expressed in two diametrically opposed tendencies in Rousseau's thought: on the one hand, *Emile ou de l'éducation* (1762) outlines a program of educational reform based on the one-on-one private relationship between student and governor; on the other hand, the *Considérations sur le gouvernement de Pologne* (1772) recommend public education aimed at indoctrination of patriotic civic virtues. These two opposing tendencies highlight the tension between the need to protect individual rights and freedom and the need to create a sense of community based on shared values. This tension is all the more important today in the context of pluralistic liberal democracies where it has become increasing difficult to safeguard the rights of individuals and minority cultures without sacrificing shared community values.

In this opening chapter, I explore the tension between the need to protect individual rights and freedoms and the need to foster common values. Specifically, I propose to explore the conflict between private, individualized education and civic education in relation to the general problem of contracts. My aim is to analyze the connection between contractual understandings of political associations and their extension into the social and moral realms. In the case of education, this means that the relationship between the individual and the state is still cast as a contractual one, which leads to deficient conceptions of responsibility. It is my contention that without an attendant conception of responsibility, the notion of a right or liberty is meaningless.

In setting up a choice between protecting an individual right or creating a sense of communal responsibility, Rousseau's theories of education fail to recognize their fundamental interconnection. It is my belief that contemporary debates in education regarding the right to home schooling, the rights of parents to determine curricula, and the demands of multiculturalism are still informed by and, to a great extent, misled by liberalism's failure to connect rights and responsibilities.

Individual Rights and Private Education

Rousseau's *Emile* inaugurated a revolutionary upheaval in the understanding of education whose influence is still felt today. This treatise on education championed the natural abilities of the child and urged learning through experience. I will explore the particulars of Rousseau's educational program in *Emile* in chapter 2, specifically with regard to the question of Emile's moral education. In the present chapter, I develop the more general question of the right to private education that the treatise implicitly sanctions.

In choosing the one-on-one relationship between student and governor to represent his ideal, Rousseau underscores the necessity of tailoring education to meet the specific needs and talents of the particular child.[2] In response to the rote memorization and sedentary approach used during the seventeenth and eighteenth centuries in France, Rousseau's natural education enables the child to develop and enhance his own innate abilities free of the constraints of ritualized, institutional education.[3] As John Dewey writes of eighteenth-century reactions to the earlier model of sedentary education, "Educational reformers disgusted with the conventionality and artificiality of the scholastic methods they find about them are prone to resort to nature as a standard."[4] This individualized approach, grounded in a conception of natural abilities, fosters individual expression and the development of specialized talents, both sorely lacking in education prior to Rousseau.

If the desire to cultivate the strengths of the particular child is laudable in contrast to the indoctrination of traditional education, it is predicated on a conception of individual freedom and rights that poses serious difficulties for liberal democracies attempting to provide public education. The right to private education and, in the case of Rousseau, the desire to provide individualized education represent an extension of the freedom in matters of individual conscience that has been a cornerstone of liberalism. The issue of religious tolerance, in particular, has shaped the political theory that has also come to tolerate private education.[5] As Judith Shklar ably summarizes the issue, "Liberalism has only one overriding aim: to secure the political conditions that are necessary for the exercise of personal freedom."[6]

The need to protect individual freedom, especially in private matters of belief, has come to be understood in contractual terms. In direct relationship to social contract theory, liberalism upholds the right to exercise personal freedom in private matters of conscience and property. As Rousseau's famous formulation states,

> "To find a form of association that may defend and protect with the whole force of the community the person and property of every associate, and by means of which each, coalescing with all, may nevertheless obey only himself, and remain as free as before." Such is the fundamental problem to which the social contract furnishes the solution.[7]

Rousseau underscores the importance of retaining the same degree of freedom within civil life that the individual enjoyed in the state of nature. What this means in practical terms is that the state both guards against violating individual rights and freedom and protects individuals' rights and freedom from being violated by other citizens. However, in the area of education, the protection of individual freedom is more problematic.

The issue really involves several interrelated questions. First, whose individual freedom and rights are being protected, the child's or the parents'? Second, whose responsibility is the education of the child, the state's or the parents'? Third, what interests need to be served in education, the state's, the parents', or the child's?

To advocate private education, as Rousseau does in *Emile*, is to construct an argument from the *Social Contract* protecting the parents' right to educate the child as an exercise of moral and therefore private authority over a minor within the realm of the family.[8] It follows, then, that education seen in this light is the parents' responsibility. This is underscored in *Emile* by the fact that Rousseau addresses himself in the "Preface" to a "good mother"[9] and at various times in the early part of the work to the parents. What remains unclear is whose interests are served in private education.

The question is answered in part by the aims of the education. Rousseau unequivocally states that his goal, in *Emile*, is to provide an education for living rather than for any specific profession:

> In the natural order, men all being equal, their common vocation is the condition of man; and whoever is well raised for that condition cannot badly fulfill the others that relate to it. Let my pupil be destined for the sword, the church, the bar, it matters little. Before the parents' vocation, nature calls him to human life. Living is the profession that I want to teach him. Upon leaving my hands, he will not be, I admit, either magistrate, or soldier, or priest; first and foremost he will be a man: all that a man must be. . . .[10]

Since the education is not designed with a specific trade or profession in mind, but rather with the business of living, it does not prepare Emile to assume a role in society.[11] In fact, Rousseau insists that Emile must be self-sufficient. This means that he understands and derives his sense of self-worth independently of others. Rousseau condemns any sense of self that derives from and/or is beholden to a broader community:

> The natural man is everything for himself; he is the numerical unity, the absolute entirety, who has no relations except to himself and to his kind. The civil man is but a fractionary unity that depends on the denominator, and whose value is in relationship with the whole, which is the social body.[12]

With his sense of self derived independently of any social body, Emile represents a self cut off from the external world. Although his education is complete insofar as his self is fully formed according to Rousseau's conception that privileges independence and autonomy, Emile has not learned any lessons that will help him to integrate into communal life.

Returning to the question of whose interests are served in this private education, it seems apparent that the interests of the state are not explicitly served. Because Rousseau does not have Emile learn a trade and, more importantly, because his education is specifically designed to make him self-sufficient, his assimilation into social life is not facilitated.[13] Clearly, Emile is not being groomed to be a good citizen. If the state's interests are not being served, neither are the parents'. Though the parents select the tutor (and Rousseau recommends that the father serve as the tutor), Rousseau's pronouncements emphasize the fact that Emile is not being educated for the vocation chosen for him by his parents. Emile is being educated according to the dictates of nature, which presumably means according to his own innate talents, strengths, and abilities.[14] While this is commendable, and all children ought to be educated in accord with their particular abilities, it says nothing about the ways in which these talents will be coordinated with the community as a whole. Emile's education in isolation says nothing about future integration into society.

Because *Emile* is not simply a treatise on education but also part of Rousseau's utopian vision, it serves the interests of that vision. In Rousseau's ideal society, men lead identical but independent lives in peace and relative isolation.[15] This vision ultimately answers the question of whose interests are served, for it highlights the fact that Emile's independence and autonomy are valued above the interests of the state and the family. It is the student's interests that are served in this private education and, thus, his freedom and rights that are protected from infringement either by the state or the family. The values that are being inculcated prepare him for a life of freedom in isolation.

Civic Education and Virtue

Diametrically opposed to this vision of independent, isolated private education in the interest of the student's freedom and rights is the vision of civic education proposed in *The Government of Poland*. The overriding concern in this text, unlike that in *Emile*, is to protect national security by promoting patriotic virtues that will provide the social cohesion lacking in Polish society. Rousseau recommends free public education in order to inculcate the kind of identification with the social body that he shunned for Emile.[16]

Rather than promote the innate talents and abilities of each individual student according to the dicates of nature, Rousseau here advocates that the government indoctrinate a love of country through the use of state-controlled institutions:

> How, then, are we to move men's hearts and make them love their fatherland and its laws? Dare I say? Through children's games, through institutions that, though a superficial man would view them as pointless, develop cherished habits that abide and attachments that nothing can dissolve.[17]

If Rousseau sacrifices the sense of self-worth and independence derived from the individualized attention Emile receives, he gains civic virtues that will not only serve as common values for the society but also help to regulate that society in the citizens' shared love of their country.

Beyond the desire for social cohesion, there is also an egalitarian impetus behind his advice to the Poles to establish free public schools:

> I do not like at all those distinctions between your schools and academies that make it so that your rich nobles are brought up differently and separately from your poor ones. All of them being equal under the State's constitution, they should be brought up together, and in the same way; and if you cannot establish entirely free public schools, you must at least put education at a price that the poor nobles can afford.[18]

Although Rousseau's egalitarianism only extends through the ranks of the nobles, it nonetheless bespeaks his desire to create a society of equals at least among the nobility.[19] Being educated together will bind the children in such a way that their individual identities will be forged together with, and as part of, a common national identity.

Most important in the program for national education is the emphasis placed on cultivating civic virtues in the future citizens. Rousseau stresses above all the need for physical exercise and competition under the public eye. Even for those educated privately at home, Rousseau insists that they compete in public games with other children. These public exercises are designed to promote virtue by "keep[ing] the children always on their toes,"[20] and rewarding them with prizes presented with proper ceremony and spectacle. It is the fact that the games are conducted in public that promotes the sense of duty and honor that Rousseau equates with civic virtue. In order to raise patriotism to its highest level, Rousseau exhorts the Poles to see to it that

> all citizens shall incessantly feel themselves to be in the public eye; that no one shall advance and succeed except by public approbation; that no post, no employment shall be filled except according to the nation's wishes; and that from the least of the nobles, or even the last of the peasants, up to the king, if it is possible, all shall depend so completely on public esteem that no one will be able to do anything, acquire anything, or achieve anything without it.[21]

Rousseau equates civic virtue with the citizen's absolute dependence on public acknowledgment for a sense of his own worth. Civic virtue means having a sense of patriotic duty and honor enforced by the gaze of the public. Individual identities are subordinate to the communal identity of the state.

Returning to the questions I posed earlier in reference to *Emile*, it is apparent that in *The Government of Poland*, public education serves the interests of the state by promoting national loyalty and patriotic zeal. Rather than protecting individual rights and freedom, the interests of the state—to be free of foreign control—require that individual rights be subordinate to state control. If citizens wish to remain Polish citizens and not Russian or Prussian, then they will learn to uphold their rights as citizens first, and then, perhaps later, as individuals. This means that the state will assume responsibility for the education of Polish youth, because the needs of national security and identity override the rights of individuals.

Contractual Obligations

The two diametrically opposed programs for education presented in *Emile* and *The Government of Poland* seem exaggerated to the point of caricature. On the one hand, in *Emile*, the individual rights and freedom of the child dictate the course of education without regard to the needs and interests of either the state or the parents. On the other hand, in *The Government of Poland*, the state's needs and interests solely determine the content of the education, subordinating individual identity—not to mention rights and freedom—to the collective interest. If these visions of education appear at first glance as gross exaggerations of possible solutions to the issue of education in liberal democracies, they nonetheless highlight the endemic problems. To devise a workable solution is to balance the gains and losses of the two alternative visions.

Let us begin with *Emile*. By safeguarding individual freedom and rights in isolated, individualized education, Rousseau has created an adult capable of individual expression. The emphasis placed on independence has secured his identity and sense of self-worth. These gains have been purchased at the expense of his sense of belonging to a wider community. His understanding of his own freedom and rights, as we will see in chapter 2, seriously hampers his ability to function as a citizen. A community composed of Emiles would not coalesce into a harmonious political body; more likely it would at best function as a number of identical, isolated units, synchronized in their movements. If common interests did not bind these units together, such a "community" would no doubt devolve into a state of nature. Because the conception of individual rights and freedom is not balanced by an attendant conception of responsibility toward the social body but only by a sense of responsibility toward the self, the rights are ultimately meaningless.

In *The Government of Poland*, however, Rousseau has engineered a sense of community by instilling patriotic civic values. In effect, he has recreated, in modern form, the Spartan republic.[22] Individual citizens experience their value only as part of the broader community. In this way, Rousseau eliminates the problem of civic responsibility, since all individuals are continually motivated to act in a socially and politically responsible manner. Their individual identities, subordinated to the collective identity of the state, can only be derived from and expressed through acts of civic virtue. Moreover, the limited form of egalitarianism helps to further bind the community in a collective spirit of cooperation and patriotic zeal.

The community spirit created by the system of public education proposed in *The Government of Poland*, while serving the interests of the state, sacrifices a great deal. There can be no individual self-expression—so carefully cultivated in *Emile*—in a state in which individual identity is subordinate to the collectivity. Furthermore, without individual expression there can be no pluralism. As with *Emile*, smooth functioning of the state depends on identical interests, here created through state-controlled public education. The worst-case scenario for this new Spartan republic would be a closed society of xenophobes infused with patriotic zeal.

If, in *Emile*, the overriding concern is to protect the rights and freedom of the individual child, then, in *The Government of Poland*, the overriding concern is to protect the interests of the state. These opposing visions are grounded in two different versions of the social contract. As I indicated above, the conception of private education as negative right is an extension of the liberal protection of the private sphere from government intervention. *Emile* represents a limit case of such a conception of individual freedom, since the individual whose rights and freedom are being protected is the child and not the parent. In this version of the social contract, the individual enters the contract in order to protect his private freedom both from the interests of the collectivity—represented by the state—and from other individuals. In this respect, the conception of the social contract more closely resembles the versions of Hobbes and Locke than it does Rousseau's own. In implying the protection of individual rights and freedom against state intervention in *Emile*, Rousseau's vision approaches that of the atomistic, possessive individuals described by Macpherson.[23] For education, this means that individuals exercise their personal freedom and rights essentially by educating themselves free of interference by the state or other citizens.

The vision of education presented in *The Government of Poland* is simply the opposing interpretation of the social contract. In this version, individuals enter into a contract forming a community which develops its own interests. In opposition to the vision described above—resembling those of Hobbes and Locke—here Rousseau remains consistent with his own conception of the *volonté générale*. Protecting the interests of the community always comes before protecting the interests of individual citizens. Indeed, according to this view, protecting the collective interest ultimately entails protecting all members of the community, since the general will is a truer expression of the common good than are private interests. In effect, the general will exercises its right to protect common interests and therefore assumes complete responsibility for education. By entering into the contract, individuals have secured their rights, not as individuals but as members of a community that looks out for their interests.

The two interpretations of the social contract presented in the two visions of education rely on one-sided conceptions of the social contract. In the version implicit in *Emile*, the state has little to do outside of protecting negative freedom and rights. All rights and responsibilities fall to the individual in the name of protecting personal freedom. Contrarily, in *The Government of Poland*, all rights and responsibilities are located in the state, which assumes complete control over education. The citizen's role is simply to be indoctrinated into the state-engineered community.

A more balanced vision of education clearly requires a more balanced distribution of rights and responsibilities. In other words, protecting individual freedom need not lead to completely privatized education. Likewise, protecting collective interests need not result in civic indoctrination. In contemporary pluralistic democracies, these issues are complicated by a multiplicity of communities to which individuals feel allegiances, often more strongly than their allegiance to the state.[24] While the solution offered by *Emile* seems ludicrous in the contemporary context, it bears a strong resemblance to the rationale given for the home-schooling movement. Individualized, isolated education is precisely what this movement promotes. The state's role in home schooling is, in effect, little more than protecting the personal freedom of individuals, although it does ensure quality control of the curriculum. This is a deficient conception of the social contract for it does not reciprocally balance rights and responsibilities between the state and the individual. If Emile is unprepared to assume a role in society, then I think it highly likely that home-schooled children will face great obstacles in integrating themselves into the broader social community. More importantly, the state has a deeper responsibility toward its citizenry than merely protecting their private freedoms. As part of a fuller conception of the social contract, the state ought to help create and protect a sense of community.

Clearly, the same criticisms are applicable to the vision in *The Government of Poland*, but in the opposite direction. The sense of community is created and protected, but without protecting the rights and freedom of individual citizens. In order to create a community where difference is tolerated, individuals need to learn to assume responsibility in the judicious exercise of their rights. A state-controlled curriculum that does not allow for the expression of individual difference and/or smaller-community difference ultimately works against its own interests. These are the criticisms that have been leveled against traditional education by proponents of multiculturalism, who contend that the creation of a collective identity has sacrificed the histories and cultures of minority populations. The interests of individuals and smaller communities within the broader contexts of national and international communities need to be balanced, yet without recourse to the extreme privatization of *Emile*. The goal of a balanced education is to yield politically and morally responsible members of various communities. This goal can only be attained in a conception of the social contract balanced by reciprocity between the community and the individual.

Notes

[1] For an overview of the individualist/collectivist debate, see Peter Gay's "Introduction," in Ernst Cassirer, *The Question of Jean-Jacques Rousseau*, ed. and trans. Peter Gay, 2d ed. (New Haven, Conn.: Yale University Press), 1989.

[2] Rousseau sharply distinguishes between public education, best exemplified by Plato's *Republic*, and what he terms domestic education. Claiming that there is no more *patrie*, he sees no need to elaborate another theory of public education. See *Emile*, in *Oeuvres complètes*, ed. Bernard Gagnebin and Marcel Raymond, 4 vols. (Paris: Gallimard, 1959–), vol. 4, pp. 250–51.

[3] See Georges Snyders, Roger Chartier, Marie-Madeleine Compère, and Dominique Julia, *La Pédagogie en France aux XVIIe et XVIIIe siècles* (Paris: Presses Universitaires de France, 1965), for a description of Jesuit education in France in the seventeenth and eighteenth centuries. The following sentence from Snyders et. al. sums up the general principles: "Immobile et toujours occupé, constamment surveillé et souvent puni, l'enfant passe à l'école le plus clair de son temps et la classe est pour lui une seconde demeure" (145). [Motionless and always occupied, constantly under surveillance and often punished, the child spends most of his time at school and, for him, class is a second home.]

[4] John Dewey, *Democracy and Education* (New York: Free Press, 1916, 1944), p. 112.

[5] See my discussion of tolerance in chapters 4 and 5.

[6] Judith N. Shklar, "The Liberalism of Fear," in *Liberalism and the Moral Life*, ed. Nancy L. Rosenblum (Cambridge: Harvard University Press, 1989), p. 21.

[7] "'Trouver une forme d'association qui défende et protege de toute la force commune la personne et les biens de chaque associé, et par laquelle chacun s'unissant à tous n'obéisse pourtant qu'à lui-même et reste aussi libre qu'auparavant?' Tel est le problème fondamental dont le contract social donne la solution." Rousseau, *Du contract social*, in *Oeuvres complètes*, ed. Bernard Gagnebin and Marcel Raymond, 4 vols. (Paris: Gallimard, 1959–), vol. 3, p. 360. Tranlations are my own.

[8]This position is consistent with the way the liberal state continues to view most matters concerning children's rights. David Archard writes as follows: "The 'liberal standard' prescribes the proper relations between State, family and children, and in some form is presently the most influential account of how the law should govern families within liberal democratic societies. It comprises three elements. First, there is a commitment to the paramountcy of the best interests of the child. Second, parents, that is, those accorded responsibility in the first instance for the welfare of particular children, are entitled, subject to standard conditions, to autonomy and privacy. Autonomy here means freedom to bring up children as they see fit; privacy means the absence of unconsented intrusion upon the family's domain. Third, there is a clear specification of the threshold of State intervention, that is, a statement of those conditions whose satisfaction would warrant the State in breaching parental rights to privacy and autonomy." Archard, *Children: Rights and Childhood* (New York: Routledge, 1993), pp. 110–11.

[9]Jean-Jacques Rousseau, *Emile ou de l'éducation* in *Oeuvres complètes*, vol. 4, p. 241.

[10] "Dans l'ordre naturel, les hommes étant tous égaux, leur vocation commune est l'état d'homme; et quiconque est bien élevé pour celui-là ne peut mal remplir ceux qui s'y rapportent. Qu'on destine mon élève à l'épée, à l'église, au barreau, peu m'importe. Avant la vocation des parents, la nature l'appelle à la vie humaine. Vivre est le métier que je veux lui apprendre. En sortant de mes mains, il ne sera, j'en conviens, ni magistrat, ni soldat, ni prêtre; il sera premièrement homme: tout ce qu'un homme doit être . . ." Rousseau, *Emile* in *Oeuvres complètes*, vol. 4, pp. 251–52.

[11]As part of his education, the tutor has him work at different trades. See Jean-Jacques Rousseau, *Emile*, Book 3, in *Oeuvres complètes*, vol. 4, pp. 458–88.

[12] "L'homme naturel est tout pour lui; il est l'unité numérique, l'entier absolu, qui n'a de rapport qu'à lui-même ou à son semblable. L'homme civil n'est qu'une unité fractionnaire qui tient au dénominateur, et dont la valeur est dans son rapport avec l'entier, qui est le corps social." Rousseau, *Emile*, in *Oeuvres complètes*, vol. 4, p. 249.

[13]The unfinished sequel, *Emile et Sophie ou les solitaires*, in *Oeuvres complètes*, vol. 4, pp. 881–924, bears this out.

[14]Many have criticized the ways in which the tutor manipulates "nature" in order to guide Emile in one direction or another. See Suzanne Gearhart, *The Open Boundary of History and Fiction: A Critical Approach to the French Enlightenment* (Princeton, N. J.: Princeton University Press, 1984), esp. pp. 271–80; and Lester G. Crocker, *Jean-Jacques Rousseau*, 2 vols. (New York: Macmillan, 1968), esp. vol. 2, pp. 132–42.

[15]For a further discussion of Rousseau's vision of the ideal society, see my analysis of the *Discourse on the Origin of Inequality*, in *Mass Enlightenment:*

Critical Studies in Rousseau and Diderot (Albany: State University of New York Press, 1995), pp. 25–43.

[16]See Jean-Jacques Rousseau, *Considérations sur le gouvernement de Pologne*, in *Oeuvres complètes*, vol. 3, pp. 966–67.

[17]"Par où donc émouvoir les coeurs, et faire aimer la patrie et ses loix? L'oserai-je dire? par des jeux d'enfans; par des institutions oiseuses aux yeux des hommes superficiels, mais qui forment des habitudes cheries et des attachemens invincibles." Rousseau, *Pologne*, in *Oeuvres complètes*, vol. 3, p. 955.

[18] "Je n'aime point ces distinctions de colléges et d'academies qui font que la noblesse riche et la noblesse pauvre sont elevées differemment et séparément. Tous étant égaux par la constitution de l'Etat doivent être elevés ensemble et de la même manière, et si l'on ne peut établir une éducation publique tout à fait gratuite, il faut du moins la mettre à un prix que les pauvres puissent payer." Rousseau, *Pologne* in *Oeuvres complètes*, vol. 3, p. 967.

[19]Elsewhere I have referred to Rousseau's repressive egalitarianism in connection with the totalitarian tendencies toward state-engineered homogeneity. See *Mass Enlightenment*, pp. 44–69; and "Militarisme et vertu chez Rousseau," in *Actes du IIe Colloque International de Montmorency, J.-J. Rousseau: Politique et nation*, ed. Robert Thiéry (Oxford: Voltaire Foundation, forthcoming).

[20] "[T]enir toujours les enfans en haleine." Rousseau, *Pologne*, in *Oeuvres complètes*, vol. 3, p. 968.

[21] " . . . [T]ous les Citoyens se sentent incessamment sous les yeux du public, que nul n'avance et ne parvienne que par la faveur publique, qu'aucun poste, aucun emploi ne soit rempli que par le voeu de la nation, et qu'enfin depuis le dernier noble, depuis même le dernier manant jusqu'au Roi, s'il est possible, tous dépendent tellement de l'estime publique, qu'on ne puisse rien faire, rien acquérir, parvenir à rien sans elle." Rousseau, *Pologne*, in *Oeuvres complètes*, vol. 3, p. 1019.

[22] Tzvetan Todorov maintains that for Rousseau, public institutions no longer exist. Citing *Emile*, he argues that modern individuals will not tolerate the kind of indoctrination that went on in Sparta: "Un événement s'est produit dans l'histoire qui sépare irrémédiablement la Sparte d'antan de la France d'aujourd'hui: les hommes ont commencé à se penser comme des individus pourvus de volonté, comme des sujets, comme des entités à part entière et non seulement comme des fractions de l'entité plus vaste qui est la communauté." [An event occurred in history that irremediably separates the Sparta of yesteryear from the France of today: men began to think of themselves as individuals endowed with will, as subjects, as individual whole entities and not only as fractions of the vaster entity that is the community.] *Frêle bonheur: Essai sur Rousseau* (Paris: Hachette, 1985), p. 35. Todorov believes

that Rousseau makes an exception for Poland because he sees it as outside of European history.

[23]See C. B. Macpherson, *The Political Theory of Possessive Individualism: Hobbes to Locke* (Oxford: Oxford University Press, 1962).

[24]For communitarian arguments on these issues, see Jean Bethke Elshtain, "Democracy and the Politics of Difference"; Diane Ravitch, "Pluralism vs. Particularism in American Education"; and Robert N. Bellah, "Community Properly Understood: A Defense of 'Democratic Communitarianism'"; all in *The Essential Communitarian Reader*, ed. Amitai Etzioni (Lanham, Md.: Rowman and Littlefield, 1998).

2: Property, Contract, and Tort: The Limits of Freedom in Rousseau's *Emile*

Je suis trop pénétré de la grandeur des devoirs d'un précepteur, et je sens trop mon incapacité, pour accepter jamais un pareil emploi de quelque part qu'il me soit offert.

—Jean-Jacques Rousseau, *Emile*

We think of ourselves as "born free," but we are, in truth, born weak and dependent and acquire equality as a concomitant of our citizenship. Liberty is learned: it is a product rather than the cause of our civic work as citizens.

—Benjamin R. Barber, "A Mandate for Liberty: Requiring Education-Based Community Service"

IN CHAPTER 1, I argued that deficient conceptions of the social contract led to one-sided distributions of rights and responsibilities in *Emile* and *The Government of Poland*. Either the social contract was interpreted as protecting individual rights and freedoms to such an extent that education was left entirely up to the individual, or collective interests completely eclipsed private interests, leaving education in the hands of the state. While the solution offered to the problem of education in *The Government of Poland* has potentially nightmarish consequences, the issues raised by *Emile* go to the heart of the difficulties in liberal conceptions of rights and responsibilities. Indeed, it is the desire to protect personal freedom understood in contractual terms that underlies the problematic conception of morality inherent in liberalism. In this chapter, I propose a reading of *Emile* that seeks to uncover the relationship between the conception of individual freedom that Rousseau's proposed form of education fosters and the deficient conception of morality to which it leads.

At the beginning of Book 1 of *Emile*, Rousseau distinguishes between three different types of education. He maintains that

> Education comes to us from nature, or from men, or from things. The internal development of our faculties and of our organs is the educa-

tion of nature; the use to which we are taught to put this development
is the education of men; and the acquired knowledge of our own experience over objects that affect us is the education of things.[1]

Of these three educations, he further asserts, we have control only over
that which comes from men (4:247). But the distinction itself is crucial
for understanding the type of education that he establishes for Emile.
Rather than reforming the education that comes from men, Rousseau's
plan for Emile involves systematically replacing the education he receives from men with an education from things. In other words, despite
the distinction between the three types of education, Rousseau's reform
of educational practice entails the effacement of the distinction between
the last two types: Education from men will be indistinguishable from
education from things. All education will seemingly emanate from objects.

The following analysis questions Rousseau's assumptions concerning the desirability of an "education from things." In particular, I focus
on the problematic relationship between, on the one hand, the development of Emile's sense of freedom and independence and, on the
other, his sense of moral autonomy. It is my contention that moral development necessarily entails both what Rousseau provides, namely, a
well-developed conception of individuality, and something that is sorely
lacking in Rousseau's project. Turning to an analysis of the preceptor's
role in Emile's education, I argue that it is precisely this type of connection and commitment to other human beings that Emile's education fails to foster. Ultimately, Emile emerges from his education
prepared to deal with other humans on one level but woefully lacking
in other skills that are necessary for moral personhood.

Freedom, Independence, and Abstract Individualism:
The "Natural" Man?

Rousseau's bias is already evident in the distinction between types of
education in the passage quoted above. Only the last type of education,
which the student acquires from "his own experience," guarantees the
solid foundation that Rousseau seeks for knowledge. Closely following
the empiricist tradition, and more specifically Locke, Rousseau maintains that

> We are born impressionable, and from our birth, we are affected in di-
> verse ways by the objects that surround us. As soon as we have con-
> sciousness of our sensations, so to speak, we are disposed to search out
> or flee the objects that produce them, first according to whether they

are agreeable or unpleasant, then according to the agreement or disagreement that we find between ourselves and the objects, and, finally,
according to judgments that we carry about them concerning the idea
of happiness or perfection that reason gives us.[2]

The education from things produces the sense impressions that stimu-
late progressively more complex responses in the individual. Only the
education from things guarantees that Emile will remain a free and independent thinker—relying solely on his own ideas, given to him by his
own reason, and judging according to his own standards. In other
words, the rationalist and empiricist traditions converge in Rousseau's
educational program to cast doubt upon any ideas not developed by
the student. Consistent with Cartesian rationalism, Rousseau traces all
ideas back to their "origin" in an indubitable ground. And borrowing
from empiricism, he maintains that the only indubitable ground for
knowledge is direct experience. All other kinds of ideas threaten
Emile's independence and freedom because they come from sources
outside himself. In Rousseau's terms, these ideas are not "natural."
Emile's education must remain faithful to "nature" if it aspires to produce a "natural" man (4:249–52).

Above all, "natural" man is free and independent. This bias in favor
of the individualized, separate development of the subject also underlies
the epistemological models of both rationalism and empiricism. Following these traditions, Rousseau seeks to offer an education that
seems to emanate from the student himself. The student "naturally"
learns at his own pace, according to the dictates of his own curiosity,
unfettered by the imposition of the assumptions, preferences, expectations, or desires of others. In this way, the student's freedom will also
be developed and preserved. Echoing his earlier distinction between
types of education, Rousseau also distinguishes between types of dependence:

> There are two types of dependence: that of things, which comes from
> nature; and that of men, which comes from society. Dependence on
> things, having no morality, does not harm liberty and engenders no
> vices; dependence on men, being disorderly, engenders all of them,
> and it is through it that the master and slave mutually deprave each
> other.[3]

Emile's education seeks to preserve natural independence and freedom
and thus to preserve natural virtue. Consistent with this distinction,
outside interference from the teacher can only be interpreted as a
stimulus to dependence on men that will inevitably engender vice. For
Rousseau, moral depravity is defined as a form of social interdepend-

ence resembling the master/slave dialectic. In place of a traditional education, he proposes an education from things that will foster only a "natural" dependence on objects and thus protect Emile's freedom and virtue.

What this education entails in practical terms defies the imagination of any parent. Rousseau advocates a delicate balance between leaving the child alone and aiding him in his endeavors:

> Maintain the child in [a state of] dependence on things only: you will have followed the order of nature in the progress of his education. Never offer to his indiscreet whims anything but physical obstacles or punishments that are born from the actions themselves and that he re-calls when the opportunity arises. Without prohibiting him from mis-behaving, it suffices to keep him from it. Only experience or impotence must hold for him the place of law.[4]

In order to direct the course of this education, the preceptor manages and orchestrates from behind the scenes. For, as Suzanne Gearhart has argued, the preceptor's role resembles that of a director or *metteur en scène* of Emile's direct experience of objects.[5] His job requires him not only to keep all harmful objects away from Emile so that he need not prohibit him from doing specific things, but also to enable certain ex-periences to occur by strategically positioning other objects and per-sons. These activities on the part of the governor ensure that Emile learns according to the dictates of his own curiosity and through direct experience.[6] But the level of manupulation behind the scenes calls into question what motivates Emile to learn: is he "naturally" attracted to some objects and repelled by others, or does the manipulation of the learning environment create an artificial staging area where Emile's "natural" curiosity can be constructed? The implications of this distinc-tion between natural and constructed curiosity become more serious when we turn from the question of the object of the lessons to what motivates Emile to learn. In other words, if it is the preceptor's ma-nipulation of the environment that produces a certain learning se-quence—a less than "natural" order for Emile's education—then it is also the preceptor who determines what and when Emile learns.

If the "natural" order of Emile's education is not dictated solely by Emile's natural curiosity, then it is also true that what motivates Emile to learn is not simply his own "natural" desires and will. Emile's free-dom, in a sense, is shaped by the constructed environment in which his education takes place. The preceptor creates a space for Emile to "freely" explore and learn, according to a pace and according to desires that only appear to be free. In effect, the manipulation of the physical environment enables the preceptor to have a rather heavy hand in determining both the pace and the objects of the lessons.

Placing the preceptor in the role of a behind-the-scenes manipulator of the learning environment enables Rousseau to maintain that Emile's education comes from things. In other words, by indirectly setting the pace and objects of lessons through manipulation of the environment, the preceptor conceals the role played by his own will in determining Emile's education. In fact, the main objective in making "natural" force, that is to say, the force that comes from objects, the only restriction on Emile's actions, and not the authority of the preceptor, is to preserve Emile's natural freedom. In other words, concealing the preceptor's will in the learning environment makes it seem as though Emile's will is uncontested by any other will. In this sense, Rousseau calls for promoting "well-regulated freedom" in place of the endless constraints imposed by the teacher in classical education:

> All the instruments have been tried, except one. Precisely the only one that can succeed: *well-regulated freedom*. One must not get mixed up in raising a child if one does not know how to lead him where one wants solely by the laws of possibility and impossibility. The sphere of the one and the other being equally unknown to him, one expands it or restricts it around him as one wishes. He is chained, pushed, restrained only with the bond of necessity, without his complaining about it: he is rendered supple and docile only through the force of things, without the seed of any vice having the opportunity to sprout in him; for never are the passions as animated as when they have no effect.[7] [My emphasis.]

As the foregoing description clearly indicates, Emile's freedom is indeed an illusion as is his "education from things." The repeated use of the pronoun *on* by Rousseau underscores the degree of invisibility he assigns to the preceptor here. Expressing simultaneously the anonymity of a diffused power out there beyond the student, the "one" of educational authority and the almost passive voice construction of lack of subjectivity (as I have chosen to translate it above), the use of *on* in the passage makes it seem as though, at the same time, everything and nothing were conspiring to push and pull Emile in various directions. As I have already suggested, the main responsibility of the preceptor is to efface any traces of his own handiwork in Emile's education by hiding behind and manipulating the objects destined to educate the student. Emile is indeed pushed, restrained, and chained, by a mysterious power that "regulates" his freedom.

The use of the phrase "well-regulated freedom" at the beginning of the passage becomes problematic in light of the fact that it is the preceptor who regulates Emile's freedom from behind the scenes. While it appears to Emile that natural obstacles stand in his path and teach him to regulate his own freedom, the use of *on* later in the passage indicates that the preceptor regulates Emile's freedom through the strategic manipulation of objects and the environment. Emile's "natural" freedom, thus, is created by the preceptor through the artificial staging of an education from things.

The "illusion of freedom," which it is the preceptor's responsibility to foster, presents further difficulties when examined from the standpoint of Emile's moral development. It is in order to prevent vice from developing that Rousseau advocates preserving the illusion of freedom. In theory, Emile's passions will not be encouraged to develop if his efforts are thwarted only by objects. In other words, it is the experience of *other people* resisting his will and failing to satisfy his desires that enables Emile's passions and vices to appear. Without the encouragement occasioned by resistance to his will by others, Emile will remain in a "natural" state free from vice.

This "natural" state is directly related to Rousseau's pronouncements on discipline. Rousseau recommends not punishing Emile precisely because of the difficulty of interpreting his actions as either good or bad. Like those of man in the state of nature, the child's actions are presumed to be good for lack of the general concept of moral value.[8] Hence, punishment is both superfluous and potentially dangerous given the child's "innocent" state:

> Do not give your pupil any kind of verbal lesson; he should not receive any except from experience: do not inflict any kind of punishment on him, for he does not know what it means to be at fault: never make him ask forgiveness, for he would not know how to offend you. Devoid of any morality in his actions, he cannot do anything that is morally bad and that merits either punishment or reprimand.[9]

Considered from the standpoint of Emile's moral development, the lack of punishment seems problematic at best. Even if the child's actions are not in and of themselves either morally good or bad, they nonetheless have consequences and would seem to require some action on the part of the preceptor. In order to *teach* the concepts of good and bad, right and wrong, it would seem necessary to impose restrictions on and sanctions against the child for certain actions according to their seriousness. Without an awareness that his actions produce certain moral consequences, Emile's moral education remains stalled.[10]

The lack of punishment ensures that Emile knows no artificial restrictions on his freedom and is designed to ensure that his will is never restricted. In a clear departure from Locke, Rousseau does not recommend teaching Emile to curb his desires.[11] In fact, he explicitly maintains that reasoning with children, as Locke advises, is a waste of time. As we have already seen, he recommends force as the only "natural" way to restrict their behavior (4:319–20). But the force must always be "naturalized" in the sense that it must appear to come from the objects themselves.[12] Thus, the child's freedom is only restricted by the "force" of "natural resistance." This formulation gives rise to numerous objections and questions. As we have seen in the analysis of passages above, the manipulation of the learning environment by the preceptor calls into question the naturalness of the forces opposed to Emile's will. Why should objects and physical forces contrived by the preceptor to subvert Emile's will provide better moral lessons than more direct manifestations of the preceptor's will? Why wouldn't it ever be appropriate to simply say "no" to a child? How would the child learn to respect the will of others if his own will only collided with "natural" objects? Ultimately, how would the child learn the difference between right and wrong without some sort of articulation of reason coming directly from the preceptor rather than indirectly through the objects?

The illusion of freedom is achieved at the cost of not restricting Emile's desires or making his will conform to reason—either his own or the preceptor's. Although he may learn to avoid certain situations or to seek out others, it remains to be seen whether the development of reason in this context would move beyond strategic manipulation of objects and forces to the well-regulated freedom that Rousseau asserts for Emile. I maintain that the price of this "natural" freedom is also Emile's moral education. It is Rousseau's peculiar conception of the nature of the social bond that leads him to delay Emile's moral education until adolescence.[13] In effect, Emile's freedom in early childhood resembles the problematic freedom of the state of nature.[14] But Rousseau himself never characterizes this type of freedom as moral. In fact, in the *Social Contract* he explicitly distinguishes between natural freedom and moral freedom. In both the *Social Contract* and the "Profession de foi du vicaire savoyard"—which appears later in *Emile*, during adolescence—he favors the latter over the former as necessary for social life. For Rousseau, moral freedom necessarily entails adherence to a self-prescribed law:

> What man loses by the social contract is his natural liberty and an unlimited right to anything that tempts him and that he can attain; what he gains is civil liberty and property in all that he possesses. . . . One could add to the preceding things that are acquired in the civil state, *moral freedom, which alone makes man truly master of himself; for the*

impulse of appetite alone is slavery, and obedience to self-prescribed law is freedom.[15] [My emphasis.]

Without establishing restrictions on Emile's will so that the student might in turn establish them for himself, Rousseau fails to provide the mechanism necessary for what Freud characterized as the development of the superego.[16] Emile cannot internalize the moral law if it is never explicitly externalized. Reliance on education from objects prevents the clear articulation of rules of conduct for Emile's reason to seize upon, understand, and give to himself. Instead, during early childhood, Emile roams "freely" in a state of detached indifference to others.[17]

Abstract Individualism and Property Rights: Morality?

Given the emphasis placed on Emile's independence and the attempt to reproduce the state of nature during his early childhood, it comes as no surprise that the only "moral" lesson that actually occurs during this period involves the concept of property. This lesson avoids the traps of teaching abstract concepts of right and wrong or interfering in Emile's "natural" development by imposing external ideas not derived from experience. It does not broach the dangerous subject of Emile's "relation" to others by articulating a rule of conduct. Instead, a situation is arranged by the preceptor in order for it to be resolved in a contractual relation between Emile and the gardener. The resolution appeals to an abstract conception of the individual in order to teach a lesson concerning justice and equity based on contractual relations.

The very appearance of the lesson on property highlights the problems in Emile's conception of self and its relation to others in early childhood. Because the lesson on property rights emphasizes abstract notions of personhood rather than concrete relations with others, it reinforces the liberal notion of self as independent and free. Consistent with Rousseau's stipulation that the governor not interfere directly with Emile's development, the lesson on property arises out of Emile's "natural" desire to imitate those around him by planting, creating, and tending a garden of his own (4:330).

The lesson begins in classic Lockean fashion with Emile learning the concept of ownership by mixing his labor with something in order to create personal property. In this case, Emile plants bean seeds in a garden. But rather than have Emile simply plant and tend his garden and then reap the fruits of his labor, Rousseau's scenario requires a loss in order for Emile to learn the lesson. As Frances Ferguson has suggested, "Rousseau's account involves substituting a vision of an infinite series of losses for Locke's vision of an infinite projection of credit."[18] After Emile plants his seeds and tends them, he returns to find his garden torn up and, according to Rousseau, experiences the feeling of injustice for the first time (4:331). Emile learns that he planted his seeds in a garden tended by someone else. Robert, the gardener, explains that Emile's beans have ruined his Spanish melons and have done him, the gardener, an irreparable wrong.[19]

The simple lesson on the concept of property quickly develops into a rather complicated lesson on torts, property rights, and contractual obligations. While Rousseau maintains that the lesson on property will explain the concept by returning to its origin and presumably to the right of first occupancy, in actuality the lesson does something quite different. Emile learns the concept of injustice based on tort—both his own and Robert's—in the form of a loss of property. The relatively uncomplicated concept of property has become the legal concept of property right through the insistence on loss. In order to resolve the dispute and right the wrongs done, Emile will now have to learn about contractual obligations through negotiation with Robert. The lesson ends with the preceptor negotiating an agreement with Robert to lease some property to the preceptor and Emile:

> Jean-Jacques: Couldn't we propose an arrangement to the good Robert? That he grant us, to my little friend and me, a corner of his garden to cultivate, on the condition that he have half of the produce.
>
> Robert: I grant it to you without condition. But remember that I will plow your beans if you touch my melons.[20]

The contract is striking on many accounts. First, if the original purpose of the lesson is to teach the concept of property by returning to its "origin" in invested labor, the contract contradicts this lesson. The terms of the contract suggest that property rights are negotiated between parties. The right of first occupancy does not obtain in this case, even assuming that Robert is the first occupant.[21] Second, the contract does not grant Emile the exclusive right to property in what he has produced with his own labor. According to the terms of the contract, he has to pay Robert for the use of the land in the form of half of his return. Thus, the concept of property here extends to Emile's labor as leased to Robert.[22] Robert has a right to the fruit of his own labor and to part of the fruit of Emile's labor, as payment for use of the real property. Through the contract, Emile acquires a civil and thus limited right to property, which restricts his natural and presumably unlimited right to property. Ironically, the contract engenders wage-dependency, which Rousseau himself elsewhere identifies as a threat to the autonomy requisite for civic virtue.[23] Third, the contract includes an enforcement clause. If Emile violates the terms of the contract by touching Robert's melons, he forfeits the fruit of his own labor in the form of property in the beans. Thus, the contract appeals to a concept of negative liberty in restricting Emile's freedom to create property through labor. In this way, it establishes the conditions and terms for dealing with any future tort disputes.

The concept of negative liberty, to which the contract appeals, bears a striking similarity to the concept of "natural" freedom that operates throughout Emile's early childhood education.[24] Rousseau's insistence on the use of force and "natural" physical consequences to teach Emile the limits of his own freedom amounts to the same thing. Emile's understanding of his own responsibility extends only as far as the concept of not harming others. Thus, the tort aspect of the lesson highlights the importance of recognizing the limit of freedom as the infringement of someone else's rights.

The parallel structure of the scenario that gives rise to the property dispute could have led to another lesson. Rather than resort to a contract that limits property rights and establishes the terms for enforcement of potential breaches, the lesson could have emphasized the similarity of feeling between Emile and Robert in their shared experience of loss and injustice. They could have agreed to cooperate and coordinate their labor in the garden for their mutual benefit in the future. But rather than lead to a feeling of solidarity, the experience of injustice prompts the creation of abstract, contractual relations between the two.[25]

From the standpoint of moral development, the recourse to legal concepts and the missed opportunity for creating another sort of bond both point to failings in the conception of self and its relation to others that Rousseau's educational program engenders. Emile's freedom and independence are achieved at the expense of the development of his moral autonomy and concrete relations to others. As an abstract individual, he contracts with other abstract individuals in order to promote the free exercise of "natural" liberty within the limits imposed by agreed-upon obligations and negative rights. He does not empathize with, or care for, concrete others according to conceptions of imperfect duty or positive freedom.[26] Instead, he treats others as he has learned to treat things—as obstacles in the path of his liberty.

Moral Education in Adolescence

The education proposed by Rousseau for Emile in early childhood parallels the existence of man in the state of nature: Emile lives a free and independent existence, virtually untouched by meaningful human contact. He has none of the vices of other humans but likewise none of the virtues. Rousseau maintains that he is simply without the artifice of other children, who have learned to appear as though they have certain feelings. Emile is "[i]ndifferent to all, outside of himself; like all other children, he takes no interest in anyone; all that distinguishes him is that he does not want to appear to take any and he is not false like they are."[27]

But without feelings of attachment to other humans, Emile cannot be a moral person with a social existence. In some sense, Rousseau postpones Emile's moral education until adolescence, a point in development that he marks with the dawning of feelings of attachment to other human beings. Rousseau distinguishes adolescence as the time when these feelings "naturally" appear. He claims about Emile that "when the first development of the senses lights the fire of the imagination in him, he begins to feel himself in his fellow creatures, to be moved by their cries and to suffer from their pains."[28] Thus, he establishes the "natural" feeling of pity to serve as the foundation for moral sentiment in *Emile* as it does in the *Discours sur l'origine de l'inégalité*. However, the relatively late appearance of pity in Emile signals some difficulties in the developmental model of moral education that Rousseau presents. If man in the state of nature feels pity when he witnesses the suffering of other sentient beings, why doesn't the young Emile?

Clearly, the notion that Emile is "indifferent" to the existence of others is related to the conceptions of independence and freedom that characterize the entire education of early childhood. Dependence on others engenders vices, as do any limitations on his freedom stemming from anything other than objects in the environment or natural forces. As a corollary to this understanding of Emile's natural independence and freedom, Rousseau distances Emile from caring about other humans. His indifference seems to signal his lack of attachment to others, understood positively as his relative independence from his tutor.

But unlike man in the state of nature, Rousseau cannot posit an isolated existence for Emile. Emile must learn to live in society. Having pity appear at the onset of adolescence—rather than early childhood— postpones a discussion of human interdependence. Having established Emile's freedom and independence in early childhood, the time of adolescence seems to allow for the shift toward a consideration of interpersonal relations that will not disturb Emile's natural freedom.

But delaying a fuller conception of morality until the moment of adolescence creates a peculiar conjunction. The emergence of a sense of human interdependence and moral relations of caring is mapped onto physical development in such a way as to make a fuller understanding of morality coincide with the appearance of sexual feelings. In other words, Emile is motivated to look beyond himself and consider other human beings as moral persons at the same time that his body also motivates him to look at other humans, and, more specifically, women, as objects of desire. Rousseau even suggests that nascent sexual feelings aid the development of moral feelings:

> Far from this fire of adolescence being an obstacle to education; it is through it that education is consummated and completed; . . . As long as he did not love anything, he only depended on himself and his needs; as soon as he loves, he depends on his attachments. [29]

Putting aside the complicated question of the relation between the sexes in Rousseau—which will be examined in detail in chapter 7 with regard to the marriage contract—it seems problematic on another level to have the appearance of the feeling of pity coincide with adolescence. Emile's lack of attachment to anyone else, including his governor, until adolescence places a heavy burden on the adolescent. Rousseau seems to suggest that the power of sexual attraction will overcome Emile's early childhood indifference to others and propel him toward moral relations of care and sympathy.

Rousseau outlines three maxims on pity in the section of *Emile* that precedes the "Profession of Faith," to summarize the appearance of a new sensibility of care in Emile. All three maxims stress the importance of the perception of suffering in the person with whom one sympathizes. Thus, they recapitulate certain aspects of the lesson on property in the gardening episode and recast them for the adolescent. Specifically, maxims two and three emphasize the potential to suffer the same fate as the one with whom we sympathize: "*One never pities in another the harms from which one believes oneself to be exempt*"; and "*The pity that one has for the injuries to another is not measured by the quantity of the injuries, but according to the feeling that one lends to those who suffer them.*"[30]

In the gardening episode with Robert, structured as we have seen around mutual loss, both Emile and Robert have experienced a wrong done to them. Both also clearly suffer from the wrong done to them. But the emphasis in that first moral lesson, as we have seen, was more on preventing Emile's future suffering by limiting his rights and freedom. The episode did little to draw comparisons between the loss suffered by Robert and that suffered by Emile. In other words, Emile was not induced to feel compassion for Robert, only to concentrate on his own hurt and loss and the creation of a contract to prevent future harm.

In Rousseau's developmental model, it would seem that Emile was too young to have feelings for others. His "natural" youthful indifference to others precluded a lesson on pity. However, during adolescence, when feelings for others appear, Emile is taught an abstract lesson on compassion summarized in maxims. Assumptions about early childhood egoism appear to condition the lesson revolving around property, while the adolescent capacity to reason enables an abstract lesson on compassion.

Several questions arise concerning Rousseau's decision to create a lesson on compassion that remains wholly abstract. First and foremost, why not stage an encounter with another being in which Emile is able to feel compassion and respond in a moral way? Why choose to summarize compassion in abstract maxims? In other words, why does Rousseau abandon his pedagogical method for the lessons on pity? As I have argued elsewhere, Rousseau's account of pity in the state of nature in the *Second Discourse* creates a situation in which the person feeling pity is not required to respond. In effect, pity is a feeling and only a feeling. Pity does not require the person to act.[31] Here in *Emile*, making pity into an abstraction summarized in a maxim keeps Emile at a distance from fellow sentient beings. It would seem that "learning by doing," or here "by feeling," has been abandoned in favor of abstract reasoning.

On another level, beyond the pedagogical inconsistency, the maxims on pity raise further difficulties. If Emile did not feel compassion during the episode with Robert, and his governor did not take the opportunity to teach a lesson on pity at that time, how can we be certain that he will feel pity now that he is an adolescent? In other words, is pity really a "natural" feeling that appears as if by magic in adolescence, or is it learned? As I shall argue in chapter 5, in which I discuss Rousseau's theoretical articulation of pity as part of a larger discussion of sympathy, feelings of compassion for other beings require nurturing over time. For now, suffice it to say that even granting the physiologically motivated appearance of pity in the adolescent, it would seem that not enough groundwork has been laid in Emile's early childhood education to support feelings of pity.

Beyond the maxims on pity introduced at this stage of moral development, there is also the "Profession of Faith of the Savoyard Vicar," aimed at teaching Emile abstract lessons concerning both morality and faith. The association of moral development with teachings on religion further complicates the understanding of the development of the moral person in Rousseau's *Emile*. As if the coincidence of pity and sexuality were not problematic enough, moral feelings for other persons—the sense of connectedness and caring that were absent in early child- hood—are also displaced onto a relationship with God. This leads to further abstractions in the understanding of moral relations.

"The Profession of Faith of the Savoyard Vicar" in many respects represents the culmination of Emile's education as he achieves an un- derstanding of the most abstract philosophical concepts. The religious lessons of "The Profession of Faith"—like the maxims on pity—mark the end of the education from things and introduce a turn toward indi- vidual conscience. Structured like a philosophical argument, "The Pro- fession of Faith" begins with epistemological and faculty psychology conceptions of the workings of the human mind and moves to broader questions of metaphysics and morality. The argument in favor of mind/body and spirit/matter dualism rests on conceptions of an active faculty psychology deriving from both Cartesian rationalist and Lockean empiricist traditions consistent with what we saw in Emile's early childhood education. In Rousseau's account, the human mind actively combines data from sense impressions and in turn forms judg- ments that motivate the will to act (4:570–76). This argument from faculty psychology to dualism culminates in a conception of the uni- verse in which a supreme intelligent being has willed matter into mo- tion. The corollary to the perception of a supreme intelligence behind the harmonious workings of the universe is a postulate concerning the harmony of all living things: "I do not know why the universe exists, but I cannot help but see how it is modified, I cannot help but perceive the intimate correspondance by which the beings that compose it lend to one another mutual aid."[32] However, this corollary concerning the mutual dependence of all things does not lead to further discussion of human interdependence. Rather, the text of "The Profession of Faith" grounds moral feelings directed toward a supreme intelligent being and toward the self more than it does those directed toward fellow sentient beings. In large part, the focus of moral examination in this section of *Emile* is on the self: "The supreme pleasure is in the contentment of oneself; it is in order to merit this contentment that we are placed on the earth and endowed with liberty, that we are tempted by passions and restrained by conscience."[33] I will return to the question of private moral conscience in greater detail in the introduction to part 2, where I examine the potential for conflicts between individual conscience and public rules of conduct. But here in Emile's moral education, and specifically in its relation to religious teachings, the difficulty of negotiating moral relations between persons is already evident. The focus on the individual's private relation to a supreme being and to himself occludes the self's relation to other humans.

Thus, the moral education of Emile in his adolescence attempts to remedy the deficiencies of his moral character, specifically his general independence from and indifference to others, by providing a basis for moral relations with others. The feeling of pity provides a foundation for relations of care. The insistence on relations of interconnectedness in "The Profession of Faith" also signals the need to extend Emile's education beyond himself. Yet, the delay in the appearance of pity until adolescence raises questions about the individual's ability to learn relations of care at this late stage. In seeming contradiction with the account in the *Discourse on the Origin of Inequality*, pity is not natural in early childhood although in all other respects Emile's education parallels the development of man in the state of nature. And, while the invocation of a moral dimension to the metaphysics of "The Profession of Faith" clearly signals the importance of moral life for Rousseau, the privileged relationships are the ones between self and self and self and God. Concrete relations of care and interdependence are still lacking in the formulations given for Emile in adolescence.

Negative Liberty, Natural Freedom, and the Duty of the Preceptor

Most ironic in the account of Emile's moral development is Rousseau's failure to provide him with the means of reproducing his education with his own children. Although the culmination of his education and the end of the book are marked by his marriage to Sophie and the news that they are expecting their first child, Emile has not learned enough to enable him to give to his own children what the preceptor has given him. In effect, his education has failed because he remains dependent on the preceptor to reproduce himself. The last paragraph of *Emile* ironically points to the level of failure in creating a program for moral education:

> After a few months, Emile came into my room one morning and said, embracing me, "My master, congratulate your child; he hopes to soon have the honor of being a father. Oh, what cares are going to be imposed on our zeal, and *how we are going to need you*! God willing, I

will not leave you to raise the son after having raised the father. God willing, such a sacred and sweet duty will never be performed by someone other than me, even though I would make as good a choice for him as was made for me! Yet remain the teacher of young teachers. Counsel us, govern us, we will be docile: *as long as I live, I will need you. I need you more than ever, now that my functions as a man begin.* You fulfilled yours; guide me so that I may imitate you. Rest yourself, it is time."[34] [My emphasis.]

Although Rousseau's text suggests that Emile will attempt to educate his own children with the preceptor guiding him from retirement, it seems doubtful at best that Emile's education has prepared him for the type of dedication and moral commitment that parenting and teaching require. He does indeed need his teacher now more than ever.[35]

For, as Rousseau conceives it, the preceptor's duty with respect to the student extends far beyond the type of moral obligation or relationship that Emile himself has been taught to honor. A close analysis of the governor's duties demonstrates that they require a moral commitment based on a concrete relation to the other. This type of imperfect duty defies reduction to an abstract contractual relation of obligation.

As we have already seen, one of the main tasks of the governor is to carefully orchestrate the eduction from things. This requires observation, planning, and, to a large extent, identification with Emile.[36] It also requires great patience and understanding. One of the things that make the job of preceptor so daunting is precisely the degree of self-effacement that it requires. Although Rousseau vacillates between the appellations of "preceptor" and "governor" for the private tutor, he prefers "governor" precisely for the indirectness that the term implies: "I call the master of this science governor rather than preceptor, because it is less a question of his instructing than leading. He must not give precepts, he must cause them to be discovered."[37] Working from behind the scenes and in such a way as to minimize his own contribution, the preceptor sacrifices his identity for the student.

The level of sacrifice required by the governor is perhaps most evident during Emile's adolescence (Book 4). Rousseau cautions that, although recognition of the preceptor's commitment and level of care is well deserved, insisting on it may lead to resentment on the part of the pupil. He advises using care in order to increase and not put at risk the authority the preceptor holds over Emile. In a passage that openly advocates the strategic manipulation of Emile's feelings, Rousseau reveals another of the problematic aspects of the relation between teacher and pupil:

If then recognition is a natural sentiment, and you do not destroy its effect through your own fault, rest assured that your pupil, beginning to see the value of your cares, will be sensitive to them, provided that you did not yourself set a value on them, and they will give you an authority in his heart that nothing can destroy. But, before assuring yourself of this advantage, refrain from taking it away by making yourself valuable to him. To vaunt your services to him is to render them unbearable to him; to forget them is to make him remember them. . . . I did not want him to be told that what was done was for his own good, before he was in a position to understand it; *in this discourse he would have only seen your dependence, and he would have taken you for his valet.* But now that he begins to feel what it is to love, he also feels what a sweet bond can unite a man to what he loves.[38] [My emphasis.]

Rousseau encourages the preceptor to continue, here at the level of his relationship to Emile, the kind of effacement of his duties that occurred during Emile's education at the level of the strategic manipulation of the environment. Rousseau seems to suggest that as long as the preceptor's relationship to Emile remains unquestioned, and, more specifically, as long as Emile is not asked to recognize the preceptor's relationship to him, a kind of "natural" recognition will develop. If the preceptor attempts to point out his own role in Emile's education, he runs the risk of being perceived as a servant. This is disturbing for a number of reasons. At the most basic level, there is a real risk of confusion here—on the part of Emile—between dependence in the form of love and dependence in the form of domestic service. This potential confusion suggests that forms of relation between people are often perceived, or run the risk of being perceived, as relations of subordination and indebtedness rather than of love and care.[39] Most of all, Rousseau wants to guard against the possibility that Emile might perceive a relationship of dependence between himself and his teacher.

While it is laudable that Rousseau seeks to avoid a situation in which Emile would perceive his preceptor as simply his servant and therefore dismiss the significance of his role, it seems unfortunate that such a risk of confusion appears in Rousseau's work at all. Why would Emile risk taking his teacher for his servant? What is it about this relationship that creates a situation that could lead to feelings of resentment or superiority on the part of the student if it is not handled delicately? Is dependence in and of itself always a dangerous thing for Rousseau? In other words, is dependence of any kind always a negative aspect of interpersonal relations?

It seems that the relationship of dependence threatens to reveal a carefully guarded secret to Emile. One possibility Rousseau suggests is that the revelation could lead to Emile's perception of his governor as his social inferior. This threatens to destroy their relationship because Emile would never learn to recognize the governor's duty for what it really is—a great moral responsibility. Instead, he would view the preceptor as someone hired to do his bidding. The preceptor's authority would be eroded and ultimately Emile's education would grind to a halt.

The risk that Emile would perceive the teacher as a hired servant is all the greater precisely because Emile has never learned any moral lessons about the bonds that tie humans together. His abstract conception of himself from early childhood, with all that it entails in the way of negative freedom and perfect duties, does not allow for anything but a contractual and abstract relation to others. Even the adolescent morality does not recognize concrete duties of care, but rather abstract maxims. Thus, Emile lacks the conceptual framework to understand the preceptor's relationship to him.

But there is another possible reading of the risk that revealing the preceptor's dependence presents. Rousseau fails to mention that the revelation of the preceptor's dependence on Emile also threatens to destroy the illusion of Emile's "natural freedom." Up to this point, Emile has believed that he is "free"—that the exercise of his liberty follows "naturally" from his condition. But the revelation of the preceptor's dependence indicates that Emile's "natural freedom" was purchased at the expense of the preceptor's "natural freedom." Since the pupil's independence requires the teacher's complete dependence, the pupil cannot be free. In other words, recognizing the preceptor's dependence on the pupil entails recognizing the pupil's reciprocal dependence on the preceptor. Emile would no longer see himself as "naturally free," but rather as "artificially free."

This other reading again points to the moral shortcomings in Emile's conception of self in relation to others. Recognizing his own dependence on the preceptor in the revelation of the preceptor's dependence on him would destroy the illusion of his entire education: His education never came from things; it came from prearranged things. He was never free; his governor carefully orchestrated the exercise of his freedom. He was never detached from and independent of other beings; he was always bound to others—and especially to his governor—by a tie founded on care and commitment. Most importantly, the recognition of Emile's dependence suggests that he ought to reciprocate his governor's commitment as a mature, moral person.

But the moral responsibility of a mutual and reciprocal commitment to care exceeds the limits of a conception of perfect duty bounded by negative rights and liberties. To care for another as a teacher or a parent requires a conception of the other as both abstract and concrete.[40] Perhaps it is for this reason that Rousseau recognized his own inability to fulfill such an awesome responsibility (I refer to my epigraph quoting from Rousseau at the beginning of this chapter).[41] Emile too is incapable of reproducing his own education, precisely because he has not been educated to understand moral autonomy as necessarily bound up with other people.[42] His conceptions of negative liberty and negative rights lead to legal-style contractual arrangements between abstract individuals, and not to the interconnected, concrete understanding of himself as intimately and necessarily tied to others.

Thus, the insistence on an education from things, designed to protect Emile's negative freedom, leaves him with a conception of self ill suited for life in a community.[43] His moral autonomy—which he understands as a right to exercise his freedom as long as it does not infringe on anyone else's rights—cannot provide a foundation for moral autonomy as Rousseau himself understood it in the *Social Contract*. Adherence to a self-prescribed law is not required of the abstract individual of liberalism. More importantly, negative liberty and abstract rights do not allow for caring relationships based on a concrete and embedded conception of the self and the other. Without these concrete relations of care, Emile will not be able to be a good parent or a good teacher and reproduce his education with his own children. Doomed by the abstract individualism of liberalism, Emile can never assume the role of governor.

As far as the political consequences of Emile's education are concerned, negative liberty and negative rights are also inadequate to prepare him for life as a member of a community. Without concrete relations of care to others, Emile cannot develop the civic virtues requisite for an active political life. His conception of self denies the possibility of his engaging in positive actions aimed at improving general conditions—even when he himself would benefit. Thus, his incapacity to assume the role of governor or parent parallels his lack of preparation to act as a responsible citizen of a democracy. Near the end of *Emile*, after Emile and his tutor have travelled to explore countries where Emile and Sophie may live and raise their family, Emile must be reminded by his tutor that he has duties toward his fellow citizens. The tutor addresses the following admonishment to Emile:

> So don't say: what does it matter to me where I am? It matters to you to be where you can fulfill all your duties; and one of those duties is

attachment to your birthplace. Your compatriots protected you when you were a child; you must love them as a man. You have a duty to live among them, or at least in a place where you could be as useful to them as you could be, and where they would know where to find you if they ever needed you.[44]

The tutor not only has to remind Emile of his patriotic duties as a citizen, he also has to spell them out explicitly. Having just summarized the main points of the *Social Contract* in the context of Emile's search to find a suitable place to live, Rousseau puts the discourse of civic duty into the mouth of the tutor to remind his self-centered student of what it means to be a part of a community. Ironically, Rousseau's account of education undermines his dearly held republican ideals in its failure to produce the requisite qualities for a citizen. His effort to preserve natural freedom destroys the possibility of creating moral autonomy.

The concept of the individual equipped with natural freedom but without true moral autonomy that emerges from *Emile* highlights liberalism's overinsistence on protecting one aspect of private life, namely, the property and freedom of economic man. What it neglects is the embodied, caring world of imperfect duties that membership in a family and a broader community ought to entail.

Having traced the contours of the individual in liberalism and the conflicts between individual life and community values in the realm of education, I turn in part 2 to questions in which the individual moral conscience finds itself in conflict with the public realm of contractual obligations in order to examine the limits of duty. Under scrutiny in part 2 are questions related to the themes of private moral conscience, tolerance, and sympathy.

Notes

[1]"[L]'éducation nous vient de la nature, ou des hommes, ou des choses. Le developement interne de nos facultés et de nos organes est l'éducation de la nature; l'usage qu'on nous apprend à faire de ce developement est l'éducation des hommes; et l'acquis de nôtre propre expérience sur les objets qui nous affectent est l'éducation des choses." Jean-Jacques Rousseau, *Emile*, in *Oeuvres complètes*, ed. Bernard Gagnebin and Marcel Raymond, 5 vols. (Paris: Gallimard, 1959–), vol. 4, p. 247. All parenthetical references to this work in chapter 2 (text and notes) cite the volume number followed by the page number. All translations are my own.

[2] "Nous naissons sensibles, et, dès nôtre naissance, nous sommes affectés de diverses maniéres par les objets qui nous environnent. Sitôt que nous avons,

pour ainsi dire, la conscience de nos sensations, nous sommes disposés à re-chercher ou à fuir les objets qui les produisent, d'abord selon qu'elles sont agréables ou déplaisantes, puis selon la convenance ou disconvenance que nous trouvons entre nous et ces objets, et enfin selon les jugemens que nous en portons sur l'idée de bonheur ou de perfection que la raison nous donne" (4:248).

[3]"Il y a deux sortes de dépendance. Celle des choses qui est de la nature; celle des hommes qui est de la societé. La dépendance des choses n'ayant aucune moralité ne nuit point à la liberté et n'engendre point de vices. La dépen-dance des hommes étant désordonnée les engendre tous, et c'est par elle que le maitre et l'esclave se dépravent mutuellement" (4:311).

[4]" Maintenez l'enfant dans la seule dépendance des choses; vous aurez suivi l'ordre de la nature dans le progrès de son éducation. N'offrez jamais à ses volontés indiscretes que des obstacles physiques ou des punitions qui naissent des actions mêmes et qu'il se rappelle dans l'occasion. Sans lui deffendre de mal faire il suffit de l'en empêcher. L'expérience ou l'impuissance doivent seules lui tenir lieu de loi" (4:311).

[5]Suzanne Gearhart, *The Open Boundary of History and Fiction: A Critical Ap-proach to the French Enlightenment* (Princeton, N. J.: Princeton University Press, 1984), esp. pp. 271–80.

[6]Of course, when we recognize the manipulative role the preceptor plays in this education, the concept of Emile's "natural" curiosity also becomes sus-pect. If the preceptor plants objects for Emile's "natural" curiosity to explore, then the curiosity itself is cultivated and formed by the one who controls the objects. Cf. Lester Crocker's discussion of *Emile* and the manipulative role as-signed to the preceptor, in Lester G. Crocker, *Jean-Jacques Rousseau*, 2 vols. (New York: Macmillan, 1968), esp. vol. 2, pp. 132–42.

[7] "On a essayé tous les instrumens hors un. Le seul précisément qui peut réus-sir; *la liberté bien réglée*. Il ne faut point se mêler d'elever un enfant quand on ne sait pas le conduire où l'on veut par les seules loix du possible et de l'impossible. La sphére de l'un et de l'autre lui étant également inconnüe, on l'étend, on la reserre autour de lui comme on veut. On l'enchaîne, on le pousse, on le retient avec le seul lien de la necessité, sans qu'il en murmure. On le rend souple et docile par la seule force des choses, sans qu'aucun vice ait l'occasion de germer en lui: car jamais les passions s'animent tant qu'elles sont de nul effet" (4:321). [My emphasis.]

[8]Cf. the formulation in the *Discours sur l'origine de l'inégalité*, Rousseau, *Oeuvres complètes*, vol. 3, p. 202, note IX.

[9] "Ne donnez à vôtre élève aucune espéce de leçon verbale, il n'en doit re-cevoir que de l'expérience; ne lui infligez aucune espéce de châtiment, car il ne sait ce que c'est qu'être en faute; ne lui faites jamais demander pardon, car il ne sauroit vous offenser. Dépourvû de toute moralité dans ses actions, il ne

peut rien faire qui soit moralement mal, et qui mérite ni châtiment ni répri-mande" (4:321).

[10]The magical transition from the state of nature to civil society parallels the magical transformation of Emile from natural child to moral adult. Since the state of nature is hypothetical, the transition from natural to moral freedom remains hypothetical as well. Rousseau's difficulty in developing a theory of moral education that allows for this crucial shift stems in part from his map-ping of the state of nature onto early childhood. Cf. Jan Marejko's discussion of the difficulty of the transition from the state of nature to civil society and the parallels to *Emile*; Jan Marejko, *Jean-Jacques Rousseau et la dérive totali-taire* (Lausanne: Editions l'Age d'Homme, 1984), pp. 83–92.

[11]See John Locke, *The Educational Writings of John Locke*, ed. John William Adamson (Cambridge: Cambridge University Press, 1922), p. 35.

[12]Occasionally he allows for the possibility that the governor himself may ap-pear as a force. See vol. 4, p. 320, where the preceptor's physical strength is opposed to his authority. This tends to teach the rather un-Rousseauian les-son that "might makes right."

[13]Sexual desire motivates sociability and therefore moral relations in *Emile*, thereby putting an undo burden on women, who must control their sexual passions in the service of society. Because of this, Rousseau fails to address the serious question of moral relations arising through relations of care. Thus, Books 4 and 5 of *Emile* further complicate the difficulty of identifying a foundation for caring ethical relations in Rousseau's social and moral theory. I discuss the moral education in the "Profession of Faith of the Savoyard Vicar" later.

[14]For a discussion of the problematic nature of freedom in the state of nature, see Roger D. Masters, *The Political Philosophy of Rousseau* (Princeton, N. J.: Princeton University Press, 1968); Marejko, *Jean-Jacques Rousseau et la dé-rive totalitaire* (Lausanne: Editions l'Age d'Homme, 1984); Alfred Cobban, *Rousseau and the Modern State* (London: George Allen & Unwin, 1964); Ju-dith N. Shklar, *Men and Citizens: A Study of Rousseau's Social Theory* (Cam-bridge: Cambridge University Press, 1969); and my *Mass Enlightenment* (Albany: State University of New York Press, 1995), chapter 1.

[15] "Ce que l'homme perd par le contract social, c'est sa liberté naturelle et un droit illimité à tout ce qui le tente et qu'il peut atteindre; ce qu'il gagne, c'est la liberté civile et la propriété de tout ce qu'il possede. . . . On pourroit sur ce qui précede ajouter à l'acquis de l'état *civil la liberté morale, qui seule rend l'homme vraiment maitre de lui; car l'impulsion du seul appetit est esclavage, et l'obéissance à la loi qu'on s'est prescritte est liberté.*" Rousseau, *Du contract so-cial*, in *Oeuvres complètes*, vol.4, p. 364–65.

[16]Sigmund Freud, *An Outline of Psycho-Analysis*, trans. James Strachey (New York: W. W. Norton, 1969).

[17]For a well-developed discussion of the Freudian implications of Rousseau's theory, see Alessandro Ferrara, *Modernity and Authenticity: A Study of the Social and Ethical Thought of Jean-Jacques Rousseau* (Albany: State University of New York Press, 1993), esp. pp. 70–86.

[18]See Frances Ferguson, "Reading Morals: Locke and Rousseau on Education and Inequality," *Representations* 6 (spring 1984), p. 81.

[19] "Vous m'avez fait un tort irréparable" (4:331). This episode bears a certain resemblance to the aquaduct incident in Book 1 of the *Confessions*, in which Rousseau and his cousin plant a willow and construct an underground aquaduct that drains water from M. Lambercier's young nut tree. See Rousseau, *Les Confessions* in *Oeuvres complètes*, vol. 1, pp. 23–24.

[20] "*Jean-Jacques.* Ne pourroit-on pas proposer un arrangement au bon Robert? Qu'il nous accorde, à mon petit ami et à moi un coin de son jardin pour le cultiver, à condition qu'il aura la moitié du produit. *Robert.* Je vous l'accorde sans condition. Mais souvenez-vous que j'irai labourer vos féves, si vous touchez à mes melons" (4:332).

[21]Of course, we do not know who owns the property in question, or whether or not Robert is the first occupant. In fact, Robert's assertion that the Spanish melons were destined for Emile (4:331) suggests that he merely works the land for someone else, perhaps even for Emile's family. We also do not know what would happen if Robert rejected the terms of the contract.

[22]This is consistent with eighteenth-century French theories of labor, which hold that its value is equal to what it produces. Thus, hired hands are like leased property, paid according to the value of the objects they produce. Labor, from a legal point of view, is considered to be a form of property. See Michael Sonenscher, *The Hatters of Eighteenth-Century France* (Berkeley: University of California Press, 1987), pp. 4–11. Compare C. B. Macpherson's account of the individual's relation to property in *The Political Theory of Possessive Individualism: Hobbes to Locke* (Oxford: Oxford University Press, 1962), esp. pp. 263–77.

[23]His position on the necessity for self-sufficiency is perhaps most pronounced in the *Projet de constitution pour la Corse*. See also Shklar's discussion of the evils of the division of labor, in *Men and Citizens*, pp. 29–30.

[24]On the concept of negative liberty, see Isaiah Berlin, "Two Concepts of Liberty," in Berlin, *Four Essays on Liberty* (Oxford: Oxford University Press, 1969).

[25]In this respect, the lesson on property resembles Rousseau's decision to represent Julie's marriage to Wolmar as inadequate in certain fundamental respects regarding connectedness. See my discussion of Julie's marriage in chapter 7. For a very different reading of the episode as the inculcation of a morality based on the social contract, see Allan Bloom, "The Education of

Democratic Man: *Emile*," in *Jean-Jacques Rousseau*, ed. Harold Bloom (New York: Chelsea House, 1988), pp. 149–171.

[26]Kant distinguishes between perfect and imperfect duties. A perfect duty is defined negatively and prohibits behaviors that infringe on others' rights, for example, "thou shalt not kill." Perfect duties must be followed at all times and with all persons. By contrast, an imperfect duty is defined positively and prescribes a particular course of behavior, for example, "act charitably." Imperfect duties cannot be followed at all times and for all persons, and thus they require the exercise of judgment. For Kant, the truly moral person fulfills both perfect and imperfect duties. See Immanuel Kant, *The Metaphysical Elements of Justice*, trans. John Ladd (Indianapolis: Bobbs-Merrill, 1965). See also my discussion of sympathy as an imperfect duty in chapter 5 and of marriage in chapter 7 for further discussion of the difficulty of translating an imperfect duty into contractual terms of obligation.

[27] "Indifférent à tout, hors à lui-même, comme tous les autres enfants, il ne prend intérêt à personne; tout ce qui le distingue est qu'il ne veut point paraître en prendre, et qu'il n'est pas faux comme eux" (4:288).

[28] " . . . [Q]uand le premier développement des sens allume en lui le feu de l'imagination, il commence à se sentir dans ses semblables, à s'émouvoir de leurs plaintes et à souffrir de leurs douleurs" (4:288).

[29] "Loin que ce feu de l'adolescence soit un obstacle à l'éducation, c'est par lui qu'elle se consomme et s'achève; . . . Tant qu'il n'aimoit rien, il ne dépendoit que de lui-même et de ses besoins; si-tôt qu'il aime, il dépend de ses attachemens. Ainsi se forment les premiers liens qui l'unissent à son espece" (4:520).

[30] "*On ne plaint jamais dans autrui que les maux dont on ne se croit pas exempt soi-même,*" and "*La pitié qu'on a du mal d'autrui ne se mesure pas sur la quantité de ce mal, mais sur le sentiment qu'on prête à ceux qui le souffrent*" (4: 507–8).

[31] See my discussion of pity, in *Mass Enlightenment*, pp. 31–35.

[32] "J'ignore pourquoi l'univers existe, mais je ne laisse pas de voir comment il est modifié, je ne laisse pas d'appercevoir l'intime correspondance par laquelle les êtres qui le composent se prêtent un secours mutüel" (4:578).

[33] "La suprême jouissance est dans le contentement de soi-même; c'est pour mériter ce contentement que nous sommes placés sur la terre et doüés de la liberté, que nous sommes tentés par les passions et retenus par la conscience" (4:587).

[34] "Au bout de quelques mois, Emile entre un matin dans ma chambre, et me dit en m'embrassant: mon maitre, félicitez vôtre enfant; il espère avoir bientôt l'honneur d'être pére. Ô quels soins vont être imposés à nôtre zéle, et *que nous allons avoir besoin de vous!* A Dieu ne plaise que je vous laisse encore élever le fils, après avoir elevé le pére. A Dieu ne plaise qu'un devoir si saint et

si doux soit jamais rempli par un autre que moi, dussai-je aussi bien choisir pour lui qu'on a choisi pour moi-même: mais restez le maitre des jeunes maitres. Conseillez-nous, gouvernez-nous, nous serons dociles: *tant que je vivrai, j'aurai besoin de vous. J'en ai plus besoin que jamais, maintenant que mes fonctions d'homme commencent.* Vous avez rempli les vôtres; guidez-moi pour vous imiter, et reposez-vous: il en est tems" (4:867–8). [My emphasis.]

[35]The incomplete manuscript *Emile et Sophie* bears out this assessment. As Marejko astutely remarks, "Le parcours d'Emile est révélateur. Elevé dans la nature, il échoue dans la société civile. L'imagination de Rousseau donne chair à ce que son intellect pressentait: même un être élevé avec le plus grand soin dans la nature et suivi avec attention dans le moment délicat du passage des champs à la ville, se révèle incapable de trouver son chemin dans un espace politique. L'histoire d'Emile suggère que, à partir de l'état de nature, il est impossible de parvenir à l'état de culture, de sorte que l'hypothèse d'une origine naturelle n'est pas propre à éclairer la naissance des sociétés civiles. Pour qu'Emile devienne un homme politique, il doit s'exiler, *tuer un autre homme*, être asservi et prendre la tête d'une révolte." [Emile's route is revelatory. Raised in nature, he fails in civil society. Rousseau's imagination gives flesh to what his intellect had a presentiment of: even a being raised with the greatest care in nature and followed with attention in the delicate passage from field to town is revealed to be incapable of finding his way in the political space. The story of Emile suggests that, from the state of nature, it is impossible to accede to the state of culture, so that the hypothesis of a natural origin is not suited to explain the birth of civil societies. In order for Emile to become a political man, he must exile himself, *kill another man*, be enslaved, and lead a revolt.] Marejko, *Jean-Jacques Rousseau et la dérive totalitaire*, p. 90.

[36]Identification represents a significant problem in Rousseau. See my discussion of pity in chapter 5 in relation to tolerance and sympathy.

[37]"[J]'appelle plutôt gouverneur que précepteur le maître de cette science, parce qu'il s'agit moins pour lui d'instuire que de conduire. Il ne doit point donner de préceptes, il doit les faire trouver" (4: 266). Amy Gutmann suggests that the association between education and governance goes back as far as Plato's *Republic*: "The identification of education and governance is total in *The Republic*. Governance *is* education in Plato's family state." See Amy Gutmann, "Undemocratic Education," in *Liberalism and the Moral Life*, ed. Nancy L. Rosenblum (Cambridge: Harvard University Press, 1989). Yet, Rousseau explicitly rejects Plato's model in *Emile*, claiming that he is not interested in public education. His choice of the word *gouverneur*, as opposed to preceptor, master, or teacher, is supposed to express the indirect form of leading suggested by the relationship to the word for a ship's rudder, *gouvernail*, from Latin *gubernaculum* and *gubernare*. See *Emile* (4: 55).

[38] "Si donc la reconnoissance est un sentiment naturel, et que vous n'en détruisiez pas l'effet par votre faute, assurez-vous que votre éleve, commençant

à voir le prix de vos soins, y sera sensible, pourvu que vous ne les ayez point mis vous-même à prix, et qu'ils vous donneront dans son coeur une autorité que rien ne pourra détuire. Mais avant de vous être bien assuré de cet avantage, gardez de vous l'ôter, en vous faisant valoir auprès de lui. Lui vanter vos services, c'est les lui rendre insupportables; les oublier, c'est l'en faire souvenir. . . . Je n'ai point voulu qu'on lui dît que ce qu'on faisoit étoit pour son bien, avant qu'il fût en état de l'entendre; *dans ce discours il n'eût vu que votre dépendance, et il ne vous eût pris que pour son valet.* Mais maintenant qu'il commence à sentir ce que c'est qu'aimer, il sent aussi quel doux lien peut unir un homme à ce qu'il aime" (4:522). [My emphasis.]

[39]This difficulty is echoed in problems associated with the marriage bond discussed in chapter 7.

[40]Compare Benhabib's argument in favor of a communicative ethic that entails recognizing the importance of both conceptions of the other. Seyla Benhabib, "The Generalized and the Concrete Other: The Kohlberg-Gilligan Controversy and Feminist Theory," in *Feminism as Critique*, ed. Seyla Benhabib and Drucilla Cornell (Minneapolis: University of Minnesota Press, 1987), pp. 77–95.

[41]Both the epigraph and his giving his children to a foundling home suggest that he felt himself to be inadequate to the task. See Rousseau, *Les Confessions*, in his *Oeuvres complètes*, vol. 1, p. 357.

[42]Carol Gilligan, *In a Different Voice: Psychological Theory and Women's Development* (Cambridge: Harvard University Press, 1993), suggests that these negative relations between individuals are gender specific, women being socialized for a more concrete and embedded conception of the other. I would like to argue that liberalism is incompatible with the ethic of care precisely because of the insistence on negative liberty and negative rights. Compare my discussion of the problem of reciprocity in marriage in chapter 7, particularly in Charrière's depiction of marriage in Isabelle de Charrière, *Lettres de Mistriss Henley publiées par son amie*, ed. Joan Hinde Stewart and Philip Stewart (New York: Modern Language Association, 1993.)

[43]Compare Marejko's analysis of the conflict between the *cité parfaite* and the *homme total* in Marejko, *Jean-Jacques Rousseau et la dérive totalitaire*, pp. 117–9, and Emile's difficult insertion into political life.

[44] «Ne dis donc pas: que m'importe où que je sois? Il t'importe d'être où tu «peux remplir tous tes devoirs, et l'un de ces devoirs est l'attachement pour le «lieu de ta naissance. Tes compatriotes te protégérent enfant, tu dois les aimer «étant homme. Tu dois vivre au milieu d'eux ou du moins en lieu d'où tu «puisses leur être utile autant que tu peux l'être, et où ils sachent où te «prendre si jamais ils ont besoin de toi» (4:858).

Part 2:
Private Moral Conscience
and Public Obligation

Part 2: Private Moral Conscience and Public Obligation

> I love man as my fellow; but his scepter, real, or usurped, extends not to me, unless the reason of an individual demands my homage; and even then the submission is to reason, and not to man. In fact, the conduct of an accountable being must be regulated by the operations of its own reason; or on what foundation rests the throne of God?
>
> –Mary Wollstonecraft, *A Vindication of the Rights of Woman*

LIBERALISM LEAVES A LOT OF ROOM for private moral conscience due to its historical association with the need to protect the rights of individual citizens against interventions by government, particularly with regard to religious freedom. In a sense, liberalism clears a legal and political space for the individual moral conscience and assumes that religion will take over from there. And certainly, to a great extent, religion did step in to regulate private life in the seventeenth and eighteenth centuries. The epigraph from Mary Wollstonecraft's *Vindication of the Rights of Woman* (1792) signals the importance of both freedom and faith within the realm of conscience to determine one's beliefs and to set limits on one's conduct.

It is precisely the paradoxical eighteenth-century understanding of moral freedom that leads to the questions addressed in the following three chapters concerning conflicts between private moral conscience and public obligations. I have already indicated briefly in the introduction to this book the complex relationship between social contract theory and Kantian ethics. Here, I would like to examine in more detail the problematic conception of moral freedom that attends these theoretical formulations. Rousseau articulates the paradox of moral freedom best in the *Social Contract* (1762) when he asserts,

> One could add to the preceding things that are acquired in the civil state, *moral freedom*, which alone makes man truly master of himself; for the impulse of appetite alone is slavery and *obedience to self-prescribed law is freedom*.[1] [My emphasis.]

Moral freedom is understood as the ability to set limits, to control one's instincts and appetites, in other words, to live according to law.

Liberalism, and specifically social contract theory, ascribes moral freedom to man and creates a form of civil and political association that allows for both the exercise of that moral freedom and adherence to the law. Rousseau's formulations of the relationship of the individual to the general will in the *Social Contract* highlight the importance of ensuring that living according to the law will not entail a loss of individual freedom. For Rousseau, living according to the dictates of the general will is, in fact, a form of moral freedom, for the individual will blends with the general will to form an agent for communal self-prescribed law. I quote the following lengthy passage in its entirety, for it encapsulates all the important relations between and among citizens and the state that are of concern here:

> From whichever side we trace back to the principle, we always arrive at the same conclusion, namely, that the social pact establishes an equality between the citizens such that they are all mutually engaged under the same conditions, and must enjoy the same rights. Thus, by the nature of the pact, any act of sovereignty, that is to say, any authentic act of the general will, obliges or favors equally all the Citizens, in such a way that the Sovereign only knows the body politic and does not distinguish any who compose it. What then properly speaking is an act of sovereignty? It is not a convention between a superior and an inferior, but a convention of the body politic with each of its members: Legitimate, because it has as its basis the social contract, equitable because it is common to all, useful because it can have no other object than the general good, and solid because it has for guarantee the public force and supreme power. *As long as subjects are submitted only to such conventions, they obey no one, but only their own will.*[2] [My emphasis.]

The initial act of association and subsequent acts of legislation understood as expressions of the general will do not and cannot contradict the individual wills of the citizens. For although the general will may be in conflict with private, particular interests, one's own good as a member of the collective is always ultimately expressed through the general will.[3] In this way, codified public law is intimately linked with the limitations the individual sets on his/her own freedom. In other words, following the law becomes an expression and exercise of the individual's moral freedom in Rousseau.[4]

This understanding of both moral freedom and the individual's relation to the social body and its laws inaugurates the rule of law. When citizens obey the law in this system they demonstrate their respect for their own moral freedom expressed in their willful self-determination. Moral and political freedom are blended to produce a respect for the law that underwrites organized and lawful social behavior by the collective.

In Rousseau's democratic republic, the rule of law rarely conflicts with individuals' interests. Rousseau favors direct democracy and minimal legislation, which both tend to minimize potential conflicts between individual citizens' interests and codified law.[5] By ensuring that citizens are actively involved in all acts of legislation, Rousseau decreases the chances that an individual or group of individuals will feel that their wills are not being expressed through the general will. Thus, the problem of conflicts between private moral conscience and public obligation—which will be the subject of the next three chapters—is not addressed in Rousseau's version of the social contract.[6] Rather, he attempts to set up a system in which these conflicts, ideally, should never arise.

In general, the moral and political theory of the late eighteenth century relies on a conception of the individual that guarantees respect for the law, both private and public. In Rousseau, Wollstonecraft, and Kant, as well as in other theorists, the free, rational, educated individual consults his/her reason, which functions as a private tribunal and judges potential actions.[7] Respect for the law functions as a kind of ultimate principle in this moral system that in turn empowers individuals to reason for themselves. In other words, as we saw in Rousseau above, moral freedom and the law are mutually and reciprocally implicating. One cannot be free without the law, for freedom necessitates "adherence to a self-prescribed law." For Kant, specifically in the *Critique of Practical Reason* (1788), this principle produces a feeling of respect before the moral law as evidence of our moral freedom:

> Thus respect for the law is not the incentive to morality; it is morality itself, regarded subjectively as an incentive, inasmuch as pure practical reason, by rejecting all rival claims of self-love, gives authority and absolute sovereignty to the law.[8]

> Respect for the moral law is therefore the sole and undoubted moral incentive, and this feeling is directed to no being except on this basis.[9]

> The consciousness of free submission of the will to the law, combined with an inevitable constraint imposed only by our own reason on all inclinations, is respect for the law.[10]

The circularity of the system ensures that free, rational individuals respect the law and, in that feeling of respect, find the proof of their own moral freedom. In exercising their moral freedom and choosing to uphold the law, they demonstrate their accountability as rational beings.

Ultimately, the feeling of respect before the moral law functions in Kant, and in Wollstonecraft and Rousseau as well, as a kind of secular faith.[11] While links to God and a kind of rational religious faith are explicit in all three theorists, it is also true that faith in reason itself can support faith in the rule of law. That is to say that while religious faith accompanies and subtends these theories, religious faith is not, strictly speaking, necessary for grounding faith in the individual's rational capacity for self-determination and morally and politically lawful conduct. Belief in the individual's freedom and capacity for reason provide the necessary grounds for faith in the rule of law. The rational being who functions according to the rule of law has a duty to God, but also to him/herself and to the community, to rationally account for his/her behavior. In cases in which the individual is in conflict with the law, the individual owes it to him/herself, God, and the community to give a rational account of his/her behavior. In such a conflict, the individual would have to choose between upholding an unjust law out of respect for the rule of law and respect for the community or breaking the law out of respect for his/her rational, moral sense of obligation. The individual who chooses to disobey the law may even justify such behavior by appealing to a respect for just law.[12] Such a justification for breaking the law—in favor of civil disobedience—would argue that respect for the law does not extend to unjust laws, and that the individual has a duty to him/herself, God, and the community to fight to rectify the law.

In the following three chapters, I examine texts in which the individual's private sense of duty and obligation—or of the spirit of the law—are in conflict with codified public expressions of obligation. Such conflicts, although rarely discussed by either eighteenth- or twentieth-century theorists of liberalism, are endemic to its conception of the inviolability of the individual's moral freedom as foundational for liberalism's political formations.

In chapter 3, I explore the conflicts and contradictions between the individual's sense of justice and the applications of the law raised in Diderot's *Entretien d'un père avec ses enfants*. Diderot's text raises fascinating problems for liberalism that parallel present-day discussions in professional ethics concerning the limits of obligation. In exploring the limits of moral and political obligation in the context of situations that highlight conflicts between individual moral conscience and public duty, Diderot's dialogue also implicitly raises the question of civil disobedience.

In chapters 4 and 5, I turn to the issue of tolerance as an extension of the problem of individual conscience in liberalism. In chapter 4, my discussion of Montesquieu's *De l'Esprit des lois* questions the limits of toleration as official policy within pluralistic democratic societies. Specific analyses of the questions of slavery and polygamy provide a context in which the question of official public policy on toleration intersects with the question of individual moral attitude. In chapter 5, the discussion returns more explicitly to the question of private moral conscience to explore the spectrum of moral attitudes—from tolerance to sympathy—toward "otherness." In this chapter, texts by Voltaire, Rousseau, and Charrière provide a context to question again the limits of moral obligation within liberalism. These texts, considered together, provide a means to examine different ways in which the relation between public obligation and private sense of justice can be configured within liberalism.

Notes

[1] "On pourroit sur ce qui précède ajouter à l'acquis de l'état civil la *liberté morale*, qui seule rend l'homme vraiment maitre de lui; car l'impulsion du seul appetit est esclavage, et *l'obéissance à la loi qu'on s'est prescritte est liberté.*" [My emphasis.] Jean-Jacques Rousseau, *Du contract social* in *Oeuvres complètes*, ed. Bernard Gagnebin and Marcel Raymond, 5 vols. (Paris: Gallimard, 1959–), vol. 3, p. 365. Translations are my own.

[2] "Par quelque côté qu'on remonte au principe, on arrive toujours à la même conclusion; savoir, que le pacte social établit entre les citoyens une telle égalité qu'ils s'engagent tous sous les mêmes conditions, et doivent jouir tous des mêmes droits. Ainsi par la nature du pacte, tout acte de souveraineté, c'est-à-dire tout acte authentique de la volonté générale, oblige ou favorise également tous les Citoyens, ensorte que le Souverain connoit seulement le corps de la nation et ne distingue aucun de ceux qui la composent. Qu'est-ce donc proprement qu'un acte de souverainté? Ce n'est pas une convention du supérieur avec l'inférieur, mais une convention du corps avec chacun de ses membres: Convention légitime, parce qu'elle a pour base le contract social, équitable, parce qu'elle est commune à tous, utile parce qu'elle ne peut avoir d'autre objet que le bien général, et solide parce qu'elle a pour garant la force publique et le pouvoir suprême. *Tant que les sujets ne sont soumis qu'à de telles conventions, ils n'obéissent à personne, mais seulement à leur propre volonté.*" *Du contract social*, in *Oeuvres complètes*, vol. 3, p. 375. [My emphasis.]

[3] For a discussion of potential conflict between particular wills and the general will, see my "Militarisme et vertu chez Rousseau," in *Actes du IIe Colloque International de Montmorency, J.-J. Rousseau: Politique et Nation*, ed. Robert Thiéry (Oxford: Voltaire Foundation, forthcoming).

⁴See Emile Durkheim, *Montesquieu et Rousseau: Précurseurs de la sociologie* (Paris: Marcel Rivière, 1953), pp. 155–57; Ernst Cassirer, *The Question of Jean-Jacques Rousseau*, ed. and trans. Peter Gay, 2d ed. (New Haven, Conn.: Yale University Press, 1989), pp. 55–60; and Allan Bloom, "Rousseau's Critique of Liberal Constitutionalism," in *The Legacy of Rousseau*, ed. Clifford Orwin and Nathan Tarcov (Chicago: University of Chicago Press, 1997), pp. 143–67.

⁵ Rousseau also minimizes potential conflicts by creating a largely homogeneous population with identical interests. See my discussion of this homogenizing tendency in Rousseau, in *Mass Enlightenment: Critical Studies in Rousseau and Diderot* (Albany: State University of New York Press, 1995), chapters 1–2. See also Jan Marejko, *Jean-Jacques Rousseau et la dérive totalitaire* (Lausanne: Editions l'Age d'Homme, 1984); and Judith N. Shklar, *Men and Citizens: A Study of Rousseau's Social Theory* (Cambridge: Cambridge University Press, 1969).

⁶ Montesquieu stands out among eighteenth-century theorists in his analysis of the relation between liberty and power. Simone Goyard-Fabre summarizes Montesquieu's views as follows: "Le vrai problème de la liberté des citoyens est celui de la *limitation du pouvoir*. Puisque aucun Etat est libre par nature, puisque aucun régime politique n'est libérateur par essence, il faut empêcher le pouvoir de se muer en instrument d'oppression. En soi, le pouvoir définit la souveraineté; il n'est, comme tel, ni bon, ni mauvais. Ce qui est mauvais, c'est l'abus du pouvoir." *Montesquieu: la nature, les lois, la liberté* (Paris: Presses Universitaires de France, 1993), p. 171. [The true problem of the freedom of the citizens is that of *the limitation of power*. Since no State is free by nature, since no political regime is liberatory by essence, it is necessary to prevent power from turning into an instrument of oppression. In itself, power defines sovereignty; it is not, in itself, either good or bad. What is bad is the abuse of power.]

⁷ See my discussion of Diderot's article, "Droit naturel," in the conclusion.

⁸ Immanuel Kant, *Critique of Practical Reason*, trans. Lewis White Beck (New York: Macmillan, 1985), pp. 78–79.

⁹ Ibid., p. 81.

¹⁰ Ibid., p. 83.

¹¹ This is not to diminish the importance of religious faith in relation to moral freedom, in Rousseau, Wollstonecraft, or Kant. See my discussion of Rousseau's "Profession of Faith of the Savoyard Vicar," in chapter 2. For a reading of Wollstonecraft that highlights the significance of faith, see Barbara Taylor, "For the Love of God: Religion and the Erotic Imagination in Wollstonecraft's Feminism," in *Mary Wollstonecraft and 200 Years of Feminisms*, ed. Eileen Janes Yeo (London: Rivers Oram Press, 1997), pp. 15–35.

[12] For an example of such a justification for civil disobedience, see Martin Luther King, Jr., *Letter from Birmingham City Jail* (Philadelphia: American Friends Service Committee, 1963).

3: Negotiating the Legal and the Moral: Diderot's *Conversation of a Father with His Children*

> ... [P]ublic affections, as well as public virtues, must ever grow out of the private character, or they are merely meteors that shoot athwart a dark sky, and disappear as they are gazed at and admired.
>
> —Mary Wollstonecraft, *A Vindication of the Rights of Woman*

> Claus, legally, this was an important victory, morally, you're on your own.
>
> —Alan Dershowitz to Claus von Bülow, in *Reversal of Fortune*

IN CHAPTER 2, I argued that the conceptions of negative liberty and negative rights that inform Rousseau's project for educational reform in *Emile* ultimately work against the republican virtues that his political philosophy elsewhere champions. Specifically, I suggested that Emile's moral lesson—involving property rights, contractual obligations, and torts—highlights conflict rather than harmony, only to draw negative boundaries delimiting individual rights and responsibilities in order to adjudicate such conflicts. This lesson and others like it, I contended, would be insufficient to produce a parent capable of undertaking the type of educational program outlined in *Emile* or to produce a responsible citizen of a democratic republic.

Leaving aside temporarily the question of education, the next three chapters, comprising part 2, will focus on conflicts between individual moral conscience and limited, more public, conceptions of obligation. In this chapter I recast the problem of the limits of contractual responsibility in the context of a reading of Diderot's *Conversation of a Father with His Children or The Danger of Setting Oneself above the Law* (1770–72).

This dialogue raises questions concerning apparent conflicts between the legal and moral spheres and between individual conscience and professional ethics. Following Diderot's lead, I again question liberalism's tendency to define moral obligation in contractual and, therefore, negative terms. In effect, I explore the limits of professional ethics as a form of contractual, legal obligation in opposition to privately held moral beliefs.

The Private Sphere of the Family

It is certainly no coincidence that Diderot chooses to raise the question of private moral conscience in conflict with codified law in the context of a family discussion.[1] After all, the traditional seat of moral values, particularly in the liberal tradition, has been the family. Moreover, in the case of Diderot's own family, the choice also encompasses the other equally important site for moral values, the church, in that Diderot's brother was a clergyman and his sister died in a convent. Thus, in his depiction of family conversation in the private, domestic sphere, he is able to invoke the powerful authority of the church as well.

In spite, or perhaps because, of his brother's and sister's affiliations with the church, Diderot depicts his father as the ultimate moral authority in his family, describing him as "a man of excellent judgment, but a pious man."[2] This familial setting with its religious overtones provides the context for raising questions concerning the limits of legal authority and legitimacy in such a way as to downplay the more radical implications of the dialogue. By staging the conversation within the confines of the family, Diderot at least implicitly offers a more traditional solution to the questions he asks, namely, that questions of value be settled within the private sphere of the family. At first glance, he seems to suggest that father really does know best. And yet, this answer seems too simplistic given the complexities of Diderot's text.

To begin our exploration of the relationships between and among the public and private spheres and legality and morality, let us consider the first situation discussed in the dialogue. It involves the father, who acted as executor of the will of the parish priest of Thivet at the behest of the priest's destitute would-be heirs. In the course of carrying out his duties, the father makes an inventory of the deceased's belongings and discovers an old will. This will names an executor, who has been dead for twenty years, and leaves all the priest's belongings to wealthy Paris booksellers. The situation presents the father with a moral and legal dilemma. He describes his dilemma as follows:

> [W]hat to do with this thing? Burn it? Why not? Didn't it bear all the signs of rejection? And the place where I had found it, and the papers it was mixed in with: didn't they testify quite strongly against it, not to mention its revolting injustice? That was what I was saying to myself; and, at the same time representing to myself the misery of those

poor defrauded heirs, their hopes denied, I gently advanced the will toward the fire. Then other thoughts crossed the first: I don't know what kind of fear of making a mistake in deciding such an important case, distrust of my own judgment, the fear of listening more to the voice of commiseration that cried at the bottom of my heart than that of justice, suddenly stopped me; and I spent the rest of the night deliberating over the iniquitous document that I held several times over the flame, uncertain as to whether I would burn it or not.[3]

The situation in which the father finds himself as executor of the curé's estate is a difficult one, for wills are slippery documents when considered from the perspective of the divide between the public and private spheres. In certain respects, wills concern the private sphere: they transfer private property either between generations or between private parties.[4] In this respect, they do not challenge either of the two ways in which the private sphere has been traditionally defined in liberalism. Wills involve private property, thus respecting the public-conceived-as-politics and private-conceived-as-civil-society version of the divide. But wills also remain within the bounds of the conception of the private sphere as the realm of the family because they usually transfer private property between family members.[5] In this case, since the curé obviously has no children to whom he can will his estate, his impoverished parishioners would seem to be the logical legal replacement for his nonexistent children.

But wills are also public documents and, as such, involve the public sphere, for they rely upon the legal sphere of the government for their execution. Executors and judges arbitrate disputes arising over the disposition of goods. Wills are, thus, in a sense, contracts between private parties executed in the public realm by a third party to the contract, the executor, and enforced by the state in much the same way that private financial contracts can become a matter for state adjudication in contract disputes. But in contrast to other economic contracts concerning the transfer of goods and/or property, wills always involve third parties and the legal system—and often involve the state as well because of inheritance taxes—in their execution. The just execution of these contracts depends in part on a social contract that binds citizens to the laws of inheritance in a particular society.

Intersecting these legal concerns and entanglements between the public and private spheres are moral issues that also seem to cross this boundary. As executor of the will, the father is morally bound to perform his duties and follow the exact wording of the will. This ethical constraint is a public one, for it involves his public role as executor. But the father also has private moral obligations as executor. First, he was chosen by the destitute parishioners to serve as executor and thus feels a sense of loyalty and responsibility toward them. By delivering the estate to the Paris booksellers, he seemingly denies this obligation. Second, as executor he keeps a promise—in this case an implicit promise since the executor named in the will has been dead for twenty years—to realize the wishes of the deceased. And third, he is also bound by his own private morality, which judges this will to be unjust, both because of the context in which he found it—among other papers that seem to have been thrown away—and because of his sense of the injustice of giving the estate to the wealthy booksellers rather than to the destitute parishioners.

In the end, the father decides to execute the will he found and deliver the estate into the hands of the wealthy Paris booksellers. He does so after consulting with a priest, who pronounces definitively that, "No one is permitted to infringe the law, to enter into the thoughts of the dead and to dispose of the goods of another."[6] Favoring public legal obligations over private moral obligations, the father, in executing the will, defines the role of executor in a strictly public way: by upholding his legal contractual obligations. He offers no interpretation of the setting in which he found the will, nor does he choose to impose his own judgment and suppress the will in accordance with his own private sense of justice. Public legality thus supersedes private morality.

Legal Obligations

As I have already suggested concerning the private sphere as defined in liberal theory, the legal realm also presents certain difficulties in the attempt to place it on one side or the other of the public sphere/state divide. According to the versions of liberalism that define the public sphere as the realm of civil society in opposition to the state, the legal realm represents an aspect of society that straddles this division.[7] The judicial system is clearly a branch of the government and, as such, represents an arm of the state. But, as I have already indicated, the judicial system functions somewhat independently of the state and, more importantly in the case at hand, serves to regulate disputes arising between private parties concerning the disposition of private property. In this role, the legal sphere partakes of civil society in a manner quasi-independent of the state, and thus it represents an aspect of the public sphere.

Further complicating the issue of this distinction between the public sphere and the state is the division between the public and private spheres. As I indicated earlier, wills straddle the traditional definitions established for the public and private spheres as well as for the state and civil society. For my purposes here, I maintain that in the case of wills, and particularly in the context of eighteenth-century French society, we are dealing with the bourgeois public sphere insofar as wills control the disposition of private property. More than other concerns, the issue of private property and, specifically, the protection of it from state inter-ference define the public sphere in the Enlightenment context. For, as Habermas argues, it is precisely the protection of private property that motivates the creation of a public sphere independent of the state dur-ing the eighteenth century:

> The social precondition for this "developed" bourgeois public sphere was a market that, tending to be liberalized, made affairs in the sphere of social reproduction as much as possible a matter of private people left to themselves and so finally completed the privatization of civil so-ciety.[8]

Insofar as the executor acts independently of the state in order to en-force the wishes of the deceased, wills represent an example of con-tractual obligations between private citizens characteristic of the bourgeois public sphere. In Habermas's terms, it is an instance of social reproduction liberated from the constraints of the state due in part to laissez-faire attitudes borrowed from the concept of the free market and applied to private contracts.[9]

Yet, insofar as executing a will raises ethical questions concerning the precise duties and obligations entailed, it points to an interesting problem area in Habermas's theory of the public sphere. If the creation of the public sphere entails the "privatization of civil society," to use Habermas's phrase, it still does not indicate where the boundary be-tween the public and private spheres lies. Since conflicts may arise be-tween the public and private spheres, as the case of the will demonstrates, it remains to be seen how such conflicts may be resolved. Is the state our only recourse in such cases of conflict? It seems ironic that matters pertaining to private property and the family should need to be adjudicated by the very authority, namely the state, whose authority the public and private spheres seek to guard against.[10] And yet even the father's choice points in the direction of the state.

The father's course of action—to adhere strictly to the letter of the law—suggests one possible solution to the dilemma. This solution re-lies on legal definitions and a strict separation between one's public re-sponsibility and one's private sense of justice. In effect, it borrows from the state—without directly invoking its authority—in order to regulate a dispute in the public and/or private sphere. It parallels another example, raised in the dialogue, of a physician who is asked if he would treat a renowned scoundrel. Dr. Bissei replies unequivocally, "My business is to heal him, not to judge him; I will heal him, because it's my profession; afterwards the magistrate will have him hanged, because that's his."[11] The parallel between the two cases suggests that the executor of the will might use the same logic as the physician and maintain a strict separation between professional, that is, public, responsibility and private morality. The use of such an argument demonstrates what Weber characterized as part of the progressive rationalization of Western culture. Specifically, the use of impersonal and formal categories to decide questions of value indicates the degree of rationalization in the realm of science in the case of the doctor and in the domain of law and morality in the case of the executor of the will.

According to Weber's theory of rationalization, the progressive differentiation and formalization of spheres coincides with the rise of experts in these fields.[12] Thus, the doctor—an expert in the domain of science—uses formal and impersonal rationality to solve problems relating to value. In this case, it enables him to treat the criminal as a patient in need of healing like any other, so the doctor is able to suspend his moral judgment in order to administer proper care. Rationality in the realm of science also enables the doctor not to hold himself morally accountable for saving the criminal's life. As he says, it is not his business to judge the patient. Thus, the doctor's status as expert clearly defines the parameters of his professional and thus moral responsibilities.

Returning to the case of the executor, and the solution to the dilemma offered by Diderot's father, he too uses the impersonal and formal obligations of the legal realm to define his moral responsibilities. Setting aside his own personal sense of justice, he carries out his duties according to an ethical code that replaces private morality with public legality in the form of rationalized social relations. In this respect he typifies bureaucracic authority as Weber described it:

> I. There is the principle of fixed and official jurisdictional areas, which are generally ordered by rules, that is, by laws or administrative regulations.

> 1. The regular activities required for the purposes of the bureaucratically governed structure are distributed in a fixed way as official duties.

> 2. The authority to give the commands required for the discharge of these duties is distributed in a stable way and is strictly delimited by rules concerning the coercive means, physical, sacerdotal, or otherwise, which may be placed at the disposal of officials.

3. Methodical provision is made for the regular and continuous fulfil-
ment of these duties and for the execution of the corresponding
rights; only persons who have generally regulated qualifications to
serve are employed.[13]

Although not all aspects of Weber's description are represented in Diderot's dialogue, and certainly many are problematized in the narrative
of the father serving as executor of the will, the father's decision to adhere to the letter of the law in his duties resembles the methodical, official, and above all rule-abiding tendencies of bureaucratic authority.
Granted, the father's authority is undermined precisely because the will
he executes does not name him as executor, but this circumstance provides an even greater incentive to discharge his duties according to the
structure provided. Because his "jurisdictional area" has not been officially established, he is all the more compelled to interpret his duties as
narrowly as possible and adhere strictly to those duties in executing the
will.

Even the priest who counsels him falls back on the logic of the strict
separation of spheres and the legal accountability imposed by the contract entailed in serving as executor of the will. The priest insists that
the executor's responsibility is to carry out and *not* to interpret the desires expressed in the will. In his insistence, he emphasizes the narrow-
est possible interpretation of the father's moral/legal responsibilities:

Father Bouin added, "And who authorized you to remove or give
sanction to documents? Who authorized you to interpret the intentions of the deceased? —But, Father Bouin, what about the box? —
Who authorized you to decide if this will had been rejected
deliberately, or if it was misplaced in error? . . . —But, Father Bouin,
the date and the inquity of the paper? —Who authorized you to
pronounce on the justice or injustice of this act, and to regard the
bequest more as an illicit gift rather than as a restitution or some such
other legitimate deed that you might imagine? —But, Father Bouin,
these immediate and impoverished heirs and this distant and rich
collateral? —Who authorized you to weigh what the deceased owed to
his close relatives, whom you don't know any better?[14]

Consistent with Weber's account of bureaucratic authority, even the
priest recommends suspending one's own sense of justice and carrying
out orders without interpreting them. The executor, according to this
account, is authorized only to execute the wishes expressed in the
written document.

In this respect, Diderot's representation of religion in the dialogue—both in the figure of the priest whom his father consulted and
in the arguments put forth by his brother—places religion on the side

of professional, formalizable ethical systems against the private morality of the individual conscience. Choosing to abide by the letter of the law as opposed to its spirit, these church officials ignore Pauline teachings in favor of a bureaucratic sense of right and wrong.[15]

And yet, Diderot's dialogue suggests that there might be a difference between behavior that is legal and behavior that is moral (see my epigraph quoting from Alan Dershowitz to Claus von Bülow). In raising the dilemmas of both the father as executor of the will and the physician treating the criminal, the dialogue highlights situations in which legal and moral systems are potentially at odds with one another. In particular, these situations are marked by a tension between professional ethics and private morality. In a historical period that gave rise to professional ethics due to increased rationalization, Diderot's dialogue pinpoints the relationship between the rise of the public sphere and the extension of formalizable principles into social relations.

Private Moral Conscience

One may well ask: "How can you advocate breaking some laws and obeying others?" The answer lies in the fact that there are two types of laws: just and unjust. I would be the first to advocate obeying just laws. One has not only a legal but a moral responsibility to obey just laws. Conversely, one has a moral responsibility to disobey unjust laws. I would agree with St. Augustine that "an unjust law is no law at all."

–Martin Luther King, Jr., *Letter from Birmingham Jail*

Not surprisingly, one finds in Diderot's representation of himself in the dialogue the voice of the individual conscience who maintains the authority to judge the legitimacy of particular laws and, therefore, whether or not to abide by them. Against the arguments of his father, his brother, and at times his sister, he asserts the primacy of the individual moral conscience against the authority of professional ethics or laws. In an argument characteristic of eighteenth-century conceptions of legitimacy derived from natural law, the Diderot character in the dialogue equates legitimate laws with moral right:[16]

Nature made good laws from time immemorial; it is a legitimate force that assures their execution; and that force, which can do anything against the wicked, can do nothing to harm the good man. I am that good man; and in these circumstances and in many others that I could detail to you, I summon that force to the tribunal of my heart, of my reason, of my conscience, to the tribunal of natural equity; I question it, I submit myself to it or I annul it.[17]

Sounding a great deal like the social contract theorists, Diderot grounds the legitimacy of conventional law in a conception of natural law. In upholding the right of individuals to question the legitimacy of particular laws, he goes further than most social contractarians in maintaining the right of individuals to nullify laws that they feel are unjust. This position is roughly consistent with provisions in social contract theory for dissolving the government,[18] but, more importantly, essential for the type of critical political thinking that eventually led to the French revolution.

With respect to the issues that I am raising here, it is significant that Diderot's argument in favor of individual conscience relies on a certain type of *reason* to adjudicate the dispute between private morality and public legality. But unlike the arguments in favor of professional ethics and the separation of spheres, in which the phenomenon of rationalization establishes ethical systems that cannot be called into question, in Diderot's argument in favor of private conscience, reason is allowed to question all the premises. In other words, there are no first principles that do not undergo some type of rational scrutiny. In an ethical extension of skepticism, the Diderot character advocates reasonably questioning the legitimacy of all laws and all ethical systems, which are ostensibly manifestations of reason itself.

The representation of Diderot's position in the dialogue echoes the Polly Baker story reproduced in Diderot's *Supplement to Bougainville's "Voyage."*[19] Significantly for the questions raised here in the *Conversation of a Father with His Children*, this story also questions the legitimacy of laws on issues pertaining to family life, and it sides unequivocally with the right of the individual. The story involves a young woman who is brought before a court in colonial Connecticut for the fifth time on charges of being pregnant outside of wedlock. Her speech to the magistrates, which Diderot "includes" in his text, stresses the illegitimacy of the law she has infringed:

> This is the fifth time, gentlemen, that I appear before you on the same charge; twice I paid onerous fines, twice I endured public and shameful punishment because I was not in a position to pay. That may be in conformity with the law, I do not contest it, but sometimes there are unjust laws, and they are abrogated; there are also some that are too severe, and the legislative power can waive their execution. I dare say that the one that condemns me is both unjust in itself and too severe with regard to me.[20]

The magistrates side with Polly: "her judges remitted her fine," and moreover her seducer makes "an honest woman of the one whom five years before he had made a whore." [21] In this case, the individual conscience speaks against the unjust law and the magistrates listen. Even the moral wrong committed by her seducer is righted. Although a fairy-tale ending, it nonetheless succinctly and forcefully asserts the right of the individual to question unjust laws, by representing a state apparatus capable of recognizing and avoiding potential injustice through a careful exercise of judicial authority.

The case of the executor of the will raises these same issues concerning the right of the individual to question legal obligations, yet without the benefit of an appearance before a tribunal. Only if the father had chosen not to execute the will as written, and the Paris booksellers subsequently initiated legal action, would a judge have had the opportunity to decide on this question.[22] By representing a situation which does not necessarily involve judicial authority, Diderot makes the central dilemma of the dialogue—the father's conflict between legal obligations and moral duties—a question that remains within the confines of the individual moral conscience.

In response to his father's decision on the will, Diderot firmly asserts that it was the only mistake his father ever made. "I would have burned that act of iniquity. It was necessary to burn it, I tell you; it was necessary to listen to your heart, which has not ceased to protest since."[23] Clearly, according to Diderot, the duty of private moral obligation to one's own principles outweighs the duty to execute a public contract or stay within the bounds of the law. Consistent with the outcome of the Polly Baker story, this position asserts the right of the individual to break an unjust law. Precursory to civil disobedience, Diderot's position invokes private moral standards based on natural law ("I summon that force . . . before the tribunal of natural equity")[24] against the illegitimacy of bad laws.

Public Legality and Private Morality

One who breaks an unjust law must do so openly, lovingly, and with a willingness to accept the penalty. I submit that an individual who breaks a law that conscience tells him is unjust, and who willingly accepts the penalty of imprisonment in order to arouse the conscience of the community over its injustice, is in reality expressing the highest respect for the law.

—Martin Luther King, Jr., *Letter from Birmingham Jail*

Against the arguments in favor of individual moral conscience, Diderot the author poses equally strong counterarguments. In response to the Diderot character's assertions, his father and brother point to the necessity of acting as a public person. The father states, "Your reasons, as private, were perhaps good; but as public, they would be bad."[25] Invoking an almost Kantian meta-ethic, they argue that abiding strictly to the law is a universalizable principle, whereas infringing it, leads to chaos. Specifically, in the case of public duties and responsibilities, obedience to the law must take precedence over other concerns. The brother argues,

> Judges hold strictly to the law, like my father and Father Bouin, and do well. Judges close their eyes, in such cases, to circumstances, like my father and Father Bouin, for fear of the difficulties that would follow, and they do well. Sometimes, against the testimony of their own conscience, they sacrifice, like my father and Father Bouin, the interest of the unfortunate and the innocent that they couldn't save without letting go the reins on an infinite number of scoundrels, and they do well. They fear, like my father and Father Bouin, passing a judgment equitable in the specific case, but disastrous in a thousand others for the multitude of disorders to which it would open the door, and they do well.[26]

This argument curtailing judicial authority asserts, among other things, that application of the law to particular cases is unproblematic, which means, that it is not a matter requiring interpretation. In a manner characteristic of bureaucratic authority and professional ethics, it maintains as its highest good the orderly conduct of society according to codified law. Such a position cannot allow for an outcome like the one in the Polly Baker story, for all infractions of the law must be punished. Ultimately, such a position makes of the judiciary merely an enforcement arm of the legislature.

Significantly, this position clearly begs the question of interpretation. Although the case of the will provides circumstances in which the father can either choose to interpret the setting in which he found the will or not to interpret the setting, not all legal conflicts entail a neat opposition between interpretation and noninterpretation. Many such disputes indeed involve interpretation by both parties.

Furthermore, arguing against this position, the Diderot character asserts that there is a difference between being an executor and being a lawyer: "[b]ut think that you were not a man of law, and that released from all judicial procedure, the only functions that you had to fulfill were those of goodwill and natural equity."[27] According to this position, even if judges are bound to uphold the law without interpreting it, as part of their role as a regulatory social institution, it is not clear that private citizens, even serving in a quasi-public capacity, ought to be bound by the same constraints. Not being a part of the legal system enables the individual to invoke a sense of justice and morality here founded on natural law. Precisely because he is a private citizen, the Diderot character maintains that his father is authorized to question the legitimacy of the law.

If the ban on interpretation by either the courts or individual citizens seems overstated, the more Kantian arguments invoking adherence to the law as the highest social good warn of the "danger of setting oneself above the law," the dialogue's subtitle.[28] Taking the two ethical principles in conflict—abiding by the law in all situations and questioning the legitimacy of laws—and applying a universalizability principle to them, the father and brother maintain that to abrogate the law is to "let go the reins on an infinite number of scoundrels."[29] As I indicated above, this Kantian meta-ethic favors obedience over moral and legal skepticism leading to disobedience.

In further defense of this position, the father and brother develop a line of argument that invokes the dangers of allowing individuals to take the law into their own hands. Using examples of people acting on their own authority to right wrongs, they demonstrate the terrifying side of vigilante justice. In one example, a cobbler from Messina, tired of witnessing crimes going untried and/or unpunished, "established a court of justice in his shop."[30] Acting on his own authority,

> Hearing of some atrocious crime, he researched it, he conducted for himself a rigorous and secret investigation. His double function of reporter and judge fulfilled, the criminal trial concluded, and the sentence passed, he would go out with a harquebus under his coat; . . . he equitably discharged five or six bullets through their bodies.[31]

While Diderot's brother, the abbé, condemns the man as "nothing but a murderer,"[32] even the Diderot character recognizes the tale as a trap. Asked how he would judge such a man, he replies, "Abbé, you are laying a trap for me and I happily fall in it. I will condemn the viceroy to take the place of the cobbler, and the cobbler to take the place of the viceroy."[33] Seemingly acknowledging that private citizens ought not to take the law into their own hands, he also recognizes the difficulty of justifying his own position regarding private moral conscience while at the same time condemning vigilantism.

Clearly, questioning the legitimacy of laws has some limits, for without them the Diderot character could not make such a distinction.

Perhaps the distinction rests on whether one is acting as a public person or as a private one. But, in that case, we still do not have a solution to the dilemma of the will, because the status of the executor partakes of both. Either the executor acts according to "good will and natural equity" as a private citizen, or he narrowly interprets and strictly adheres to the letter of the law as a public person.

Most important for the questions that I raise here is the fact that, in Diderot's representation, the argument in favor of the authority of the private citizen is made by Diderot the *philosophe*, and the argument in favor of limits on the authority of the public person is made by the two representatives of the private sphere: the father and the brother. Ironically, it is the representatives of the church and the family who argue in favor of bureaucratic authority in imitation of the state. This representation allows the argument in favor of individual moral conscience to be made without the traditional appeals to the family or the church as sites of moral value. Rather, it seems to invoke a conception of the private citizen taking responsibility for the law in a critical manner.

The formal aesthetic of the dialogue also pushes in favor of the Diderot character's position, against the arguments in favor of always abiding by the law. The dialogue form requires an active reading practice that is able to bear all arguments in mind. In a sense, the dialogue form invites participation in the conversation and encourages the reader to agree or disagree with the characters in the dialogue. Moreover, the various interruptions within the dialogue create a formal structure in which parallels are implicitly made. As the dialogue is interrupted by a series of visitors, the examples multiply. Each story varies to some degree from the previous one, creating a structure of analogies. Overall, this formal aesthetic places a large amount of responsibility on the reader, who must sort through, compare, and contrast the various cases and examples.

The active reading practice is fully consistent with Diderot's desire for an active reader of the *Encyclopédie*, someone who will be able to create his/her own *renvois* between articles.[34] And, as I have argued elsewhere, it typifies Diderot's materialist hermeneutics.[35] In the case of the *Conversation of a Father with His Children*, the necessity for active interpretation on the part of the reader tips the scales in favor of the Diderot character's position: it requires personal responsibility on the part of the reader.

In addition to the active reading practice that the dialogue sets in motion, the paralogical structure resembles case law as opposed to codified law. Insofar as the reader compares and contrasts, for example, the father's position when facing the dilemma of the will and the doctor's position when curing a scoundrel, the reader becomes a judge. The reader's job is to sort out the relevant facts and to rule based on analogy. This process, again, is active and speaks in favor of interpretation and a more fluid conception of law than the codified forms of law—related to professional ethics—that are discussed in the dialogue. In other words, the case law model which the dialogue structure imitates, reintroduces the question of interpretation in matters of law against the notion that law represents an unproblematic application of a general rule to a specific case.

Thus, the aesthetic of the dialogue, argues in favor of the duty of the individual moral conscience to question the application of the law. Within the body of the dialogue, it is not altogether clear that the Diderot character presents the strongest arguments. Reading the aesthetic of the dialogue as an additional facet of the argument, it would seem that the strongest case is made for individual moral responsibility.

The final exchange of the dialogue returns to a cautionary mode concerning the right to disobey unjust laws, and it echoes similar lines in the *Supplement to Bougainville's "Voyage"*:

> When it was my turn to wish him a good night, kissing him, I said in his ear, My father, in the end there are no laws for the wise man. — Speak more softly. —All being subject to exceptions, it is his duty to judge the cases where it is necessary to submit oneself or to break free from them. —I would not be too angry, he responded to me, if there were one or two citizens like you in the town; but I wouldn't live there if they all thought like you."[36]

The father's remarks suggest that even critical reason has its limits and that lawfulness is a good in itself. Earlier in the dialogue, the father points to the restlessness that accompanies his son's position: "My son, my son, reason is a good pillow, but I find my head rests even more peacefully on that of religion and law, and no retort on that, because I don't need insomnia."[37] Opting for the peace of mind that abiding by the law can offer, instead of the constant turmoil of critical reflection and self-doubt, the father's comments also point to the social stability that professional ethics and legality provide.

Laws and professional ethics keep the fabric of society together by providing norms for behavior, by establishing a sort of public accountability. But the Diderot character could always counter, in Habermasian fashion, that such norms, in order to be truly legitimate, must be put to the challenge of reason in open critical debate. Such laws and norms do indeed provide legal and moral accountability, but if they cannot be challenged, they run the risk of perpetuating injustice. Legal and moral accountability are only desirable with respect to just laws. Bureaucratic authority represents a limited form of responsibility bounded by contractual relations. If the grounds of these relations go unchallenged, then the legal system cannot be just. Returning to the rhetoric of social contract theory, when the government "becomes incompatible with the public good,"[38] or "the legislators endeavor to take away and destroy the property of the people, or to reduce them to slavery under arbitrary power, they put themselves into a state of war with the people who are thereupon absolved from any further obedience."[39] Although the case at hand hardly represents an example of government incompatible with the public good or legislators taking away and destroying private property, recognizing these events when they occur requires the exercise of reason. In short, the social contract depends on the exercise of reason to determine the public good and ensure that it is pursued and protected.

Such a conception of the duties of the citizen is not incompatible with bureaucratic authority, but it does point to the limits of contractual understandings of responsibility. My reading of Diderot's *Conversation of a Father with His Children* has highlighted some problem areas concerning the boundaries between the state and the public and private spheres, and specifically the difficulty of adjudicating disputes that arise at the boundaries of these spheres. Citizens of a liberal democratic state have a responsibility to question the legitimacy of laws, but this responsibility must be balanced against the danger of dissolving the social fabric through civil disobedience and lawlessness.

At the risk of invoking a transcendental subject, I finally ask how we reconcile our own deeply held moral beliefs with rational ethical systems that do not always seem legitimate. Without recourse to the family or the church—which Diderot's dialogue guards against—or natural law doctrine, might it be possible to ground private moral conscience as a safeguard against the tyranny of the bureaucratic zeal of strict adherence to the law?

In the chapters 4 and 5, I turn to the problem of tolerance as another exemplary situation in which private moral conscience finds itself in conflict with public obligations. Having just seen a defense, in Diderot's dialogue, of the duty to uphold the private, moral conscience against what I have characterized as zealous adherence to the letter of the law, we find that the case of tolerance turns the tables. Because the private moral conscience in matters concerning tolerance usually corresponds to the intolerant person, in these cases I argue in favor of public obligations. In other words, whereas in Diderot's text, private moral conscience represented the side of greater moral obligation, in matters of tolerance, the side of moral conscience usually involves the condemnation of behaviors regarded as different and morally unacceptable. In these cases, the side of public obligation holds individuals to moral standards appropriate for the community.

In chapter 4, I consider tolerance pursued as a state policy and examine weak and strong versions of tolerance in Montesquieu's *De l'Esprit des lois*. Chapter 5 moves the discussion of tolerance back toward the private realm of individual conscience to consider representations of sympathy alongside more formal defenses of tolerance. These two chapters echo the themes of the discussion of Diderot's dialogue, moving between private morality and public legality.

Notes

[1] I am indebted to Suzanne Pucci for very insightful comments on this point.

[2] "[H]omme d'un excellent jugement, mais homme pieux" (465). All parenthetical references to this work in the notes to chapter 3 are to Denis Diderot, *Entretien d'un père avec ses enfants*, in *Oeuvres complètes*, ed. Herbert Dieckmann, Jacques Proust, Jean Varloot, et. al., 25 vols. (Paris: Hermann, 1975–, vol. 12, pp. 465–96), and cite the volume number followed by the page number. Translations are my own.

[3] "[Q]ue faire de cette pièce? La brûler? pourquoi non? N'avait-elle pas tous les caractères de la réprobation? et l'endroit où je l'avait trouvée, et les papiers avec lesquels elle était confondue et assimilée, ne déposaient-ils pas assez fortement contre elle, sans parler de son injustice révoltante? Voilà ce que je me disais en moi-même: et me représentant en même temps la désolation de ces malheureux héritiers spoliés, frustrés de leur espérance, j'approchais tout doucement le testament du feu; puis d'autres idées croisaient les premières, je ne sais quelle frayeur de me tromper dans la décision d'un cas aussi important, la méfiance de mes lumières, la crainte d'écouter plutôt la voix de la commisération, qui criait au fond de mon coeur, que celle de la justice, m'arrêtaient subitement; et je passai le reste de la nuit à délibérer sur cet acte inique que je tins plusieurs fois au-dessus de la flamme, incertain si je le brûlerais ou non" (12:468).

[4] Rights of inheritance were normally included in seventeenth- and eighteenth-century conceptions of natural law. See C. B. Macpherson, "Natural Rights in Hobbes and Locke," *Political Theory and the Rights of Man*, ed. D. D. Raphael (Bloomington: Indiana University Press, 1967), p. 6.

[5] Feminist critics of liberalism have paid much attention to drawing the boundary between the public and private spheres. See Susan Moller Okin, "Humanist Liberalism," in *Liberalism and the Moral Life*, ed. Nancy L. Rosenblum (Cambridge: Harvard University Press, 1989), pp. 39–53.

[6] "[I]l n'est permis à personne d'enfreindre les lois, d'entrer dans la pensée des morts et de disposer du bien d'autrui" (12:475).

[7] See Jürgen Habermas, *The Theory of Communicative Action*, vol. 2, trans. Thomas McCarthy (Boston: Beacon Press, 1987, pp. 309–10); and Jürgen Habermas, *Between Facts and Norms: Contributions to a Discourse Theory of Law and Democracy*, trans. William Rehg (Cambridge: MIT Press, 1996).

[8] Jürgen Habermas, *The Structural Transformation of the Public Sphere: An Inquiry into a Category of Bourgeois Society*, trans. Thomas Burger with the assistance of Frederick Lawrence (Cambridge: MIT Press, 1992), p. 74.

[9] The state clearly has an interest in overseeing even uncontested wills since inheritance taxes continue to be a source of revenue. Thus, even these uncontested private contracts require state authorization through the court system.

[10] Feminist critiques of liberalism have pointed in this direction. Susan Okin asserts, in "Humanist Liberalism," that "the liberal state *has* regulated and controlled the family, in innumerable ways, and in such ways as to reinforce patriarchy," (p. 42). I will return to these questions in part 3, chapters 6 and 7.

[11] "Mon affaire est de le guérir, non de le juger; je le guérirai, parce que c'est mon métier; ensuite le magistrat le fera pendre, parce que c'est le sien" (12:469).

[12] See Max Weber, "Science as a Vocation," in *From Max Weber: Essays in Sociology*, trans. H. H. Gerth and C. Wright Mills (New York: Oxford University Press, 1958). See also Jürgen Habermas, "Modernity: An Unfinished Project," in *Critical Theory: The Essential Readings*, ed. David Ingram and Julia Simon-Ingram (New York: Paragon House, 1991).

[13] Weber, "Bureaucracy," in *From Max Weber: Essays in Sociology*, p. 196.

[14] "Le père Bouin ajouta: 'Et qui est-ce qui vous a autorisé à ôter ou à donner de la sanction aux actes? Qui est-ce qui vous a autorisé à interpréter les intentions des morts? —Mais, père Bouin, et le coffre? —Qui est-ce qui vous a autorisé à décider si ce testament a été rébuté de réflexion, ou s'il s'est égaré par méprise? . . . —Mais, père Bouin, et la date et l'iniquité de ce papier? —Qui est-ce qui vous a autorisé à prononcer sur la justice ou l'injustice de cet acte, et à regarder le legs universel comme un don illicite, plutôt que comme une restitution ou telle autre oeuvre légitime qu'il vous plaira d'imaginer? —Mais, père Bouin, et ces héritiers immédiats et pauvres, et ce collatéral éloigné et riche? —Qui est-ce qui vous a autorisé à peser ce que le défunt devait à ses proches, que vous ne connaissez pas davantage?" (12:474–75).

[15] This representation of religion in the dialogue suggests a critique of organized Christian religion as opposed to a critique of Christian doctrine per se. Diderot's text seems to make indirect reference to Paul's *Letter to the Romans*, and *Letters to the Corinthians*.

[16]This position is consistent with Diderot's article for the *Encyclopédie*, "Droit naturel," in which he defends a conception of natural law founded on the human capacity for reason. Diderot, *Oeuvres complètes*, vol. 7, pp. 24–30. See my discussion of this article in the conclusion.

[17] "La nature a fait les bonnes lois de toute éternité; c'est une force légitime qui en assure l'exécution, et cette force qui peut tout contre le méchant ne peut rien contre l'homme de bien. Je suis cet homme de bien, et dans ces circonstances et beaucoup d'autres que je vous détaillerais, je la cite au tribunal de mon coeur, de ma raison, de ma conscience, au tribunal de l'équité naturelle; je l'interroge, je m'y soumets et je l'annule" (12:484).

[18]Cf. John Locke, *The Second Treatise of Government*, ed. Thomas P. Peardon (Indianapolis: Bobbs-Merrill, 1952), pp. 119–39; and Jean-Jacques Rousseau, *Du contract social*, in *Oeuvres complètes*, ed. Bernard Gagnebin and Marcel Raymond, 5 vols. (Paris: Gallimard, 1959–), vol. 3, pp. 421–23.

[19]According to P. N. Furbank, in Denis Diderot, *This Is Not a Story and Other Stories*, trans. P. N. Furbank (Columbia: University of Missouri Press, 1991), the story originally appeared in the *London Magazine* in April 1747, authored by Benjamin Franklin.

[20] "Voici la cinquième fois, Messieurs, que je parais devant vous pour le même sujet; deux fois j'ai payé des amendes onéreuses, deux fois j'ai subi une punition publique et honteuse parce que je n'ai pas été en état de payer. Cela peut être conforme à la loi, je ne le conteste point; mais il y a quelquefois des lois injustes, et on les abroge; il y en a aussi de trop sévères, et la puissance législatrice peut dispenser de leur exécution. J'ose dire que celle qui me condamne est à la fois injuste en elle-même et trop sévère envers moi." Denis Diderot, *Supplément au "Voyage" de Bougainville* in his *Oeuvres complètes*, vol. 12, pp. 614–15.

[21] "[S]es juges lui remirent l'amende," and, "une honnête femme de celle dont cinq ans auparavant il avait fait une fille publique." Ibid., vol. 12, p. 616.

[22] The text speculates about the outcome of such a suit, if one had been brought. Although the Diderot character at first asserts that the magistrates would have sided with justice, he capitulates to the position of his brother and father, that the judges would have been constrained by law to uphold the will.

[23] "J'aurais brûlé cet acte d'iniquité. Il fallait le brûler, vous dis-je, il fallait écouter votre coeur, qui n'a cessé de réclamé depuis" (12:486–87).

[24] "[J]e la cite . . . au tribunal de l'équité naturelle" (12:484).

[25] "Tes raisons, comme particulières étaient peut-être bonnes, mais comme publiques, elles seraient mauvaises" (12:489).

[26] "Les juges s'en tiennent strictement à la loi, comme mon père et le père Bouin, et font bien. Les juges ferment, en pareil cas, les yeux sur les circon-

stances, comme mon père et le père Bouin, par l'effroi des inconvénients qui s'ensuivraient, et font bien. Ils sacrifient quelquefois contre le témoignage même de leur conscience, comme mon père et le père Bouin, l'intérêt du malheureux et de l'innocent qu'ils ne pourraient sauver sans lâcher la bride à une infinité de fripons, et font bien. Ils redoutent, comme mon père et le père Bouin, de prononcer un arrêt équitable dans un cas déterminé, mais funeste dans mille autres par la multitude de désordres auxquels il ouvrirait la porte, et font bien" (12:488).

[27] "[M]ais songez que vous n'étiez point l'homme de la loi, et qu'affranchi de toute forme juridique, vous n'aviez de fonctions à remplir que celles de la bienfaisance et de l'équité naturelle" (12:487).

[28] "[D]anger de se mettre au-dessus des lois."

[29] "[L]âcher la bride à une infinité de fripons" (12:488).

[30] "[E]tablit une cour de justice dans sa boutique" (12:492).

[31] "Au bruit de quelque délit atroce, il en informait, il en poursuivait chez lui une instruction rigoureuse et secrète. Sa double fonction de rapporteur et de juge remplie, le procès criminel parachevé et la sentence prononcée, il sortait avec une arquebuse sous son manteau; . . . il vous leur déchargeait équitablement cinq ou six balles à travers le corps" (12:492).

[32] "[C]et homme n'était qu'un meurtrier" (12:493).

[33] "L'abbé, vous me tendez un piège et je veux bien y donner. Je condamnerai le vice-roi à prendre la place du savetier, et le savetier à prendre la place du vice-roi" (12:493).

[34] See Denis Diderot, "Encyclopédie," in Oeuvres complètes, vol. 7, pp. 221–23.

[35] See my Mass Enlightenment (Albany: State University of New York Press, 1995), pp. 103–22. For other discussions of the active reading practice that is urged by Diderot's style, see Wilda Anderson, Diderot's Dream (Baltimore: Johns Hopkins University Press, 1990), pp. 42–76; Jacques Proust, "Diderot et le système des connaissances humaines," Studies on Voltaire and the Eighteenth Century 256 (1988), pp. 117–27; Georges Benrekassa, "La Pratique philosophique de Diderot dans l'article 'Encyclopédie,'" Stanford French Review 8, nos. 2–3 (fall 1984), pp. 189–212; and Pierre Saint-Amand, Diderot Le Labyrinthe de la relation (Paris: Vrin, 1984), pp. 24–49, 68–82.

[36] "Lorsque ce fut à mon tour de lui souhaiter la bonne nuit, en l'embrassant je lui dis à l'oreille: Mon père, c'est qu'à la rigueur il n'y a point de lois pour le sage. —Parlez plus bas. —Toutes étant sujettes à des exceptions, c'est à lui qu'il appartient de juger des cas où il faut s'y soumettre ou s'en affranchir. — Je ne serais pas trop fâché, me répondit-il, qu'il y eût dans la ville un ou deux citoyens comme toi; mais je n'y habiterais pas s'ils pensaient tous de même" (12:495).

[37] "Mon fils, mon fils, c'est un bon oreiller que celui de la raison, mais je trouve que ma tête repose plus doucement encore sur celui de la religion et des lois, et point de réplique là-dessus, car je n'ai pas besoin d'insomnie" (12:489).

[38] "[D]evient incompatible avec le bien public," Rousseau, *Du contract social*, in his *Oeuvres complètes*, vol. 3, p. 435.

[39] Locke, *The Second Treatise of Government*, p. 124.

4: Value Neutrality and the Virtue of Tolerance: Montesquieu's Contribution to Liberalism

Here I am, proud as Greek god, and yet standing debtor to this blockhead for a bone to stand on! Cursed be that moral inter-indebtedness which will not do away with ledgers. I would be free as air; and I'm down in the whole world's books.

—Herman Melville, *Moby Dick*

TOLERATION REMAINS one of the most significant contributions of the liberal political tradition in the realm of ethics. Born out of the religious wars and persecutions of the sixteenth and seventeenth centuries, which continued throughout the eighteenth century, the desire to theorize toleration and pursue it as an official state policy is evident in the major thinkers of liberalism, among them Locke, Voltaire, and Montesquieu, to name only the best known. Whether defending the rights of Huguenots, Quakers, Presbyterians, or Jews, the liberal tradition, following Locke, asserted the right of individual conscience in personal matters against the interference and persecutions of the state.

But the scope of the question of tolerance has been enlarged considerably over the last two hundred years by the appearance of democracies with far from homogeneous populations. Whereas Locke's *Letter Concerning Toleration* could extend Christian arguments of tolerance beyond the case of Anglicans to include various Protestant sects, these arguments bear little resemblance to the kinds of questions posed by the coexistence of an almost infinite variety of religious, cultural, linguistic, and social practices in contemporary pluralistic democracies.[1]

While in the eighteenth-century context this type of diversity is unknown within a single state, the eighteenth-century theoretician is not unfamiliar with the question. Since the sixteenth century, the European reader had been confronted with the diversity of cultural practices in the form of travel narratives. This popular genre provided detailed (and often fanciful) accounts of cultures from all over the world. Confronted with the diversity of cultural, religious, and social practices around the globe, the eighteenth-century traveler/reader was faced, at least implicitly, with the question of tolerance as different cultures came into contact with one another.[2]

Therefore, in order to examine the question of tolerance from the perspective of contemporary notions of cultural difference, I feel it necessary to explore this issue in the context of a work that accounts for a more contemporary conception of diversity, albeit in an international and transhistorical context. For this reason I turn first to the work of Montesquieu to examine the virtue of tolerance.

My reading of Montesquieu's *De l'Esprit des lois* (1748) in this chapter focuses on different conceptions of tolerance and toleration at two distinct, but interrelated, levels. At the broadest level, I look at Montesquieu's attempt at value neutrality as a methodological position. At the level of particular cultural practices, I concentrate on his pronouncements concerning toleration as a political policy to be pursued. Specifically, I argue that the pragmatic conception of toleration that emerges from the question of state policy leads to a weak conception of tolerance closely related to the notion of the balance of powers. Finally, a careful reading of specific cultural practices condemned by Montesquieu reveals his conception of the limits of toleration within a republican democracy. From the intersection of Montesquieu's methodological value neutrality conceived as a kind of tolerance, toleration as a pragmatic political policy, and the limit cases of tolerance, I seek to defend both weak and strong conceptions of political and ethical tolerance in Montesquieu's work.

Methodological Tolerance

Montesquieu's *De l'Esprit des lois* contributed a significant new dimension to the study of political science, and he is often credited with inaugurating the new fields of sociology and anthropology.[3] His comparative, historical approach to law broadens the eighteenth-century understanding of what constitutes law and, therewith, the methodology appropriate for studying political formations.[4] In contrast to the more deductive Lockean method, Montesquieu's interweaving of general statements with anecdotal histories and ethnographic narratives creates a methodological approach that stresses an almost scientific value neutrality with respect to the subject matter. In spite of the numerous value judgments in *The Spirit of the Laws*, there is a will to explore comparative politics from a value neutral position.

Montesquieu's methodology is best understood from the perspective that he lays out in the "Préface." *De l'Esprit des lois* represents twenty years of the study of men, "First, I studied men."[5] His object, as he explicitly states it, is to enlighten. One might expect that what Montesquieu means by enlightenment, given the scope and magnitude of his study, is an enriched understanding of all possible laws and political formations, across cultures and across histories. But that is not the type of enlightenment that Montesquieu envisages. Rather, as it is for the Persian travelers in his popular novel, knowledge of other cultures is ultimately a privileged (yet clearly flawed for Usbek) means of access to knowledge of the self. In other words, studying other cultures will enable an enriched understanding of French culture.[6] Thus, Montesquieu's explicit aim in writing De l'Esprit des lois is in correcting and dispelling what he calls prejudices.

> It is not immaterial that the people be enlightened. The prejudices of magistrates began as the prejudices of the nation. . . . I would believe myself to be the happiest of mortals, if I could enable men to cure themselves of their prejudices. I call here prejudice not that which causes us not to know certain things, but that which causes us not to know ourselves.[7]

But Montesquieu goes one step further in his hopes for his study. Beyond enlightenment, Montesquieu expresses, albeit ambiguously, his desire to cultivate a love of humanity: "It is in seeking to instruct men that one can practice that general virtue that includes the love of all."[8] It is unclear in the formulation whether it is Montesquieu himself who practices the love of humanity in seeking to enlighten his readers, or if the "one" extends to humanity in general. In either case it is clear that the virtue of comparative political science resides in dispelling prejudices, which in turn encourages a general love of humanity. Thus, the virtue of the study, whether conceived solely from the author's point of view, or from the reader's point of view as well, is to promote the virtue of tolerance by eliminating the prejudices that are the result of a blind lack of self-knowledge.

In order to study man in all cultures and throughout history, and all the systems that regulate his behavior, Montesquieu is driven to redefine his conception of law. Rather than follow the narrow conception of law as codified rules of behavior within established political bodies, Montesquieu seeks to examine what he calls "l'esprit des lois." As he clearly states, "Several things govern men: climate, religion, laws, maxims of government, precedents, morals, manners; out of which is formed a general spirit that is the result of them."[9] Studying the spirit of the law in all of its manifestations requires looking objectively at the material, historical, and cultural determinants of social and political formations rather than simply constructing ideal political models.

The inductive methodology and the broadening of the object of study of political science are in effect interrelated. In abandoning the deductive methodology of the day in favor of comparative politics, Montesquieu opens the field to explore what he terms quite broadly "necessary relations," by which he means all relationships between things.[10] And inversely, by choosing to look at other cultures, he is committed to an open-minded methodology that will enable rather than disable such an undertaking.

Nonetheless, methodological tensions persist in *De l'Esprit des lois.* As Tzvetan Todorov has observed in his reading of *Lettres persanes,* at the same time that Montesquieu advocates tolerance, and therefore cultural relativism, he writes passages suggesting that he believes that absolute values do exist.[11] Continuing in the context of *Lettres persanes,* Todorov maintains that Montesquieu establishes a criterion for distinguishing legitimate forms of power as an absolute principle in contradiction to his cultural relativism: "The only thing that can legitimate an instance of power is, paradoxically, its partial abandonment: legitimacy can be acquired *a posteriori* by the fact that the holder of power has consented to share it with others, to impose limits on himself."[12] In distinguishing between legitimate and illegitimate forms of power—and Todorov's reading of *Lettres persanes* rightfully underscores the important lessons learned by Usbek about the power he exercises (or cannot ultimately exercise) in the harem—Montesquieu abandons his methodological neutrality in favor of a value judgment that partakes of the absolute. In the context of *De l'Esprit des lois,* Todorov notes the same tension between tolerance and absolute values.[13] According to Todorov, legitimate shared power in *Lettres persanes* appears as moderation. Todorov here elaborates Montesquieu's celebrated conception of the balance of powers in the British constitution, which I will examine in more detail below. For now, suffice it to say that moderation in the form of the balance of power also appears as an absolute value in contradiction to the methodological value neutrality advocated by Montesquieu in his general appeal for tolerance.

I turn now to Montesquieu's analyses of specific cultural practices to examine toleration as a practice that he advocates in relation to the tolerance he practices in the guise of his methodology.

Commerce and Tolerance

Although there is a difference between methodological tolerance and toleration pursued as a political policy, there is a connection between the two. In effect, the choice of methodological tolerance tacitly asserts the moral superiority of the value neutral position. As we saw above in the "Préface," Montesquieu implicitly argues that comparative analytical politics requires abandoning moral prejudices so that objective scientific judgments will inform the nascent social science, not chauvinism and ethnocentrism. The abandonment of prejudices, or what Montesquieu terms the enlightenment of self-knowledge, is required both of the author and of the reader. But this argument can be extended into the realm of political policy. Accordingly, the state that pursues, for example, religious tolerance is morally superior to the state that despotically enforces adherence to one religion.

Montesquieu makes the argument in favor of toleration as a policy most explicitly in connection with his discussion of commerce in Book 20.[14] Commerce brings different states with different customs into contact with one another, motivating tolerance between the negotiating parties:

> Commerce cures destructive prejudices; and it is almost a general rule that wherever there are moderate manners there is commerce; and everywhere there is commerce there are moderate manners. Let us not be surprised, then, if our morals are less ferocious than they once were. Commerce has made it so that the knowledge of the manners and morals of all nations has penetrated everywhere: they have been compared to one another, and great benefits have been the result.[15]

In much the same way that comparative politics requires a value neutral perspective, trade brings people of different cultural backgrounds together. The mere exposure to different manners and morals helps to dislodge prejudices and encourage more moderate behavior. In other words, according to Montesquieu's understanding of prejudices, the trading partners become more self-aware because of their exposure to cultural difference. This self-awareness in turn promotes moderation, as both cultures gain an enriched understanding of their own practices.

But commerce does more than simply promote interaction between different peoples and increase knowledge of different cultures; it also motivates tolerance: trade requires that nations cooperate in order to negotiate. Montesquieu goes so far as to maintain that commerce naturally leads to peace:

> The natural effect of commerce is to lead to peace. Two nations that
> negotiate together make themselves reciprocally dependent: if one has
> an interest in buying, the other has an interest in selling; and all the
> unions are founded on mutual need.[16]

Thus, the trade relationship not only encourages tolerance of the trading partner's manners and morals but also fosters a deeper understanding of reciprocal dependency and mutual need. In other words, tolerance developed in the context of trade leads to a more sophisticated moral position than simply "you scratch my back, I'll scratch yours."[17] The understanding of mutual dependence and reciprocity heightens awareness of the similarities between cultures rather than the differences. Ultimately, for Montesquieu, commerce leads to a recognition of those things that cultures hold in common rather than the differences that separate them. It is for this reason that, in spite of Montesquieu's avowed relativism, Todorov nonetheless sees him as a universalist. For it is in the establishment of common ground and understanding and, thus, in universal principles, that commerce leads to peace.

The type of tolerance encouraged by commerce goes beyond the methodological value neutrality of comparative politics. This type of tolerance suggests a moral position that recognizes that manners and morals differ with time and place. It also suggests that we must learn to respect these differences while at the same time recognizing underlying similarities. It is this moral position, extolling tolerance as a virtue, that Montesquieu seemingly recommends as a political policy to be pursued by democratic republics.

Toleration as State Policy

Not surprisingly, Montesquieu addresses the question of toleration as state policy specifically with respect to religion. For states that house several religions, he recommends ensuring tolerance amongst the various religions, as well as safeguarding the state from interference from any or all of them:

> When the laws of a State have deemed it necessary to tolerate several
> religions, it is necessary that they also oblige them to tolerate each
> other. . . . It is therefore useful that the laws require of these diverse
> religions not only that they do not interfere with the State, but also
> that the religions not interfere with each other. A citizen does not fulfill the laws in contenting himself not to agitate the body of the State;
> it is further necessary that he not interfere with any citizen whatsoever.[18]

The form of toleration recommended here with respect to religion resembles the methodological value neutrality of *The Spirit of the Laws* more than it does the conception of tolerance as virtue that develops as a result of trade. Here, tolerance is a matter of adopting an attitude that will enable differences to peacefully coexist; it is not unlike what Michael Walzer describes as the "state neutrality and voluntary association" model found in Locke's *Letter Concerning Toleration*.[19] Unlike the situation described between trading partners who interract and develop a universal sense of their shared humanity, here the state stands back and simply permits different religious practices. The pragmatic focus on keeping interference with the state at a minimum places the state in a value neutral position with respect to religions rather than in a morally superior one. In other words, Montesquieu advocates religious toleration as a state policy in order to keep order and not because it fosters mutual respect and understanding between different religious groups.[20]

Toleration of this sort is consistent both with Montesquieu's understanding of political liberty and with his belief in the efficacy of the separation of powers. This weaker version of tolerance founded in pragmatic concerns protects both the state and individual citizens' rights from being infringed by other citizens' religious practices. Grounded in the traditional liberal conception of negative liberty that I analyzed in detail in chapter 2 with respect to Rousseau, Montesquieu ensures that each citizen feels secure, protected from harm by other citizens.[21]

> Political liberty for a citizen is that peace of mind that comes from the opinion that everyone has of his own security; and in order to have this freedom, it is necessary that the government be such that a citizen cannot fear another citizen.[22]

Toleration conceived in terms of negative liberty allows for different religious practices, so long as they do not interfere either with the rights of other citizens or with the state. Very much like that of Locke, this restricted notion guarantees the citizen freedom from bodily harm or confiscation of property in his free exercise of private conscience.[23] This conception of political liberty is intimately related to the issue of the separation of powers and, in fact, it appears in connection with Montesquieu's celebrated discussion of the British constitution. According to Montesquieu, power needs to be balanced, as if it were a physical force. The abuse of power can only be avoided when power is balanced in this way. "So that power cannot be abused, it is necessary that, through the disposition of things, power stops power."[24] The best way to balance power is to ensure its separation in different branches of the government (2:396–97). Hence, Todorov's conclusion, mentioned earlier, that moderation stands as an absolute value in Montesquieu, contradicting his cultural relativism.

Like the conception of the balance of power, religious tolerance pragmatically relies on defining and limiting the extension of a citizen's freedom and rights to the point at which they interfere with another citizen's freedom or rights, or with the smooth functioning of the state. In other words, each citizen's religious freedom is balanced against every other citizen's religious freedom and limited by its interference with the state. Montesquieu suggests that this balance can be achieved through a careful distribution of jurisdictional responsibilies among the various types of legislative authority. Like the balance between the executive, legislative, and judicial branches of government, the application of the appropriate authority's law in a particular context balances the powers of religious authorities, thereby solving the problem of tolerance. In this way, religious authority over particular practices only extends so far that it does not interfere either with other citizens' freedom and rights or with the state's smooth functioning.

Let us take a contemporary example, the case of the orthodox Jewish students who do not want to live in the Yale dormitory because they feel that dormitory life interferes with their ability to practice "a life with modesty and privacy and a sense of sexual ethics," and who are disputing "Yale's requirement that all freshmen and sophomores live on campus."[25] In this case, Montesquieu would most likely side with Yale, taking the position that as the local authority with jurisdiction over students who attend the university, Yale has a right to determine their conduct. Yale does not interfere with the state by requiring first- and second-year students to live on campus. Because these students have chosen to attend Yale, they forfeit the right to violate the laws they have voluntarily accepted in attending that university.[26] For Montesquieu, jurisdictional authority will always be invoked to regulate conflicts between different religious and cultural practices. He believes that disputes between religious and state authority can be avoided if this policy of balanced toleration is pursued.[27]

Because Montesquieu recognizes various types of law, not limited to codified legislation, but also including customs, manners, and morals, he must explain how these different types of law relate to one another. As I have suggested, he relies on a conception like the separation of powers and maintains that there are jurisdictional boundaries separating the various domains:

Men are governed by diverse kinds of laws: by natural law; by divine law, which is religious law; by ecclesiastical law, otherwise called canon law . . . by the right of peoples, which can be considered as the civil law of the universe, in the sense that each nation is a citizen; by general political law, which has as its object the human wisdom that founded all societies; by particular political law, which concerns each society; by the law of conquest . . . by the civil law of each society, by which a citizen can defend his goods and his life against any other citizen; finally, by domestic law, which comes from the fact that society is divided into diverse families that need individual government. *There are, therefore, different orders of laws; and the sublimity of human reason consists in knowing to which of these orders the things about which one must legislate relate, and in not adding confusion to the principles that must govern men.*[28] [My emphasis.]

If human reason works in the sublime way that it is supposed to, then jurisdictional disputes will not arise. Tolerance will be promoted by the separation and balance of power between state, religious, and local authorities.

Jurisdictional Conflicts

The pronouncements concerning jurisdictional boundaries notwithstanding, Montesquieu's comparative inductive method supplies him with numerous examples of conflicts between the various orders of law. The remainder of Book 16 is devoted to examining precisely these conflicts between divine and human law, civil and natural law, and so on. From the perspective of the question of toleration as state policy, two interrelated issues in particular shed light on the limits of Montesquieu's conception of tolerance. Polygamy—understood by Montesquieu as domestic slavery—and civil slavery both represent practices that conflict with the ideals of the democratic republic as Montesquieu defines it. In his discussion of these specific practices, Montesquieu reveals the limits of toleration as state policy in democratic republics, and in so doing offers grounds for adjudicating disputes between different kinds of laws that jurisdictional checks and balances cannot otherwise prevent.

In his examination of the relationship between domestic slavery, that is polygamy, and climate in Book 16, Montesquieu attempts to examine the question from a value neutral perspective. As he states, "In all of this I do not justify the practices, but I give the reasons for them."[29] In *Lettres persanes* he had already made his position on polygamy and its relation to despotism abundantly clear.[30] The chaos that ensues in the harem during Usbek's prolonged absence and Roxane's resultant treachery and suicide clearly illustrate the interdependence between this domestic arrangement and despotic power: unshared power cannot be legitimate and, therefore, will always falter.

In spite of Montesquieu's efforts to examine polygamy objectively, that is to say, in the various contexts in which it arises and in relation to these contexts, he cannot refrain from commenting on the practice *in general:*

> To look at polygamy in general, independently of the circumstances that can make it somewhat tolerable, it is not useful to the human race, nor to either of the two sexes, either to the one who abuses, or to the one who is abused. Nor is it useful to children.[31]

Montesquieu cannot refrain from passing judgment on the practice of polygamy, for which he can find no use. The use of the verb *"abuser"* in this context, although not as strongly negative in French as in English, nonetheless makes that abundantly clear. In addition to the difficulties it poses for traditional family relationships of affection (2:512), it also has the paradoxical effect of creating a desire for more and more women (2:513). Most nefarious of all is the separation between the sexes that polygamy requires. Drawing the same conclusions as those he makes evident in *Persian Letters*, Montesquieu asserts that the cloistering of harem women results in the same type of extreme subordination as that required by despotic forms of government:

> In a government, in which above all tranquility is required, and in which extreme subordination is called peace, it is necessary to cloister the women; their intrigues would be fatal to their husbands. A government that does not have the time to examine the conduct of its subjects considers their conduct to be suspect, merely for appearing and making itself felt.[32]

Montesquieu contrasts this absolute subordination of women in harems and subjects of despotic governments to the political liberty required in a republic. Expanding from the conception of political liberty as the individual citizen's security from harm, Montesquieu asserts that "In a republic, the condition of citizens is limited, equal, mild, moderate; the effects of public liberty are felt in everything."[33] This freedom born of equality depends on moderation in manners and morals. Polygamy would only undermine the stability of a republic founded on equality between citizens and sustained by moderate behavior. Thus, this particular domestic arrangement—or even "domestic government" as Montesquieu calls it—proves to be incompatible with political formations other than monarchical or despotic. By extension, and unstated in Montesquieu's text, is the argument that republics must legislate against polygamy in order to protect the order upon which they are founded. Thus, the laws of the state must take priority over domestic laws and religious laws.[34]

Bearing a striking resemblance to his analysis of polygamy, Montesquieu's discussion of civil slavery in Book 15 of *The Spirit of the Laws* also attempts a value neutral analysis of the phenomenon in relation to climate. But before examining numerous possible origins of the practice of slavery consistent with his value neutral methodology, Montesquieu emphatically pronounces the practice to be morally harmful:

> Slavery, properly speaking, is the establishment of a right that renders a man to such an extent the property of another man that he is the absolute master of his life and of his goods. It is not good in its nature: it is neither useful to the master nor to the slave; to the latter because he can do nothing out of virtue; to the former because he contracts with his slaves all sorts of bad habits, and without knowing it he becomes accustomed to lacking all of the moral virtues, so that he becomes proud, hasty, harsh, angry, voluptuous, and cruel.[35]

Stronger than his condemnation of polygamy in the following book, Montesquieu's assessment of slavery finds that it is antithetical to all moral virtues. Although tolerable under a despotic regime because it is virtually indistinguishable from that form of power, according to Montesquieu slavery can only destroy monarchies and aristocratic and democratic republics.

After discussing several possible origins of the practice of slavery, Montesquieu returns to the idea that slavery is useless and must be prohibited in virtually all parts of the globe (2:496). His final argument against slavery in chapter 9 of Book 15 invokes an argument similar to John Rawls's veil of ignorance to demonstrate in an impartial and objective manner the undesirability of the practice.[36] Montesquieu proposes something like Rawls's original position in order to consider the practice of slavery:

> [T]aking another point of view, none of those who compose the small portion of each nation that is rich and voluptuous would want to draw straws to determine who would form the part of the nation that would be free, and the part that would be slave. Those that speak out most in favor of slavery would find it most horrible, and the poorest would likewise find it horrible.[37]

Montesquieu's conclusion, that even proponents of slavery would abhor the idea that they themselves might be slaves under the new political arrangement, leads him to believe that slavery is simply "the cry of luxury and voluptuousness"[38] and ought not to be tolerated in the interests of public happiness. Again, as Todorov asserts, the absolute value of moderation triumphs over Montesquieu's cultural and methodological relativism.[39]

Montesquieu's pronouncements against polygamy and slavery, in spite of his attempts at methodological neutrality, suggest that he thinks that, in questions of jurisdictional overlap between types of law, the state is justified in prohibiting and ought to prohibit certain practices. His recommendation against toleration in the cases of polygamy and slavery suggests that a greater good supersedes the virtue of tolerance; in the case of slavery, Montesquieu indicates that "public happiness" (2:497) represents a greater common good.

Returning to my discussion of the rise of tolerance in conjunction with the development of trade, I will argue that a stronger conception of tolerance as virtue underlies these pronouncements against polygamy and slavery than either the value neutrality of Montesquieu's methodology or the weak form of tolerance that relies on the separation and balance of power demonstrated in jurisdictional boundaries between types of laws.

Tolerance as Civic Virtue

As I argued above, Montesquieu's derivation of the value of tolerance from the rise of trade relations established more than simply a value neutral perspective to be adopted by the state for the purposes of preserving domestic order and peace. The stronger version of tolerance suggests that it is founded upon the recognition of reciprocal dependence and mutual need that is discovered through contact with other cultures as a result of commerce.[40] Very much like the love for all that ideally develops from the shedding of prejudices in the process of enlightenment, commerce promotes a universal value. This version of tolerance recognizes difference at the same time that it recognizes underlying similarities.[41] As a virtue, it clearly relates to Montesquieu's conception of virtue within a democratic republic.

Montesquieu's circular discussions of virtue within a republic require close analysis. To begin with, Montesquieu distinguishes between the guiding principles underlying the three types of government that interest him. While political virtue is the guiding principle in republics (2:251), honor underlies monarchies (2:256), and fear motivates subjects' actions under despotic rule (2:258). In further discussions of republican virtue, Montesquieu maintains that, "Virtue, in a republic, is something very simple: it is love of the republic." He adds, "Love of the republic, in a democracy, is for democracy; love of democracy is love of equality." [42]

In contrast to the honor underlying monarchical rule, democratic republican virtue involves a love of country founded on equality.[43] Montesquieu continually insists on the necessity of moderation in manners and morals for democratic republics, to the point of recommending extreme frugality to promote equality (2:275–76). This almost repressive egalitarianism is justified as promoting democratic republican virtues. Any difference between citizens could lead to inequalities and a return to the system of honor that relies on precisely these distinctions.[44]

If virtue in republics is closely associated with equality, then it depends on a recognition of sameness between citizens. The introduction of difference in the form of wealth or privilege would only disrupt the democratic republic, leading to its downfall. Thus, virtue amounts to recognizing the equal position in which all citizens of a democratic republic find themselves with respect to each other and to the state.

Tolerance within such a republic most often could be defined in the weak ways that I have indicated above. That is to say, egalitarian democratic republics of this type would usually need to have recourse to either the value neutral perspective of Montesquieu's inductive methodology or to a conception of jurisdictional boundaries and separation of powers to deal with problems of difference. In other words, if differences are kept to a minimum, then the balance and separation of powers and the state's neutrality with respect to religious matters will suffice to deal with cultural differences between citizens.[45] But it is also tautological to claim that minimizing cultural differences will create social harmony. Homogeneity only creates a very limited form of tolerance, with limited claims for civil liberties, in such a context. The pragmatic adoption of an indifferent attitude to cultural differences will in most cases enable the state to function smoothly and citizens to exercise these limited civil liberties because few real test cases will arise. And, theoretically, the balance of powers will provide for the maintenance of jurisdictional limits that will help to effectively adjudicate whatever disputes arise.

But we have already seen two issues on which Montesquieu deems it necessary for the state to intervene and prohibit certain practices in the interests of public happiness. One possible reason for outlawing polygamy and slavery in democratic republics might be that they represent practices that work against equality. Montesquieu seems to suggest as much in reference to slavery when he calls it "the cry of luxury and voluptuousness" (2:497), and clearly the same could be said of polygamy. Both practices encourage and/or abet the accumulation of wealth and property. Therefore, the democratic state would be justified in outlawing cultural practices that interfere with the established equality within the society.[46] Outlawing polygamy and slavery helps to foster the absence of difference and sense of a shared goal necessary for the equality that underpins this type of democratic society.[47] Thus, tolerance is more easily practiced in a society in which difference is at a minimum and, therefore, the extension of universal principles is less problematic.

But this argument seems inadequate due to its circularity. Equality and peace are maintained due to a minimum of cultural difference. The homogeneous society guarantees that questions of tolerance never present themselves. By legislating moderation and equality, this type of democratic republic in effect outlaws significant cultural difference and eliminates the problem. In an argument very similar to the more xenophobic strands in Rousseau, this line of argumentation answers the question of tolerance by in effect begging the question.

I believe, however, that Montesquieu also provides another answer for the twentieth-century context. Using the stronger version of tolerance developed as a result of trade relationships, another line of argumentation may be developed to explain why the practices of slavery and polygamy ought to be banned in democratic republics. The stronger version of tolerance in Montesquieu indicates that it is founded simultaneously on a recognition of sameness in difference and difference in sameness. The recognition of reciprocal dependence and mutual need that arises out of trade relations requires that differences be respected because of fundamental, underlying similarities. In the dialogical encounter, tolerance is founded upon shared recognition of the reciprocal relation.[48] In fact, it is as a result of the dialogical encounter required in trade relations that such a universal understanding is able to develop, eliminating the prejudices that once blinded individuals and societies to their own cultural practices.

Within a democratic republic, such a shared recognition is possible between citizens, but it goes beyond the conception of the negative liberty of the individual or the separation and balance of powers. Tolerance conceived in this way defends the other's right to practice a different religion, or to wear different clothes, or to speak a different language, on the basis of recognized shared values. To be tolerant in this way is to be virtuous, for it entails recognizing an other's fundamental similarity through and because of cultural difference.

The strong version of tolerance only makes sense, however, when it is able to draw limits. Unlike the weak version of tolerance, which is largely procedural, the stronger version of tolerance is substantive.[49] That is to say, that because it is founded on recognition across and through difference, it must not extend to all practices. Practices that violate the very principle upon which tolerance is founded cannot be tolerated. Slavery and polygamy are two such examples. Not only do they undermine equality in democratic republics by introducing differences of wealth and status, but they also violate the fundamental principles of a democratic republic: equality between citizens. With their close affinity to the despotic rule of fear, polygamy and slavery work against the republican virtues of equality, democracy, and most importantly, tolerance. Slavery and polygamy as practices undermine the very principle of tolerance in their failure to recognize the sameness underlying the difference that enables the relationships.

Thus, Montesquieu's contribution to a present-day understanding of the question of tolerance goes a long way toward resuscitating an attenuated version of universalism. His methodological relativism stops short of nihilism to invoke universal values that do not suffer from ethnocentrism. In his use of the trade relationship as a paradigmatic case for the shedding of prejudices and the development of peace through understanding, he points the way out of a cultural relativism that cannot draw important distinctions. The recognition of reciprocal needs achieved through dialogue anticipates the Habermasian communicative ethic that refuses to abandon the ideals of the Enlightenment.[50] Thus, Montesquieu sidesteps the pitfalls of universalizing a European male subject and, through comparative sociological political science, achieves a blend of relativism and universalism that still resonates today in proceduralist revisions of liberalism emphasizing the participatory process.

Notes

[1]See John Locke, *A Letter Concerning Toleration in Focus*, ed. John Horton and Susan Mendus (New York: Routledge, 1991). For a defense of Locke's position see Susan Mendus, *Toleration and the Limits of Liberalism* (London: Macmillan, 1989).

[2] This is not to say that travel narratives promoted tolerance, for many of them reinforced cultural stereotypes, feelings of European superiority, and xenophobia. See, among others, Tzvetan Todorov, *On Human Diversity: Nationalism, Racism, and Exoticism in French Thought*, trans. Catherine Porter (Cambridge: Harvard University Press, 1993); and Michel de Certeau, *Heterologies: Discourse on the Other*, trans. Brian Massumi (Minneapolis: University of Minnesota Press, 1986).

[3] See Emile Durkheim, *Montesquieu et Rousseau: Précurseurs de la sociologie* (Paris: Marcel Rivière, 1953); and Judith N. Shklar, *Montesquieu* (Oxford: Oxford University Press, 1987).

[4] For a discussion of Montesquieu's methodological debt to Aristotle and Newton, see Simone Goyard-Fabre, *Montesquieu: la nature, les lois, la liberté* (Paris: Presses Universitaires de France, 1993), pp. 1–18.

[5] "J'ai d'abord examiné les hommes." Charles-Louis Secondat, Baron de Montesquieu, *Oeuvres complètes*, 2 vols. (Paris: Gallimard, 1949–51), vol. 2, p. 229. All parenthetical references to this work in chapter 4 (text and notes) are to this edition and cite the volume number followed by the page number. All translations are my own. In the current chapter, I have retained the sexist language of Montesquieu. To translate "les hommes" as humanity or people elides the fact that for the most part Montesquieu is only speaking about men in his study.

[6] Early anthropology stated this goal explicitly. Margaret Mead writes, for example, as follows: "We know that our subtlest perceptions, our highest values, are all based upon contrast; that light without darkness or beauty without ugliness would lose the qualities which they now appear to us to have. And similarly, *if we would appreciate our own civilization*, this elaborate pattern of life which we have made for ourselves as a people and which we are at such pains to pass on to our children, *we must set our civilization over and against other very different ones.*... But if we step outside the stream of Indo-European culture, the appreciation we can accord our civilization is even more enhanced." *Coming of Age in Samoa* (New York: William Morrow, 1928), pp. 7–8. [My emphasis.] For a critical assessment of the constructed authority of anthropological texts see Deborah Gordon, "The Politics of Ethnographic Authority: Race and Writing in the Ethnography of Margaret Mead and Zora Neale Hurston," in *Modernist Anthropology: From Fieldwork to Text*, ed. Marc Manganaro (Princeton, N. J.: Princeton University Press, 1990), pp. 146–62; and James Clifford, "On Ethnographic Authority," in Clifford, *The Predicament of Culture: Twentieth-Century Ethnography, Literature and Art* (Cambridge: Harvard University Press, 1988), pp. 21–54.

[7] "Il n'est pas indifférent que le peuple soit éclairé. Les préjugés des magistrats ont commencé par être les préjugés de la nation.... Je me croirois le plus heureux des mortels, si je pouvois faire que les hommes pussent se guérir de leurs préjugés. J'appelle ici préjugés, non pas ce qui fait qu'on ignore de certaines choses, mais ce qui fait qu'on s'ignore soi-même" (2:230).

[8] "C'est en cherchant à instruire les hommes, que l'on peut pratiquer cette vertu générale qui comprend l'amour de tous" (2:230).

[9] "Plusieurs choses gouvernent les hommes: le climat, la religion, les lois, les maximes du gouvernement, les exemples des choses passées, les moeurs, les manières; d'où il se forme un esprit général qui en résulte" (2:558).

[10] "[L]es rapports nécessaires" (2:232).

[11]See Todorov, *On Human Diversity*, p. 361. See also Henry Puget, "L'Apport de l'*Esprit des lois* à la Science Politique et au Droit Public"; and P. Barrière, "L'Humanisme de *l'Esprit des lois*," both in *La Pensée politique et constitutionnelle de Montesquieu. Bicentenaire de l'Esprit des lois 1748–1948* (Paris: Faculté de Droit de Paris. Recueil Sirey, 1952).

[12] Todorov, *On Human Diversity*, p. 362.

[13] According to Simone Goyard-Fabre, it is the dichotomy established between moderate and immoderate forms of power that enables the shift from factual to normative judgments. See *Montesquieu: la nature, les lois, la liberté*, pp. 260–69.

[14] In the following analysis, I argue in favor of the existence of weak and strong versions of tolerance in Montesquieu. The weak version of tolerance is consistent with *doux commerce* theory, but the strong version of tolerance represents a departure from the moderation characteristic of Montesquieu and of the *doux commerce* theorists in general. For an overview of *doux commerce* theory, see Helena Rosenblatt, *Rousseau and Geneva: From the First Discourse to the Social Contract, 1749–1762* (Cambridge: Cambridge University Press, 1997), pp. 52–60.

[15] "Le commerce guérit des préjugés destructeurs; et c'est presque une règle générale, que partout où il y a des mœurs douces, il y a du commerce; et que partout où il y a du commerce, il y a des mœurs douces. Qu'on ne s'étonne donc point si nos mœurs sont moins féroces qu'elles ne l'étoient autrefois. Le commerce a fait que la connoissance des mœurs de toutes les nations a pénétré partout: on les a comparées entre elles, et il en a résulté de grands biens" (2:585).

[16] "L'effet naturel du commerce est de porter à la paix. Deux nations qui négocient ensemble se rendent réciproquement dépendantes: si l'une a intérêt d'acheter, l'autre a intérêt de vendre; et toutes les unions sont fondées sur des besoins mutuels" (ibid.).

[17]See Lawrence Kohlberg, *Child Psychology and Childhood Education: A Cognitive-Developmental View* (New York: Longman, 1987). Kohlberg would characterize such a moral position as preconventional (stage 2), because it is characterized by "individualism, instrumental purpose and exchange." In this preconventional stage, an individual follows "rules only when it is to [his/her] immediate interest" and acts "to meet [his/her] own interests and needs and let[s] others do the same" (*Child Psychology*, p. 284). Compare Michael Walzer's discussion of different forms of toleration under different political regimes in *On Toleration* (New Haven, Conn.: Yale University Press, 1997), esp. chapter 2.

[18]"Lorsque les lois d'un Etat ont cru devoir souffrir plusieurs religions, il faut qu'elles les obligent aussi à se tolérer entre elles. . . . Il est donc utile que les lois exigent de ces diverses religions, non seulement qu'elles ne troublent pas l'Etat, mais aussi qu'elle ne se troublent pas entre elles. Un citoyen ne satisfait

point aux lois, en se contentant de ne pas agiter le corps de l'Etat; il faut encore qu'il ne trouble pas quelque citoyen que ce soit" (2:744). The language
adopted in the *Constitution de 1791* for the *Déclaration des droits de l'Homme
et du Citoyen du 26 août 1789*, article 10, protecting the rights to matters of
private conscience including religious belief, similarly excludes practices that
disturb the public order: "Nul ne doit être inquiété pour ses opinions, même
religieuses, pourvu que leur manifestation ne trouble pas l'ordre public établi
par la loi." [No one must be troubled for his opinions, even religious opinions, provided that their display does not disturb the public order established
by law.] See Bernard Rudden, *A Source-Book on French Law: Public Law—
Constitutional and Administrative ·Law: Private Law—Structure, Contract.*
Ed. Otto Kahn-Freund, Claudine Lévy, and Bernard Rudden. 3d revised
edition (Oxford: Oxford University Press, 1991), p. 46.

[19] Walzer, *On Toleration*, p. 4.

[20] Compare Rousseau's pronouncements concerning religious tolerance at the
end of the *Social Contract*, where he insists that intolerant religions must not
be tolerated: "Maintenant qu'il n'y a plus et qu'il ne peut plus y avoir de Religion nationale exclusive, on doit tolérer toutes celles qui tolerent les autres,
autant que leurs dogmes n'ont rien de contraire aux devoirs du Citoyen. Mais
quiconque ose dire, *hors de l'Eglise point de Salut*, doit être chassé de l'Etat; à
moins que l'Etat ne soit l'Eglise, et que le Prince ne soit le Pontife. Un tel
dogme n'est bon que dans un Gouvernement Théocratique, dans tout autre il
est pernicieux." *Du contract social*, Book 4, chapter 8, in *Oeuvres complètes*,
vol. 3, p. 469. [Now that there are no more and can be no more exclusive
national Religion, we must tolerate all those that tolerate others, as long as
their dogma has nothing contrary to the duties of the Citizen. But whoever
dares to say, *outside of the Church no salvation*, must be banished from the
State, unless the State is the Church and the Prince is the Pontiff. Such a
dogma is only good in a Theocratic Government; in all others it is perni-
cious.]

[21]See Isaiah Berlin, in Berlin, "Two Concepts of Liberty," *Four Essays on Liberty* (Oxford: Oxford University Press, 1982); pp. 118–72 and chapter 2 of
this book, pp. 50-52, 57-62.

[22] "La liberté politique dans un citoyen est cette tranquillité d'esprit qui
provient de l'opinion que chacun a de sa sûreté; et pourqu'on ait cette liberté,
il faut que le gouvernement soit tel qu'un citoyen ne puisse pas craindre un
autre citoyen" (2:397)

[23]Protection of property is the motivating ground for government in Locke:
"the supreme power cannot take from any man part of his property without
his consent; for the preservation of property being the end of government
and that for which men enter into society, it necessarily supposes and requires
that the people should have property; without which they must be supposed
to lose that, by entering into society, which was the end for which they en-

tered into it—too gross an absurdity for any man to own." John Locke, *The Second Treatise of Government*, ed. Thomas P. Peardon (Indianapolis: Bobbs-Merill, 1952), p. 79.

[24] "Pourqu'on ne puisse abuser du pouvoir, il faut que, par la disposition des choses, le pouvoir arrête le pouvoir" (2:395).

[25]William Glaberson, "Five Orthodox Jews Spur Moral Debate over Yale's Housing Rules," *New York Times* (Sunday, September 7, 1997), p. 45.

[26]Locke's position on voluntary associations and state neutrality would probably yield the same judgment in this case. However, whereas Locke's argument would turn on the important issue of "voluntary association," claiming that the students freely chose to attend Yale University, Montesquieu's argument would rather underscore Yale's authority to determine rules of conduct within the limits of that voluntary association based on the concept of jurisdiction.

[27] Montesquieu mentions religious crimes specifically as offenses that ought not to be prosecuted by the state but rather should be left to religious authorities and, ultimately, God. See *De l'Esprit des lois*, Book 12, chapter 4. See also Judith Shklar, *Montesquieu.*

[28] "Les hommes sont gouvernés par diverses sortes de lois: par le droit naturel; par le droit divin, qui est celui de la religion; par le droit ecclésiastique, autrement appelé canonique, . . . par le droit des gens, qu'on peut considérer comme le droit civil de l'univers, dans le sens que chaque peuple en est un citoyen; par le droit politique général, qui a pour objet cette sagesse humaine qui a fondé toutes les sociétés; par le droit politique particulier, qui concerne chaque société; par le droit de conquête, . . . par le droit civil de chaque société, par lequel un citoyen peut défendre ses biens et sa vie, contre tout autre citoyen; enfin par le droit domestique, qui vient de ce qu'une société est divisée en diverses familles, qui ont besoin d'un gouvernement particulier. *Il y a donc différents ordres de lois; et la sublimité de la raison humaine consiste à savoir bien auquel de ces ordres se rapportent principalement les choses sur lesquelles on doit statuer, et à ne point mettre de confusion dans les principes qui doivent gouverner les hommes*" (2:750–51). [My emphasis.]

[29] "Dans tout ceci je ne justifie pas les usages, mais j'en rends les raisons" (2:511).

[30]See Montesquieu, *Oeuvres complètes*, vol. 1, esp. letters 2, 3, 4, 7, 9, 15, 20, 21, 22, 62, 64, 149–161.

[31] "A regarder la polygamie en général, indépendamment des circonstances qui peuvent la faire un peu tolérer, elle n'est point utile au genre humain, ni à aucun des deux sexes, soit à celui qui abuse, soit à celui dont on abuse. Elle n'est pas non plus utile aux enfants." (2:512).

[32] "Dans un gouvernement où l'on demande surtout la tranquillité, et où la subordination extrême s'appelle la paix, il faut enfermer les femmes; leurs intrigues seroient fatales au mari. Un gouvernement qui n'a pas le temps

d'examiner la conduite des sujets, la tient pour suspecte, par cela seul qu'elle paroît et qu'elle se fait sentir" (2:515).

[33] "Dans une république, la condition des citoyens est bornée, égale, douce, modérée; tout s'y ressent de la liberté publique" (514).

[34]Compare Michael Walzer's discussions of suttee and genital mutilation both in the context of immigrant societies and in the context of international toleration. *On Toleration*, pp. 60–66.

[35] "L'esclavage, proprement dit, est l'établissement d'un droit qui rend un homme tellement propre à un autre homme, qu'il est le maître absolu de sa vie et de ses biens. Il n'est pas bon par sa nature: il n'est utile ni au maître ni à l'esclave: à celui-ci, parce qu'il ne peut rien faire par vertu; à celui-là, parce qu'il contracte avec ses esclaves toutes sortes de mauvaises habitudes, qu'il s'accoutume insensiblement à manquer à toutes les vertus morales, qu'il devient fier, prompt, dur, colère, voluptueux, cruel" (2:490).

[36]See John Rawls, *A Theory of Justice* (Cambridge: Harvard University Press, 1971). "In justice as fairness the original position of equality corresponds to the state of nature in the traditional theory of the social contract. This original position is not, of course, thought of as an actual historical state of affairs, much less as a primitive condition of culture. It is understood as a purely hypothetical situation characterized so as to lead to a certain conception of justice. Among the essential features of this situation is that no one knows his place in society, his class position or social status, nor does any one know his fortune in the distribution of assets and abilities, his intelligence, strength and the like." *Theory of Justice*, p. 12.

[37] "[P]renant un autre point de vue, qu'aucun de ceux qui la [la petite partie riche et voluptueuse de chaque nation] composent voulût tirer au sort pour savoir qui devroit former la partie de la nation qui seroit libre, et celle qui seroit esclave. Ceux qui parlent le plus pour l'esclavage l'auroient le plus en horreur, et les hommes les plus misérables en auroient horreur de même" (2:497).

[38] "[L]e cri du luxe et de la volupté" (ibid.)

[39]See Todorov, *On Human Diversity*, pp. 377–83.

[40]This position is similar to Charles Taylor's politics of recognition elaborated in conjunction with the debates concerning multiculturalism. See Charles Taylor, *Multiculturalism: Examining the Politics of Recognition*, ed. Amy Gutmann (Princeton, N. J.: Princeton University Press, 1994). For a defense of Montesquieu along similar lines, see Isaiah Berlin, *Against the Current: Essays in the History of Ideas* (New York: Viking, 1955), pp. 130–61.

[41]I explore this issue of emphasizing difference versus sameness in questions of tolerance in chapter 5.

[42] "La vertu, dans une république, est une chose très simple: c'est l'amour de la république," and "L'amour de la république, dans une démocratie, est celui de la démocratie; l'amour de la démocratie est celui de l'égalité" (2:274).

[43] Compare this conception of equality to Rousseau's repressive egalitarianism in *Le Projet de constitution pour la Corse* in *Oeuvres complètes*, vol. 3, pp. 901–50.

[44] See Taylor's brief discussion of Montesquieu in *Multiculturalism*, p. 27.

[45] In this respect, Rousseau follows Montesquieu's lead in recommending that democracies limit themselves to small, homogeneous populations. See *Du contract social*, in Rousseau, *Oeuvres complètes*, vol. 3, pp. 386, 439, on the need for social unanimity and the preference for a small state.

[46] Ironically, from the perspective of liberalism, this position would lead to trade restrictions and a regulated market economy to protect the equality of the society. In this respect, it would resemble Rousseau's advice on restricting trade in Corsica in the *Projet de constitution pour la Corse*, in *Oeuvres complètes*, vol. 3, pp. 905–18.

[47] Compare Taylor's discussion of Rousseau in *Multiculturalism*, pp. 44–51.

[48] This does not go as far as what Charles Taylor calls the politics of equality and dignity that he finds in Rousseau and Kant. See Taylor, *Multiculturalism*, pp. 44–51 and Taylor, *Sources of the Self: The Making of the Modern Identity* (Cambridge: Harvard University Press, 1989), pp. 85–88. For a discussion of Rousseau and Taylor, see H. D. Forbes, "Rousseau, Ethnicity, and Difference," in *The Legacy of Rousseau*," ed. Clifford Orwin and Nathan Tarcov (Chicago: University of Chicago Press, 1997), pp. 220–45.

[49] See Ronald Dworkin, *Taking Rights Seriously* (Cambridge: Harvard University Press, 1977), for a defense of substantively based justice as a protection against the blindness of proceduralism. On this point, I disagree with Todorov's ultimate assessment of Montesquieu's position.

[50] Habermas supports the contention that legitimate democracy depends upon rational will formation and not a predetermined set of shared beliefs. Will formation, in turn, relies upon both communicative presuppositions— Habermas's discourse ethic—and also certain procedures to ensure fairness. For a discussion of Habermas's discourse theory of democracy, see *Between Facts and Norms: Contributions to a Discourse Theory of Law and Democracy*, trans. William Rehg (Cambridge: MIT Press, 1996), pp. 278–79, 295–302.

5: From Tolerance to Sympathy

IN CHAPTER 4, I examined strong and weak versions of tolerance in Montesquieu's *De l'Esprit des lois*, arguing that in spite of his relativism, universal values inhere in Montesquieu's conception of toleration and suggest grounds for determining the limits of tolerance in a democratic republic. In this chapter I focus on the spectrum of ethical reactions from tolerance to sympathy, but, rather than focus on the state, I shift my attention to the individual. The spectrum of moral attitudes under examination runs from a purely negative conception of tolerance conceived in terms consistent with contractual notions of obligation (reminiscent of the weaker form found in Montesquieu) to a positive conception of duty towards others that does not fit neatly within the liberal framework but nonetheless uneasily coexists with it in eighteenth-century discourses of morality.

Beginning with Voltaire's *Traité sur la tolérance* (1763), I establish a minimalist account of tolerance that I then contrast with versions of sympathy found in Rousseau's accounts of *pitié* in both the *Discours sur l'origine de l'inégalité* (1755) and the *Essai sur l'origine des langues* (1781)[1] and finally with representations of sympathy and compassion in Isabelle de Charrière's *Caliste ou lettres écrites de Lausanne* (1785–87).[2] I argue that although it is problematic with respect to liberal notions of duty and obligation, an analysis of sympathy offers an alternative eighteenth-century ethical vision to the limited contractual understanding of obligation, conceived in negative terms, that tolerance usually entails. This fuller conception, which entails imperfect duties and a concrete conception of the other, fills in the gaps in the otherwise atomistic picture of human relations and provides grounds for community.

Voltaire on Tolerance

In his *Traité sur la tolérance*, Voltaire argues in favor of religious tolerance in the wake of the execution of Jean Calas in Toulouse for the alleged murder of his son, Marc-Antoine. In one of the most infamous cases of religious persecution in France during the eighteenth century, a Protestant father was convicted of murder and condemned to die on the wheel for the hanging of his own son, who supposedly intended to convert to Catholicism in order to set up a legal practice. Along with the father, the other son and a young friend of the family (also a Protestant) were also condemned for what was in fact an obvious suicide. As is well known, Voltaire made "L'Affaire Calas" his own, campaigning and writing indefatigably until the Calas name was cleared two years after Jean Calas's execution.[3]

Although the argumentation in the *Traité sur la tolérance* is far from linear, and Voltaire for the most part takes the well-worn path of biblical citation and example to plead for religious tolerance between Christians, he does advance some general arguments in favor of religious toleration that are consistent with liberal natural rights theory. In so doing, he establishes in the eighteenth-century French context a rational argument for ceasing religious persecution, not unlike Locke's strategies in the *Letter on Toleration*.[4] Addressing himself as Locke did to the intolerant themselves, Voltaire cloaks his condemnation of the kind of religious fanaticism that leads to persecution under a more general Enlightenment plea for greater use of reason to combat superstition: "Philosophy, only philosophy, that sister of religion, disarmed the hands that superstitution had for so long bloodied; and the human spirit, waking from its drunkenness, surprised itself with the excesses to which fanaticism had driven it." [5] Within this general appeal to the public to use its capacity to reason in order to curtail the impulses of superstition and fanaticism, he invokes arguments concerning both national interest and a notion of natural morality to bring religious persecution to an end.

Voltaire's first argument in favor of toleration invokes examples that resemble what Michael Walzer characterizes as a form of toleration found in multinational empires.[6] Walzer describes this political organization, which maintains tolerance in the interests of peace, in the following terms:

> The oldest arrangements are those of the great multinational empires—beginning, for our purposes, with Persia, Ptolemaic Egypt, and Rome. Here the various groups are constituted as autonomous or semi-autonomous communities that are political or legal as well as cultural or religious in character, and that rule themselves across a considerable range of their activities. The groups have no choice but to coexist with one another, for their interactions are governed by the imperial bureaucrats in accordance with an imperial code . . . which is designed to maintain some minimal fairness, as fairness is understood in the imperial center.[7]

Consistent with Walzer's description, Voltaire writes, "Go to India, to Persia, to Tartary, you will see there the same tolerance and the same tranquility. Peter the Great encouraged all cults in his vast empire;

trade and agriculture benefited from it and the body politic never suffered because of it."[8] This purely pragmatic argument for tolerance, both in the interests of peace, as Walzer suggests, and in the interests of national prosperity, calls on the public's ability to discern rationally what is to be gained by allowing differences to peaceably coexist. Although France is clearly not a vast empire with numerous religious and cultural subgroups, and this point makes the argument less relevant to the French context, nonetheless Voltaire hopes to show that "enlightened despotism" has something to offer by way of example. His main point is that civil war—which is what religious persecution amounts to—can only serve to weaken the nation as a whole: "Finally this tolerance never provoked a civil war; intolerance covered the earth with carnage. Let us now judge between the two rivals, between the mother who would have her son's throat slit and the mother that surrenders him provided that he live!"[9] According to Voltaire, it is not possible rationally to choose intolerance from the perspective of national interest.

In partial response to the anticipated charge that France does not have the kind of diversity present in Peter the Great's empire, and as a corollary to the argument in favor of national peace and prosperity, Voltaire advances the further claim that the more numerous the sects, the less powerful each one is individually. Echoing the famous description of the stock exchange in London from the *Lettres philosophiques*,[10] he writes:

> We have Jews in Bordeaux, in Metz, in Alsace; we have Lutherans, Molinists, Jansenists: can't we suffer and control the Calvinists under roughly the same conditions by which Catholics are tolerated in London? *The more sects there are, the less dangerous each one is; their multiplicity weakens them*; all are checked by just laws that prohibit tumultuous assemblies, insults, and sedition and that are always enforced by the coactive force of the community.[11]

Again fully consistent with Walzer's analysis of tolerance in multinational empires, Voltaire makes no claims about any value to society derived from religious diversity. Religious diversity simply helps to prevent one group from gaining too much power. The groups hold each other in check in much the same way that Montesquieu recommends for democratic republics.[12]

But as Voltaire's argument advances, he adds another dimension to the pragmatic concerns of peace and prosperity for the nation. He pleads with a more insistent and personal rhetoric for basic rights to be granted to disenfranchised groups, but most particularly to Calvinists. Invoking natural law, he asks that they be allowed to live in peace:

> We know that several fathers of families, who have made great for-
> tunes in foreign countries, are ready to return to their homeland; all
> they ask for is *the protection of natural law*, the validity of their mar-
> riages, the right to inherit from their fathers, the enfranchisement of
> their persons; no public temples, no right to municipal offices or dig-
> nities. . . . It is not a question any longer of giving immense privileges
> and secure positions to a faction, but of *allowing a peaceful people to
> live.*[13] [My emphasis.]

Using a rhetoric aimed at stirring up sympathy for persecuted groups
by emphasizing the basic rights at stake in such disputes, Voltaire
claims to seek the protection of natural law for these people. However,
the rights he lists are not natural rights at all but civil rights, with the
possible exception of the right of inheritance, viewed by natural rights
theorists following Locke as a natural right.[14] These people are already
married within their own church; what they seek is civil recognition of
the marriage ceremony performed outside the Catholic Church. In
spite of the claims of the natural rights theorists, the right to inherit
follows directly from having the marriages recognized by the state,
since the distribution of property after death requires that the heirs be
legitimate heirs. But it is the tone of the passage, the appeal to natural
law, and, above all, the basic nature of the rights being asked for that
allow Voltaire to argue as though it were a question of natural law.

After the granting of these basic rights by the state, the form of tolerance advocated by Voltaire simply requires that the intolerant desist
from persecution of religious minorities and grant them some basic
rights and freedoms. He clearly does not advocate making them full-
fledged citizens since he does not include the right to hold public office. He simply wants Protestants to be allowed to live peacefully.

From the intolerant person, this would simply require ceasing to
cause harm to members of religious minorities. The state would have to
make the appropriate legal changes to recognize Protestant marriage
ceremonies and thereby make inheritance possible. These are requirements of a negative conception of liberty and rights at the most basic
level: freedom from harm. Since Voltaire's plea does not include recognizing Protestants as citizens capable of holding public office, it does
not include any positive duties on the part of the state—aside from recognizing Protestant marriages—and certainly not on the part of fellow
citizens.[15]

While this appears on the surface to be a fairly simple and straight-
forward request, the intolerant person probably does not see it this
way. As many have pointed out, from the perspective of intolerance,
the practices that are not tolerated usually evoke more than a simple

feeling of dislike or distaste. Susan Mendus summarizes the stronger intolerant point of view as one of moral condemnation in the following terms:

> Many of the truly difficult cases in which the question of toleration arises are cases in which the tolerator disapproves morally of the thing tolerated. . . . [A]mongst the most problematic cases of toleration are those in which what is tolerated is believed to be morally wrong (not merely disliked) and where it is held that there are not compensating virtues associated with the thing tolerated. Religious examples are amongst the most obvious here.[16]

Thus, although Voltaire's demands on behalf of the Protestant community seem fairly unproblematic, to the intolerant person it is an injunction to allow things that s/he judges to be morally wrong. Asking the state to recognize Protestant marriages[17] and allow for Protestants' rights of inheritance may appear to some to be a request to tolerate or even condone sinful and perhaps even corrupting behavior.[18]

In spite of the moral difficulty involved in requiring tolerance in problematic cases where the tolerated behavior is viewed as morally wrong, Voltaire's plea on behalf of Protestants still amounts to only a limited form of obligation. Toleration would require simply leaving Protestants alone to conduct their lives and business in peace. It would not involve positive measures to allow them to participate fully in the community—by holding public office or opening places of worship—and certainly would entail nothing like the arguments in favor of affirmative action or preferential hiring that require compensatory behavior from a discriminatory society.[19] Insofar as Voltaire sticks to basic civil rights and freedoms—even though they are couched in the language of natural law—he does not go beyond a minimal conception of duties and obligations toward religious minorities based on a purely negative conception of freedom and rights. Tolerance amounts to the simple maxim, "live and let live."

Pitié in Rousseau

The argument in favor of tolerance in Voltaire's *Traité*, like the weak form of tolerance in Montesquieu discussed in chapter 4, highlights differences between individuals and groups of individuals. By calling upon intolerants to desist from harming or persecuting Protestants—especially with a plea that reinscribes their difference by not advocating their full political participation—Voltaire underscores the fact of difference as the most significant issue under debate. Unlike later liberal arguments in favor of diversity, like John Stuart Mill's in *On Liberty*, arguing that diversity is good in pluralistic societies, this type of minimal argument in favor of toleration merely acknowledges difference and prescribes rules of behavior for dealing with it, namely, noninterference. It stops short of granting full rights to minority groups, and it certainly does not valorize the existence of minority subcultures as a bonus to societies. The most that can be said of the minimalist position of "live and let live" is that it establishes some negative rights and liberties for religious or cultural minorities and condemns persecution as irrational.[20] It ultimately rests, however, on a fundamental recognition and reinscription of difference.

To shift from the question of tolerance to eighteenth-century formulations and representations of sympathy requires a shift in emphasis from difference to sameness. Mirroring the fundamental tension between the two competing notions of tolerance in Montesquieu, the concepts of tolerance and sympathy rest upon opposing attitudes toward other persons: while minimalist accounts of tolerance tend to underscore difference, accounts of sympathy require seeing beyond superficial differences to a sameness beneath. In my examinations of Rousseau's and Charrière's versions of sympathy, I develop an alternative moral reaction to difference that goes beyond the negative conception of rights and liberties central to Voltaire's argument and more closely resembles the recognition of sameness entailed in Montesquieu's strong version of tolerance.

In Rousseau's *Discours sur l'origine de l'inégalité*, pity plays a central role in providing a social predisposition in an otherwise asocial or even antisocial account of man in the state of nature. As I have argued elsewhere, Rousseau's description of pity in the state of nature seems superfluous given the isolation of natural man's existence.[21] Pity provides a foundation for later moral life by establishing an almost instinctual connection between not only members of the same species but all sentient beings. Prior to reason, it springs from a recognition of pain and suffering in fellow sentient creatures. Using Mandeville against himself, Rousseau writes:

> It is with pleasure that one sees the author of the fable, *The Bees*, forced to recognize man as a compassionate and sensitive being, to leave in the example that he gives of it his cold and subtle style to offer us the pathetic image of a man enclosed who perceives outside a ferocious beast tearing a child from its mother's breast, breaking under its murderous teeth the frail limbs and tearing with its claws the throbbing entrails of the child. What atrocious agitation must this witness not feel because of an event in which he has no personal interest?

What anguish must he not suffer at its sight, for not being able to bring any aid to the mother who has fainted, nor to the dying child? Such is the pure movement of nature, prior to all reflection: such is the force of natural pity.[22]

Natural pity causes man to feel emotional stirrings when confronted with the suffering of other creatures. In this way, Rousseau provides a foundation for later social life insofar as man is naturally predisposed to some feelings of attachment to his fellow creatures.

By attributing pity to man in the state of nature, Rousseau sidesteps the issue of how persons come to feel such strong feelings of emotional identification with other feeling beings. "Naturalizing" pity also avoids the problem of prescribing such behavior. In opposition to the minimalist account of tolerance in Voltaire—which relies on negative conceptions of rights and freedom and the perfect duty not to cause harm to others different from ourselves that can easily be translated into a contractual form of obligation—pity defies such easy definition. Recourse to Nature in effect naturalizes behaviors that cannot easily be put into contractual terms.

Rousseau's account of *pitié* in the *Discourse on Inequality* also fails to confront other difficulties in theorizing human feelings of compassion for other sentient creatures. The desire to attribute feelings of pity to natural man prior to significant intellectual development causes Rousseau not to question the psychological mechanisms that foster feelings of pity. That is to say, because his account of natural man remains quite animalistic—without the intellectual capacity for abstraction or comparison—his account of pity also remains sketchy at best.[23] In the *Essai sur l'origine des langues*, Rousseau again confronts the question of pity, this time developing a significantly more nuanced explanation of the mental operations involved.

Whereas in the *Second Discourse* Rousseau attributes pity to man before he has developed the capacity to reason and certainly before he participates in any type of social existence with his fellow creatures, in the *Essay on the Origin of Language* Rousseau must concentrate on a fundamentally social phenomenon: language. In his account of pity in the *Essay*, he reiterates that pity exists natually, before the development of our reasoning capacities, but he nuances his account to claim that without intellectual development, pity would remain essentially inactive:[24]

Social affections only develop in us with our capacity for understanding. Pity, although natural in the heart of man, would remain eternally inactive without the imagination that sets it in motion.[25]

The imagination is now required for pity to function where it was absent in the *Second Discourse*. In the description of pity that follows, Rousseau stresses all the mental operations that contribute to the feeling of pity, contradicting his earlier account:

> How do we allow ourselves to be moved by pity? In transporting ourselves out of ourselves; in identifying with the suffering being. We only suffer as much as we judge that he suffers; it is not in ourselves, it is in him that we suffer. When one thinks how much acquired knowledge this transport presupposes! How would I imagine ills that I don't have any idea of? How would I suffer in seeing the suffering of another if I don't even know that he suffers, if I don't know what we have in common, the two of us? The person who has never reflected can be neither merciful nor just nor pitiable; nor can he be mean or vindictive. The person who imagines nothing feels only himself; he is alone in the middle of the human race.[26]

In spite of the passivity that characterizes the introductory question ("How do we allow ourselves to be moved by pity?"/"Comment nous laissons-nous émouvoir à la pitié?"), in this account of pity Rousseau enumerates all the mental operations needed to feel compassion for another. Imagination is required because in the process of identification we must transport ourselves out of ourselves and suffer along with the suffering being. We must be able to imagine the suffering of the person for whom we feel compassion at the same time that we imagine ourselves suffering the same fate. In addition to imagination, this also requires judgment: we judge that another being suffers, and although Rousseau does not say it, we also judge the degree to which he suffers. But most importantly, the sympathy described by Rousseau hinges on a fundamental recognition of what the two beings hold in common, "what we have in common, the two of us."[27] In fact, the mental process of identification, which requires judgment, imagination, knowledge, and understanding, presupposes this recognition of commonality. Without it there would be no sympathy.[28]

It is quite clear in the *Discourse on Inequality* that the basis for identification is the ability to experience pain. In the *Essay*, the further development of the type of identification needed for compassion suggests that the recognition of commonality goes beyond the simple ability to experience pain to a more fundamental recognition of common humanity. The end of the quotation above ("The person who imagines nothing feels only himself; he is alone in the middle of the human race") indicates that those who do not experience identification with other humans lead their lives essentially in isolation.

It should be clear from my discussion of Rousseauean pity in relation to the minimalist version of toleration endorsed by Voltaire that the significant difference between the two moral attitudes lies in their focus. While tolerance requires restraint from doing harm in the face of difference, pity asks the one who pities to bridge the gap of difference by identifying with the one who suffers. In other words, tolerance reinscribes difference while compassion tends to efface it.

But it is also true that Voltaire's rhetoric attempts to engage our sympathy. In asking for basic civil rights for Protestants, Voltaire appeals to our sympathy for people experiencing religious persecution and then uses it to support a modest claim for tolerance. Be that as it may, his appeal still reinscribes the difference that his rhetoric initially effaces: tolerated Protestants will still be viewed as fundamentally different. This is perhaps nowhere more evident than in Voltaire's reformulation of the Golden Rule as "Do not do unto others what you would not have them do unto you."[29] This formulation falls squarely within the bounds of negative freedom. In contrast, Rousseau writes, "Do unto others as you would have them do unto you," but also, "Do what is good for yourself with the least possible amount of harm to others."[30] The first, classical formulation clearly requires identification and empathy as each person is asked to put himself in the place of the other. But even Rousseau's second formulation goes beyond the negative duty of Voltaire's formulation. Going about our business with care to do the least amount of harm to others still requires placing ourselves in the other's position. We must see the world as the other sees it in order to determine which course of action will do another the least amount of harm.[31]

From these various formulations of the Golden Rule, it is evident that even a minimalist account of pity requires a positive obligation in the form of some sort of identification with the other. It is precisely this type of obligation that is difficult, if not impossible, to translate into terms of contractual obligation. In the next section I turn to Isabelle de Charrière's depictions of compassion in *Caliste ou lettres écrites de Lausanne* in order to formulate what this imperfect duty entails.

Charrière's Compassion

Teasing a theory of compassion out of a novel at first glance appears difficult enough without the added burden of comparing such a reconstructed theory to formulations, such as Voltaire's and Rousseau's, that were originally written as theoretical formulations. And yet, such a reading, as I argued in the introduction, is invited by the literary theory of the period that posits serious moral effects, both positive and negative, from the reading of novels. The more serious difficulty, or even impossibility, as I have suggested, resides in the formulation of a theory of compassion in terms of contractual obligation.

Rousseau's versions of pity in the *Second Discourse* and the *Essay on the Origin of Language* give an inadequate account of the type of relationship entailed when compassion or sympathy is invoked. Mostly, this is due to the fact that Rousseau describes pity, particularly in the *Discourse on Inequality*, in such a way that it does not require moral action; he identifies it only as a "natural" feeling. Likewise, in the *Essay*, the focus is less on the type of moral relationship instantiated between the two people and more on the fact of sociability and the psychological and intellectual prerequisites for it. For these reasons, Rousseau's accounts of pity fall short of offering a sketch of the moral relationship that ensues. My discussion of *Emile* in chapter 2 has also raised a fundamental difficulty in Rousseau in theorizing ongoing relations of care to which I will return in the context of marriage in chapter 7. For Rousseau early childhood education should scrupulously avoid any attention to relations of care, and the education of adolescence teaches compassion through abstract maxims. This combination of avoidance in early childhood and teaching through abstraction in adolescence seems both inconsistent with Rousseau's general philosophy of education and at odds with his pronouncements about the "naturalness" of *pitié*. Moreover, the centrality of the conception of compassion to his moral theory requires a more fully elaborated description of the relationship that compassion creates between individuals. Despite the difficulties involved, I believe that an analysis of Charrière's representations of compassion is warranted in order to establish a fuller account of the moral obligation that compassion entails.

I would like to make it clear at the outset that I do not mean to imply a gendered separation of duties by my choice of texts in this chapter. Although, clearly, the eighteenth century often recognized a gendered division of labor in moral matters, I am not arguing for such a separation. As Lieselotte Steinbrügge and others have argued, there was often a distinction in Enlightenment thought between reason and sentiment that followed the gender divide. According to Steinbrügge,

> Morality based on sentiment did not, after all, dispense with the functions of reason. In Enlightenment moral philosophy, both elements—instinctive, spontaneous moral feeling and the rational weighing of interests—were necessary for moral action. But the shift in emphasis from reason to sentiment was extended to women. The contradictory relations between calculating reason and compassionate feeling, be-

tween private and public morality, were borne unequally by men and women. The greater emphasis on "natural foundations"—only one tendency in the anthropological discourse of the time—is magnified in the case of women. Women become the "moral sex."[32]

Consistent with Steinbrügge's characterization, Charrière's female characters display more compassion than their male counterparts. However, Rousseau's and other theorists' formulations concerning *pitié* or sympathy demonstrate the degree to which it was understood as foundational for moral behavior. I would like to leave aside the gendered subtext of this discussion, all the while acknowledging the implied gendered division of labor that it suggests, to focus rather on the critical implications of Charrière's representation of compassion.[33]

To complicate matters further, Charrière's *Caliste ou lettres écrites de Lausanne* has a double narrative structure that enacts sympathy at a number of different levels, but it is precisely for this reason that I have chosen it to stand in as/for a theoretical discussion of sympathy. My analysis of the novel will proceed from the level of represented events toward a consideration of form and reader positioning in order to reconstruct a theory of compassion.

At the most basic level, Charrière's novel provides scenes that demonstrate acts of compassion and sympathy as the characters interact with one another. Clearly influenced by Rousseau,[34] Charrière places her characters in situations that allow for other characters to approve (or even disapprove) of compassionate acts. In this way, her narrative clearly valorizes particular acts as fundamentally moral. For example, when Cécile learns of a servant who is dying of consumption, she asks her mother to speak to him in English to make sure his needs are being met:

> [Cécile] sees some milk being carried out of the kitchen and learns that it is to a sick person that it is being taken, to a Negro dying of consumption, that the English people, whose servant he was, left in the house. . . . Cécile came to find me with this information, and begged me to go with her to the Negro, to speak English to him, to learn from him if we could do anything that would be pleasing for him. "I was told, Mama, that he doesn't know any French. Who knows," she said, "if these people, in spite of all their good will, guess his needs?" We went to him.[35]

The fact that the act of compassion is for a servant and a person of color only strengthens the representation. Charrière, by using the example of a black servant, emphasizes, more than Voltaire or Rousseau, the extent of difference—here racial, class, and cultural—that can and needs to be bridged in the act of sympathy. The mother's aid in Cécile's project and her recounting of the incident within the epistolary narrative—a structure I shall return to—serves as approbation and valorization of the act itself. The mother's assistance and approval of Cécile's actions frame the scene as a moral example.

In a similar vein, Cécile's care for a lost, tired dog also illustrates the kind of moral act of compassion that the narrative endorses and teaches through example. Overcoming her own fear, and reaching out instinctively to the exhausted animal, she demonstrates that compassion is not limited to creatures of her own species:

> At the moment when they were going to leave us, here's a beautiful Great Dane who comes to us, grazing his muzzle over the snow-covered ground; it was a last effort, a pile of snow stops him; he searches with a worried look, stumbles, and falls at Cécile's feet. She lowers herself. Milord cries out and wants to hold her back; but Cécile, maintaining to him that it's not a rabid dog, but a dog who has lost its master, a poor dog half dead of fatigue, hunger, and cold, persists in petting him.[36]

While Milord tries to stop her, Cécile attends to the dog. Identifying with an animal, she recognizes the dog's needs—just as she wanted to be certain of the servant's—and nurses him back to health.

Having narrated the scene of compassion between Cécile and the dog, the mother summarizes:

> Instead of reasoning, instead of moralizing, give something to love to someone who loves; if loving is the person's peril, loving will be her safeguard; if loving is her misfortune, loving will be her consolation; for the person who knows how to love, it is the only occupation, the only distraction, the only pleasure of life.[37]

The mother's commentary highlights one of the main difficulties in theorizing compassion: Whereas tolerance requires desisting from certain activities, compassion not only requires positive action but also seems to require, an ability to love, as the narrator puts it here. Following Rousseau's general advice in *Emile*—but not his specific advice with respect to compassion—she allows her child to grow and learn by doing. She has given Cécile something to love and now Cécile is capable of love. Teaching compassion cannot be reduced to the simple formula of Voltaire's *Traité*: do not do unto others as you would not have them do unto you. Teaching compassion seems to be a slow process of growth and development over time that has to be modeled and emulated.

The end result in the behavior of people who are not taught to be compassionate is evident in the negative example offered in the parallel narrative of the novel. The story of the fallen woman, Caliste, illustrates the victimization of a woman whose undeserved reputation prevents her from enjoying what is clearly presented in the Cécile portion of the narrative as the greatest pleasure in life: the love between parent and child. William's recounting of his missed opportunity to wed Caliste and raise a family with her underscores his lack of compassion and sympathy. This inability to empathize leads not only to Caliste's demise but to his own state of regret and despair. Having chosen to listen to the advice of his family, and having allowed himself to be swayed by the force of public opinion, William demonstrates his own lack of humanity by not marrying Caliste. Echoing the equation of compassion and love from the Cécile portion of the narrative, William insists on Caliste's great gift in this area and his own inadequacy as he describes his loss and regret upon her death. In a letter full of "should haves," William associates love with compassion:

> at least, for the price of such a long and tender passion, to give her the pleasure of seeing me while she was dying, to see that she hadn't loved an unfeeling automaton and that, if I hadn't known how to love her in the way that she deserved, I would know how to mourn her? But it's too late, my regrets also came too late, and she does not know about them. She did not know about them, I should say: I must finally have the courage to believe her dead. If there had been any return of hope, she would have wanted to soften the impression of her letter, because she, she knew how to love. Here I am then, alone on the earth.[38]

Even on her deathbed, he imagines her having enough compassion for his suffering that she would have disabused him of his belief that she was dying, had it not been true. He finds himself alone, as Rousseau predicts in the *Essay* ("The person who imagines nothing feels only himself; he is alone in the middle of the human race") because he did not know how to love. From the position of hindsight, having lost his true love because of a lack of compassion, he finally shows some evidence that he is not an "unfeeling automaton." Having suffered, he has learned the lesson of sympathy, but too late. However sensitive and special William may be because of his early connection to his twin brother, his role in the Caliste narrative underscores his inadequacy in the moral realm of personal relations because his realization comes too late and at the cost of Caliste's life.

It is clear from William's formulations and Cécile's mother's formulations, as well from the dog episode, that for Charrière, loving means having compassion for another. This compassion reaches beyond

public opinion and creates a bond between people that is a defining
feature of their common humanity.

The double narrative structure of Charrière's novel invites a comparison between the love relationship in the first half of the novel (Cécile and her mother) and the failed love relationship in the second half
of the novel (Caliste and William). What the structure suggests, and
what is clearly underscored in pointed passages, is that truly moral relations of care and compassion exist more often between parents and
children than between lovers or marriage partners. Deserving women—
from a moral perspective—like Caliste find themselves victimized by the
lack of compassion of those around them.[39] In a similar way, underscoring the lack of foundation for true relations of love and care, Cécile
also finds herself rejected by her potential suitor, Édouard, at the end
of the novel.

The focus on parent-child relations foregrounds an important aspect
of Charrière's understanding of the bond of compassion that I have already mentioned: it develops slowly over time. Moreover, compassion
has to be learned. It cannot be prescribed. In this respect, the epistolary
structure of the novel plays an important role in theorizing about compassion as well. The epistolary format allows the reader to voyeuristi-
cally become the mother's destinatee but also, in a sense, her
child/pupil as well. Reading the mother's narrative of Cécile's experience as it unfolds in her letters, as well as hearing her approve or disapprove of Cécile's behavior, teaches judgment as well as sympathy. In
effect, Charrière capitalizes on the eighteenth-century aesthetic of theatricality to teach moral lessons both about and through scenes of sympathy.[40]

Both the double narrative structure of the novel and the epistolary
form enable the creation of a reader position that fosters moral teaching. The double narrative structure invites active comparison between
the Caliste story as told by William and the story of Cécile's moral education as told by her mother. The epistolary form creates narrative levels that frame the moral tale in such a way as to place the reader at the
same level as the inscribed writer/narrator, Cécile's mother. That is to
say, because the letters are destined for a specific interlocutor, Madame
la Marquise de S., the reader usurps this position and occupies the ex-
tra-textual space created by the epistolary fiction.[41] The fact that the
destinatee possesses high moral character is inscribed in the dedication,
which pushes the reader also to assume the perspective of unquestion-
able moral authority:

> If, instead of a mix of passion and of reason, of weakness and of virtue
> such as one ordinarily finds in society, these letters only painted pure

virtues such as one sees in you, the editor would have dared to orna-
ment them with your name and thus do you great honor.[42]

The explained omission of the fictitious destinatee's name only further
encourages the reader to slip into her position and occupy the space of
"pure virtue." Because the reader does not possess such pure virtue,
occupying the destinatee's position becomes a process of apprentice-
ship: reading the letters will teach the moral lessons that the fictitious
destinatee already knows and that the real reader will now seek to
emulate. Thus, positioned in the moral space created by the dedication,
the reader judges the acts depicted in the novel, with the narrator's
gentle guidance, and learns the moral lesson of compassion.

Contractual Obligations and Imperfect Duties: From Tolerance to Sympathy

As I suggested at the beginning of my discussion of Charrière's novel,
reducing compassion to a contractual formulation requires overcoming
a series of obstacles. Most serious among these are the difficulties associated with the nature of the relationship created in the bond of sympathy. While tolerance requires desisting from certain behaviors and
practices and, as I have already suggested, can be easily stated in terms
of negative freedom and rights, compassion entails an imperfect duty to
bridge the gap of difference, identify with another human being, and
be moved to certain feelings toward this fellow person. Charrière's
novel also suggests, and this constitutes a further obstacle to a contractual formulation, that feelings of compassion need to be developed
over time through example and experience. In other words, compassion is a learned behavior.

To characterize these differences between tolerance and sympathy in
another way, tolerance is a moral attitude that can be fairly easily legislated. Its boundaries are fairly clear. Voltaire's negative formulation ex-
emplifies the ease with which tolerance can be put into a formula that
makes all parties' obligations and responsibilities clear. Although,
clearly, learning tolerance from one's parents, for example, might fa-
cilitate later moral behavior, such learning is not stricly required. Sympathy, on the other hand, while it is also a moral attitude, cannot be so
easily legislated. Even the positive formulation of the Golden Rule, "do
unto others as you would have them do unto you," on close inspection
reveals a lack of precision regarding the duties that it entails. Not to
mention the added difficulty that as a piece of legislation it would be
meaningless.

To take an example from Charrière that I have already analyzed, the duty to feel compassion for another's suffering compels Cécile to persuade her mother to speak English with the black servant dying of consumption in order to ensure that all his needs are being met. Why should the Golden Rule compel such behavior? Cécile is prompted to make an inquiry when she sees milk being taken from the kitchen, which leads to her discovery of the servant and her subsequent actions. But why not simply allow the people who are already caring for the dying man to continue? Why should she extend herself in this set of circumstances? She could just as easily conclude that his needs are being met, that she herself would desire no more in like circumstances, and that, therefore, according to the Golden Rule, her obligations have been met even without becoming personally involved.

Looking at the Kantian formulation,[43] if Cécile had decided not to help the dying man by asking her mother to speak English with him, and had tested her decision according to the categorical imperative, I believe this omission would not be subject to condemnation under that formulation either. If all others acted in this case as Cécile could have acted, that is, knowing that the man was being cared for, and chose not to get involved, this, as a general principle of behavior, would not lead to moral chaos. In other words, the duty to act in this case as Cécile acted seems to go beyond what is required for a general rule of behavior. This is not to say that acts of sympathy cannot be made consistent with the categorical imperative, because clearly they can. Putting oneself in the other's position and acting as one would want to be treated fits the criteria of the categorical imperative inasmuch as such conduct would constitute an appropriate general rule of behavior. However, the problem lies in the fact that as a rule of behavior, compassion remains as empty and formal as the categorical imperative itself. Are we to be minimally decent human beings when it comes to compassion, or are we to go the extra mile and strive to be extraordinarily compassionate, and thus moral, beings as Cécile does?

Charrière's novel, insofar as it establishes Cécile as an example, models compassionate behavior that goes beyond the strict requirements of the categorical imperative. Testing what one ought to do according to the principle of generalizability will not answer the question of how far one should go in acts of compassion.

To look at the question another way, perhaps the question of compassion really amounts to an issue of justice and fairness, as Rawls would contend.[44] But even imagined from the perspective of the original position, distinterestedness and rationality do not establish limits of compassion but rather minimal standards for decency. Like the categorical imperative, the Rawlsian conception of justice yields a conception of appropriate moral behavior, based on fairness, that cannot tell us how far to go in acts of compassion. In these abstract formulations, as in the formulations of tolerance, the lines are drawn according to minimal and therefore negatively conceived models of behavior. Sympathy does not function according to the negative model.

To raise another difficulty, acts of compassion and sympathy, even in Rousseau, are dependent on the *feeling* of identification with another being. One is moved by a "natural" feeling according to Rousseau, or a learned feeling according to Charrière, but it is nonetheless a feeling. How does one prescribe or legislate a feeling? In this regard, the categorical imperative or Rawls's original position are weak prescriptive versions of compassion that dictate the parameters of moral behavior to ensure justice and fairness but stop short of prescribing feelings. They serve as guides to making judgments that will be just and fair, but they cannot tell us how to feel toward others that are different from ourselves.

In this regard it is significant that Charrière stages her novel within the confines of the mother/daughter relationship. By representing family relations, she creates a context for the bond of sympathy that goes beyond the impersonal relations between strangers that Kant and Rawls have in mind. This is not to suggest that Cécile does not have feelings of sympathy for strangers, for clearly she does, but only that the mother/daughter relationship enables those feelings of sympathy to develop. Charrière suggests that it is from the context of family relations that children learn to extend feelings of care and compassion outward to the external world.

Now, my analysis in chapter 2 revealed that it was precisely these feelings of connectedness that were missing from Emile's moral education. Emile's moral autonomy was created within the fiction of his natural freedom, which concealed his dependence on his tutor and the human community more generally. Lacking the family structure as support for his development, I argued, Emile's self-conception would be inadequate for future participation as a citizen of a republic (which would represent a broader community) or as a parent. The negative contractual obligation that was established between Emile and Robert the gardener would be closer to Voltaire's formulation of tolerance than to Charrière's conception of compassion for others.[45] And as we will see in chapter 7, the marriage contract also provides an occasion for a glimpse into an area where contractual obligation is inadequate to the task of defining duties in interpersonal relationships within the family.

The family context, conveniently located in the private sphere, functions in liberalism to compensate for the lack of connectedness that is theorized in negative terms in the public sphere. In other words, contractual obligations prescribe minimal standards of decency for human interaction between relative strangers while the family is designated as a site for moral development of a fuller type. The messiness of compassion, therefore, need not be rendered theoretically, for it resides within the sphere of familial relations into which contractual relations are not supposed to intrude.[46] For this reason also, the strongest depictions of sympathy often reside in novels and not in treatises on morality.

But, as I have suggested, this neat separation does not really answer the questions at hand. Questions of justice and fairness require not only negative prescriptions of minimal standards of moral decency but also an equal measure of identification. As Voltaire's rhetoric makes clear, being motivated to tolerance often requires appeals to sympathy. Identification with others can only aid the causes of tolerance, justice, and fairness by creating bonds between members of communities.[47]

In part 3 of this book, I turn to questions concerning the private sphere as it is represented and theorized in French liberalism of the eighteenth century. Using the works of Sade, Rousseau, and Charrière, I explore the limits of liberal conceptions of human relations as they are played out in the private sphere of marriage and the family.

Notes

[1] Jean-Jacques Rousseau's *Essai sur l'origine des langues où il est parlé de la mélodie et de l'imitation musicale* was published posthumously in 1781. It was most likely written in 1761. For the composition and publication history of the *Essai*, see Jean Starobinski's discussion in the Gallimard edition (Paris: Gallimard, 1990), pp. 193–200.

[2] Isabelle de Charrière's *Caliste* and *Les Lettres écrites de Lausanne* were originally published independently.

[3] For the details of "L'Affaire Calas" and Voltaire's involvement, see David D. Bien, *The Calas Affair: Persecution, Toleration and Heresy in Eighteenth-Century Toulouse* (Princeton, N. J.: Princeton University Press, 1960).

[4] For a modern defense of Locke's arguments, see Susan Mendus, *Toleration and the Limits of Liberalism* (London: Macmillan, 1989), esp. pp. 22–43.

[5] "La philosophie, la seule philosophie, cette soeur de la religion, a désarmé des mains que la superstition avait si longtemps ensanglantées; et l'esprit humain, au réveil de son ivresse, s'est étonné des excès où l'avait emporté le fa-

natisme" (96). Voltaire, *Traité sur la tolérance* (Geneva: Editions du cheval ailé, 1948). All parenthentical citations to this work in the notes to chapter 5 are to this edition. Translations are my own.

[6]Michael Walzer, *On Toleration* (New Haven, Conn.: Yale University Press, 1997), pp. 14–19.

[7] Ibid., p. 14.

[8] "Allez dans l'Inde, dans la Perse, dans la Tartarie, vous y verrez la même tolérance et la même tranquillité. Pierre le Grand a favorisé tous les cultes dans son vaste empire; le commerce et l'agriculture y ont gagné, et le corps politique n'en a jamais souffert" (98).

[9] "Enfin cette tolérance n'a jamais excité de guerre civile; l'intolérance a couvert la terre de carnage. Qu'on juge maintenant entre ces deux rivales, entre la mère qui veut qu'on égorge son fils, et la mère qui le cède pourvu qu'il vive!" (101).

[10]See Voltaire, *Lettres philosophiques*, (Paris: Garnier-Flammarion, 1964), sixth letter, p. 47.

[11] "Nous avons des juifs à Bordeaux, à Metz, en Alsace; nous avons des luthériens, des molinistes, des jansénistes: ne pouvons-nous souffrir et contenir des calvinistes à peu près aux mêmes conditions que les catholiques sont tolérés à Londres? *Plus il y a de sectes, moins chacune est dangereuse; la multiplicité les affaiblit*, toutes sont réprimées par de justes lois qui défendent les assemblées tumultueuses, les injures, les séditions, et qui sont toujours en vigueur par la force coactive" (103–4). [My emphasis.]

[12]This was the position adopted in the *Déclaration des droits de l'Homme et du Citoyen* as well. See article 10 on religious freedom.

[13] "Nous savons que plusieurs chefs de famille, qui ont élevé de grandes fortunes dans les pays étrangers, sont prêts à retourner dans leur patrie; ils ne demandent que *la protection de la loi naturelle*, la validité de leurs mariages, la certitude de l'état de leurs enfants, le droit d'hériter de leurs pères, la franchise de leurs personnes; point de temples publics, point de droit aux charges municipales, aux dignités. . . . Il ne s'agit plus de donner des priviléges immenses, des places de sûreté à une faction, mais de *laisser vivre un peuple paisible*" (104). [My emphasis.]

[14]C. B. Macpherson, speaking of Locke, asserts on this point, "The natural right of children to inherit the possessions of their parents is deduced from the 'strong desire' men have 'of propogating their kind, and continuing themselves in their posterity.' If this desire is to be fulfilled, children must be allowed to have a right to a share of their parents' property." See C. B. Macpherson, "Natural Rights in Hobbes and Locke," *Political Theory and the Rights of Man*, ed. D. D. Raphael (Bloomington: Indiana University Press, 1967), p. 7. The internal citation is from John Locke, *First Treatise of Government, Two Treatises of Government*. The difficult line between natural

rights and civil rights is recognized in the Constitution of 1791 in the *Déclaration des droits de l'Homme et du Citoyen*. The right to property is listed among the natural rights (article 2), but no specific mention is made of the right of inheritance. Given the explicit motivation to outlaw the distinction of nobility and the practices that go along with it, the right to inheritance, after the revolution, was most likely understood as a civil right.

[15]D. D. Raphael distinguishes between rights of action and rights of recipience as well as between positive and negative obligations in the context of the question of human rights. He argues that there is a "real and important difference among human rights. Some are rights to liberty, rights to be *allowed* something, while others are rights to opportunity or more than opportunity, rights to be *given* something. When a man has a right to liberty, the obligation of those against whom he has the right is a *negative* obligation, an obligation to leave him alone, to leave him free to do as he thinks fit. But when he is said to have a right to participate in government, or a right to work, and even more when he is said to have a right to social security, the obligation of those against whom he has the right is a *positive* obligation, an obligation to provide him with something which he could not achieve by himself" "Human Rights Old and New," in *Political Theory and the Rights of Man*, pp. 60–61. On the whole, the rights claimed for Protestants by Voltaire amount to negative rights of liberty insofar as they demand only that Protestants be left alone, with the possible exception of the recognition of their marriages and therewith their rights of inheritance.

[16] Mendus, *Toleration*, p. 18.

[17]Protestant marriages were officially permitted and recognized in France by the Edict of Toleration of 1787. See James F. Traer, *Marriage and the Family in Eighteenth-Century France* (Ithaca, N. Y.: Cornell University Press, 1980), pp. 67–68; and Lynn Hunt, *The French Revolution and Human Rights: A Brief Documentary History* (Boston: Bedford Books, 1996), pp. 40–43.

[18]The closest example one finds today of this type of intolerance—outside of religious intolerance—is of homosexuality. Mendus makes this point in *Toleration*, pp. 3–5. Abundant evidence of the persistence of intolerance toward homosexuality exists in the debates over gay marriage both in the United States and in other countries.

[19]See Duncan Kennedy, *Sexy Dressing Etc.: Essays on the Power and Politics of Cultural Identity* (Cambridge: Harvard University Press, 1993), pp. 34–84, for a very strong case for affirmative action in view of promoting cultural pluralism. See also Ronald Dworkin's discussion of reverse discrimination in *Taking Rights Seriously* (Cambridge: Harvard University Press, 1977), pp. 223–39. On the question of preferential hiring, see, for example, Amy Gutmann's critique of Michael Walzer's position in "Justice Across the Spheres," in *Pluralism, Justice, and Equality*, ed. David Miller and Michael Walzer (Oxford: Oxford University Press, 1995), pp. 99–119.

[20]For a defense of this type of argument in relationship to the type of argument advanced by Mill in *On Liberty*, see Susan Mendus's reading of Locke's *Letter on Toleration* alongside of Mill, in Mendus, *Toleration and the Limits of Liberalism*.

[21]See my *Mass Enlightenment: Critical Studies in Rousseau and Diderot* (Albany: State University of New York Press, 1995), pp. 31–35. See also the discussion of the problem of sociability in the introduction to Part 1.

[22] "On voit avec plaisir l'auteur de la fable des *Abeilles*, forcé de reconnaître l'homme pour un être compatissant et sensible, sortir, dans l'exemple qu'il en donne, de son style froid et subtil, pour nous offrir la pathétique image d'un homme enfermé qui aperçoit au-dehors une bête féroce arranchant un enfant du sein de sa mère, brisant sous sa dent meurtrière les faibles membres, et déchirant de ses ongles les entrailles palpitantes de cet enfant. Quelle affreuse agitation n'éprouve point ce témoin d'un événement auquel il ne prend aucun intérêt personnel? Quelles angoisses ne souffre-t-il pas à cette vue, de ne pouvoir porter aucun secours à la mère évanouie, ni à l'enfant expirant? Tel est le pur mouvement de la nature, antérieur à toute réflexion: telle est la force de la pitié naturelle." Rousseau, *Discours sur l'origine de l'inégalité* in *Oeuvres complètes*, vol. 3, pp. 154–55.

[23]Elsewhere I have argued that his account of pity seeks to maintain natural man's freedom by ensuring that feelings of pity never compel him to act. See *Mass Enlightenment*, pp. 31–35.

[24] In this respect, the account of pity in the *Essay on the Origin of Language* is consistent with the relatively late appearance of pity in Emile, after Emile's capacity for reason and judgment has developed. See my discussion of pity in *Emile* in chapter 2.

[25] "Les affections sociales ne se dévelopent en nous qu'avec nos lumières. La pitié, bien que naturelle au coeur de l'homme resteroit éternellement inactive sans l'imagination qui la met en jeu." Rousseau, *Essai sur l'origine des langues*, p. 92.

[26] "Comment nous laissons-nous émouvoir à la pitié? En nous transportant hors de nous-mêmes; en nous identifiant avec l'être souffrant. Nous ne souffrons qu'autant que nous jugeons qu'il souffre; ce n'est pas dans nous c'est dans lui que nous souffrons. Qu'on songe combien ce transport suppose de connoissances acquises! Comment imaginerois-je des maux dont je n'ai nulle idée? comment souffrirois-je en voyant souffrir un autre si je ne sais pas même qu'il souffre, si j'ignore ce qu'il y a de commun entre lui et moi? Celui qui n'a jamais réfléchi ne peut être ni clément ni juste ni pitoyable; il ne peut pas non plus être méchant et vindicatif. Celui qui n'imagine rien ne sent que lui-même; il est seul au milieu du genre humain." Ibid.

[27] "[C]e qu'il y a de commun entre lui et moi." Ibid.

[28]Because the recognition of commonality is not present in the account in the *Second Discourse*, it is difficult at best to understand what pity really means in that context. Natural man, not yet having developed a sufficient amount of self-understanding to recognize, much less sympathize, with a fellow human is, according to the description in the *Essay*, not yet ready to have such feelings. See *Discours sur l'inégalité*, pp. 152–56.

[29] "*Ne fais pas ce que tu ne voudrais pas qu'on te fît*" (108).

[30] "*Fais à autrui comme tu veux qu'on te fasse*," and "*Fais ton bien avec le moindre mal d'autrui qu'il est possible*" (156).

[31]This articulation very nearly approaches a utilitarian calculus like that of Bentham's.

[32] Steinbrügge, *The Moral Sex: Woman's Nature in the French Enlightenment*, trans. Pamela E. Selwyn (Oxford: Oxford University Press, 1995), p. 107.

[33] For a discussion of the question of gender in relation to morality in eighteenth-century thought, see the introduction to part 3.

[34]See Nadine Bérenguier, "From Clarens to Hollow Park, Isabelle de Charrière's Quiet Revolution," *Studies in Eighteenth-Century Culture* 21 (1991), pp. 219–43; and my discussion of the *Lettres de Mistriss Henley* in chapter 7.

[35] "[Cécile] voit porter du lait hors de la cuisine et elle apprend que c'est à un malade qu'on le porte, à un nègre mourant de consomption, que des Anglais, dont il était le domestique, ont laissé dans cette maison. . . . Cécile vint me trouver avec cette information, et me supplia d'aller avec elle auprès du nègre, de lui parler anglais, de savoir de lui si nous ne pouvions rien lui donner qui lui fût agréable. —On m'a dit, maman, qu'il ne savait pas le français; qui sait, dit-elle, si ces gens, malgré toute leur bonne volonté, devinent ses besoins? Nous y allâmes" (105–6). Isabelle de Charrière, *Caliste ou lettres écrites de Lausanne* (Paris: Editions des Femmes, 1979). All parenthetical references to this work in notes in this section of chapter 5 are to this edition. Translations are my own.

[36] "Au moment où ils allaient nous quitter, voilà un beau chien danois qui vient à nous rasant son museau la terre couverte de neige; c'était un dernier effort, un monseau de neige l'arrête; il cherche d'un air inquiet, chancelle, et vient tomber aux pieds de Cécile. Elle se baisse. Milord s'écrie et veut la retenir; mais Cécile, lui soutenant que ce n'est pas un chien enragé, mais un chien qui a perdu son maître, un pauvre chien à moitié mort de fatigue, de faim et de froid, s'obstine à le caresser." (104–5).

[37] "Au lieu de raisonner, au lieu de moraliser, donnez à aimer à quelqu'un qui aime; si aimer fait son danger, aimer sera sa sauvegarde; si aimer fait son malheur, aimer sera sa consolation; pour qui sait aimer, c'est la seule occupation, la seule distraction, le seul plaisir de la vie" (105).

[38] "[A]u moins, pour prix d'une passion si longue et si tendre, lui donner le plaisir de me voir en mourant, de voir qu'elle n'avait pas aimé un automate

insensible, et que, si je n'avais pas su l'aimer comme elle le méritait, je saurais la pleurer? Mais c'est trop tard, mes regrets sont aussi venus trop tard, et elle les ignore. Elle les a ignorés, faut-il dire: il faut enfin bien avoir le courage de la croire morte. S'il y avait eu quelque retour d'espérance, elle aurait voulu adoucir l'impression de sa lettre; car elle, elle savait aimer. Me voici donc seul sur la terre" (180).

[39]Her own mother sold her to the theatre, which led to her becoming a kept woman (114). Her real moral worth is never questioned by William.

[40]For the importance of the theatrical aesthetic and its relation to sympathy, see David Marshall, *The Surprising Effects of Sympathy: Marivaux, Diderot, Rousseau, and Mary Shelley* (Chicago: University of Chicago Press, 1988); for a more general discussion of the aesthetic, see also Michael Fried, *Absorption and Theatricality: Painting and Beholder in the Age of Diderot* (Berkeley: University of California Press, 1980); and Jay Caplan, *Framed Narratives: Diderot's Genealogy of the Beholder* (Minneapolis: University of Minnesota Press, 1985).

[41]On narrative structure and reader positioning in the eighteenth-century French epistolary novel see Janet Altman, *Epistolarity: Approaches to a Form* (Columbus: Ohio State University Press, 1982).

[42] "Si, au lieu d'un mélange de passion et de raison, de faiblesse et de vertu tel qu'on le trouve ordinairement dans la société, ces lettres ne peignaient que des vertus pures telles qu'on les voit en vous, l'Éditeur eût osé les parer de votre nom, et vous en faire hautement hommage" (21).

[43]Immanuel Kant, *Critique of Practical Reason*, trans. Lewis White Beck (New York: Macmillan, 1985), pp. 30–31.

[44]See John Rawls, *A Theory of Justice* (Cambridge: Harvard University Press, 1971), pp. 184–92, where he discusses the impartial spectator position as a "sympathetic being" and a "perfect altruist."

[45]See chapter 2, pp. 50-52, 57-62.

[46]Iris Marion Young argues that considerations of the body, including need, affectivity and desire, have been left out of the conception of the civic public from Rousseau through Habermas, precisely because of their potential to disrupt. See Young, "Impartiality and the Civic Public: Some Implications of Feminist Critiques of Moral and Political Theory," in *Feminism as Critique*, ed. Seyla Benhabib and Drucilla Cornell (Minneapolis: University of Minnesota Press, 1987), pp. 57–76.

[47] Charles Taylor points to the fragmentation of contemporary society as a form of "soft despotism" that he relates to a breakdown of compassion. "The danger is not actual despotic control, but what I am calling fragmentation, that is, a people less and less capable of forming a common purpose and carrying it out. This fragmentation comes about partly through a weakening of the bonds of sympathy." See Taylor, "The Dangers of Soft Despotism," in

The Essential Communitarian Reader, ed. Amitai Etzioni (Lanham, M. D.: Rowman and Littlefield, 1998), pp. 50–51.

Part 3:
The Public and Private Spheres

Part 3: The Public and Private Spheres

THE FINAL PART of *Beyond Contractual Morality* examines representations of the private sphere, where, as we have seen, liberalism
often locates morality. In part 1, particularly with reference to Emile's
domestic education, we have seen that Rousseau argues for a divided
vision of society in which the abstract relations of the public sphere are
offset by more particularized and specific moral relations in the private
sphere.[1] In part 2 as well, both with respect to the private sphere of individual moral conscience and with respect to the realm of sympathy
and compassion, it has been made clear that a stronger, albeit messier,
form of morality exists within the private sphere. In chapters 6 and 7, I
focus on the private sphere of domestic relations to explore the ways in
which contractual relations permeate the understanding of moral relations now as well as in the eighteenth century.

My focus in chapters 6 and 7 is less on the realm of the family than
on the relation between the sexes in the private sphere. Having already
examined, in part 1, the question of children from the perspective of
education, in part 3 I turn to sexual relations and marriage in the context of the politics of liberalism.

Many feminist critics of liberalism have pointed to the exclusion of
women from the social contract. Feminist critiques of social contract
theory and liberalism have questioned the split between the public and
private spheres that liberalism creates, raising concerns about the exclusion of women from the realm of government and politics. As Iris
Marion Young has argued, women are excluded from the civic public
of Rousseau's social contract in order to prevent the disruption of political life by the introduction of specific needs and desires:

> Rousseau conceived that this public realm [the civic public] ought to
> be unified and homogeneous, and indeed suggested methods of fos-
> tering among citizens commitment to such unity through civic cele-
> brations. While the purity, unity and generality of this public realm
> require transcending and repressing the partiality and differentiation of
> need, desire and affectivity, Rousseau hardly believed that human life
> can or should be without emotion and the satisfaction of need and de-
> sire. Man's particular nature as a feeling, needful being is enacted in
> the private realm of domestic life, over which women are the proper
> moral guardians.[2]

The need to stabilize the public sphere in effect works to lock women into the domestic sphere of the family. There, they provide the kind of affective relations that are banned from the space of public deliberation.

But the divide enacted in social contract theory between the public and private spheres is not that simple. While it is true that women are excluded from the civic public, the creation of the private sphere in social contract theory is also complicated by an economic interest fueling liberalism. Women are clearly excluded from the civic public of contract theory, but they are also excluded, in the seventeenth and eighteenth centuries, from the economic private sphere of contractual relations. Carole Pateman raises, in the following terms, the definitional question of the private sphere in her discussion of social contract theory:

> The meaning of "civil society" in the contract stories . . . is constituted through the "original" separation and opposition between the modern, public—civil—world and the modern, private or conjugal and familial sphere: that is, in the new social world created through contract, everything that lies beyond the domestic (private) sphere is public, or "civil," society. Feminists are concerned with *this* division. In contrast, most discussions of civil society and such formulations as "public" regulation versus "private" enterprise presuppose that the politically relevant separation between public and private is drawn *within* "civil society" as constructed in the social contract stories.[3]

On this reading, the private sphere signals both the domestic space and the realm of commercial and economic transactions. Women's legal status in France prior to the revolution largely prohibited them from participation in the economic/legal realm of financial transactions and property. Thus, women were denied access both to the "civic public" and to one aspect of the private sphere, namely, the world of economic relations.

This double meaning of the private sphere within liberalism creates interesting consequences both for the status of women and the status of the domestic realm of the family. The division between the sphere of public regulation and the sphere of private enterprise is used most often in liberal and libertarian discourse to promote laissez-faire policies. The blurring of the division between the realm of private enterprise and the realm of the family facilitates the application of these discourses to shield the domestic sphere from government regulation. In other words, the confusion between the two senses of "private sphere" enables arguments in the service of laissez-faire capitalism and free markets to be employed by civil libertarians to champion the rights of the individual in the "private sphere" of both business and the family. This slippage makes the task of arguing in favor of government or public regulation of issues within the sphere of the family doubly difficult, for it needs to engage powerful rhetoric that protects both the family and private enterprise.

Where women are concerned, the double meaning of the "private sphere" creates a double disenfranchisement: Women are excluded from both the civic public and the realm of private enterprise *and*, within the family, women, although central to the functioning and power of the domestic sphere, are cut off from access to the means of improving their condition. In other words, without access to either the civic public or the economic sphere, women are imprisoned within the family under conditions created by men.

The difficulty for women within the private sphere of the family becomes clearer when we understand how the rhetoric employed to protect the sphere of private enterprise is used to block public or governmental access to the sphere of familial relations. Pateman argues as follows:

> The liberal opposition between private and public (like the patriarchal opposition between the sexes) appears in a variety of guises: for example, society, economy and freedom stand against state, public and coercion. Liberals see these dualities as posing important problems of freedom, since the private sphere of civil society must be protected from the coercive intrusions of the state.[4]

By extension, the familial and domestic sphere must also be protected from "the coercive intrusions of the state." Combined with the rhetoric of protecting the right to privacy and/or freedom of conscience, this discourse against intrusion in the "private sphere" effectively erects a barrier around conditions within the family.

During the eighteenth century, the division between the public sphere and the domestic sphere, together with women's isolation in the private sphere, created a gendered division of labor: men used abstract contractual relations and instrumental rationality to work in the public sphere and the realm of private enterprise while women used sensibility and "natural morality" to work in the domestic sphere. It was during this period and in direct relation to the emergence of the public/private sphere distinction that the discourse of women as the "moral sex" was fully elaborated.[5]

According to this eighteenth-century view, the problems I have raised with respect to what I have called "contractual morality," would stem from overreliance on a masculine type of reason—intended for the public sphere and the realm of private enterprise—in the private realm. In other words, the attempt to conceive all moral relations according to contractual models of obligation and duty would be consistent with masculine rationality. This masculine rationality exercises instrumental calculation in the economic realm and invokes an abstract, generalized notion of the other in the political realm in the creation of contractual relations.[6] Opposed to the masculine rationality would be feminine sensibility, or what Rousseau views as female practical reason, better suited to relations with concrete others.[7] Women's natural morality both necessitates their exclusion from the public sphere—their natural sensibility tends to disrupt abstract, rational deliberation—and justifies their confinement to the domestic sphere of familial relations. Within the private sphere of the family, according to Enlightenment thought, they use their natural sensibility to raise children and offer a haven from the rigors of overly abstract public life.

However, although eighteenth-century thought has tendencies toward this gendered division of labor with regard to morality, it is an oversimplification to reassert women's "natural moral sensibility" in the face of men's abstract contractual obligations. Although gender plays an important role in the creation of the discourse of morality in the eighteenth century, it would be a mistake to return to the eighteenth-century dichotomy and assert that it is a question of gender that underlies the entire problem. Rather, gender is merely one facet of a complex network of problems associated with the rise of bourgeois democratic society during the eighteenth century. Gender relations tell only part of the story. It is important not to reassert the gender divide that the eighteenth century erected.[8]

Many women of the period, most notably Mary Wollstonecraft, already perceived the contradictions and double-binds created for women within the new bourgeois system that excluded them from rationality but not from the important tasks of being wives and mothers. Clearly, for Wollstonecraft, being a good wife and mother necessitated the exercise of reason. Part of the solution, for Wollstonecraft, lay in an appeal to government—A Vindication of the Rights of Woman is addressed to Talleyrand—to create public coeducational schools. The Vindication rejects the moral double standard created in part by liberalism, in favor of an abstract universal conception of virtue that goes beyond the gendered division of labor. For Wollstonecraft, the solution lies in educating women to exercise their reason so that they may contribute in a morally meaningful way to the betterment of society.[9] Wollstonecraft's solution to the division created within liberalism is to assert liberalism's universal political and moral values for all persons—including women—in order to allow women free access to both the public sphere and the sphere of private enterprise.

Chapters 6 and 7 address the question of the private domestic sphere under liberalism from two different perspectives. In chapter 6, I examine the consequences of the Marquis de Sade's radical libertarian politics for domestic and sexual relations. In this chapter, the focus is on the relation between the sexes within the private sphere under political conditions that represent an extreme end of the liberal spectrum. I will argue that radical deregulation of the public sphere—and the sphere of private enterprise as well—results in strict regulation of the domestic sphere by agents other than the government. This dialectic between public deregulation and private regulation raises concerns for feminists that I believe have not been adequately addressed by current debates.

Chapter 7 shifts the focus away from the dialectic between the public and private spheres and focuses on the contractual understanding of marriage among the bourgeoisie. In readings of Rousseau's *Julie ou la nouvelle Héloïse* and Charrière's *Lettres de Mistriss Henley*, I examine the conceptions of commitment and obligation that subtend the marriage bond. I argue that the marriage contract, as it is reworked by the bourgeoisie, entails a stronger form of commitment on the part of the wife and ultimately amounts to a form of imprisonment within the isolation of the new bourgeois domestic sphere.

This chapter raises concerns about the contemporary debate between liberals and communitarians on marriage, specifically with regard to the endorsement of covenant marriage among some communitarians.[10] The urge to strengthen the marriage bond in the face of increasing divorce rates and "broken families" seems to echo the bourgeois impulse of the eighteenth century to further bind the nuclear family together. I would argue, against the communitarian position on covenant marriage, that although the institution of the family needs to be strengthened, covenant marriage is not the solution. As we shall see in chapter 7, strengthening the commitment of marriage only leads to depression and isolation on the part of partners who feel trapped in the commitments they have made.

Notes

[1] On the separation of the sexes in Rousseau, see Jean-Jacques Rousseau, *Emile ou de l'éducation*, Book 5, and *Lettre à d'Alembert*, both in his *Oeuvres complètes*, ed. Bernard Gagnebin and Marcel Raymond, 4 vols. (Paris: Gallimard, 1959–); Mary Wollstonecraft, *A Vindication of the Rights of Woman* (London: Penguin, 1992); Nicole Fermon, *Domesticating Passions: Rousseau,*

Woman, and Nation (Hanover, N. H.: Wesleyan University Press, 1997); Joan B. Landes, *Women and the Public Sphere in the Age of the French Revolution* (Ithaca, N. Y.: Cornell University Press, 1988), pp. 66–89; Susan Moller Okin, *Women in Western Political Thought* (Princeton, N. J.: Princeton University Press, 1979), pp. 99–194; Carole Pateman, *The Disorder of Women: Democracy, Feminism and Political Theory* (Stanford, Calif.: Stanford University Press, 1989), pp. 33–57; and Pateman, *The Sexual Contract* (Stanford, Calif.: Stanford University Press, 1988).

[2] Iris Marion Young, "Impartiality and the Civic Public: Some Implications of Feminist Critiques of Moral and Political Theory," in *Feminism as Critique,* ed. Seyla Benhabib and Drucilla Cornell (Minneapolis: University of Minnesota Press, 1987), p. 65.

[3] Carole Pateman, "The Fraternal Social Contract," in Pateman, *The Disorder of Women*, p. 34.

[4] Ibid., p. 47.

[5] See Lieselotte Steinbrügge, *The Moral Sex: Woman's Nature in the French Enlightenment*, trans. Pamela E. Selwyn (Oxford: Oxford University Press, 1995).

[6] See Seyla Benhabib, "The Generalized and the Concrete Other: The Kohlberg—Gilligan Controversy and Feminist Theory," in *Feminism as Critique*.

[7] See Rousseau, *Emile*, in *Oeuvres complètes*, vol. 4, pp. 720, 728–33.

[8] Some feminist theory reinscribes the gender divisions that the eighteenth- and nineteenth-century discourses constructed, leading to a revaluation of traditionally feminine characteristics. Although this strategy can be politically effective, I do not believe that it ultimately achieves the goals of feminism. In the area of ethics, there is a danger in ascribing the "ethics of care" to women, thereby locating them in the domestic sphere.

[9] See Wollstonecraft, *A Vindication of the Rights of Woman*.

[10] See Amitai Etzioni, ed., *The Essential Communitarian Reader* (Lanham, Md.: Rowman and Littlefield, 1998).

6: Contractual Minimalism:
Disciplinary Power and Liberalism in Sade

Il n'y a de *droit* que lorsqu'il y a une loi pour défendre de faire telle chose, sous peine de punition. Avant la loi, il n'y a de *naturel* que la force du lion, ou le besoin de l'être qui a faim, qui a froid le *besoin* en un mot. . . . non, les gens qu'on honore ne sont que les fripons qui ont eu le bonheur de n'être pas pris en flagrant délit.

—Stendhal, *Le Rouge et le noir*

You is sharks, sartin; but if you gobern de shark in you, why den you be angel; for all angel is not'ing more dan de shark well goberned.

—Herman Melville, *Moby Dick*

DURING THE 1996 Republican National Convention held in San Diego, there was a great deal of talk about "small" government and tax reduction. In an effort to remake himself in the image of Reagan Republicans, Bob Dole called for a 15 percent, across-the-board tax cut and chose Jack Kemp as his running mate to signal his seriousness about the proposal. In spite of his thirty-year voting record in the Senate favoring a different brand of fiscal conservatism, Dole attempted to recast himself as a proponent of supply-side economics. In keeping with the strategy of cutting taxes, there was a great deal of rhetoric at the convention advocating cutting back the activites of government, particularly social welfare programs.

Alongside the classic Republican rhetoric—sounding even libertarian at times—of cutting taxes and social programs and, therefore, the government was the Republican platform position on abortion. Contradicting the rhetoric extolling greater freedom through less government was the strong support for a constitutional amendment to ban abortions. In spite of the tolerance plank of the Republican Party platform, and the compromise "Personal Responsibility Plank" proposed by Governor Pete Wilson of California expressing a more moderate view on abortion, the party officially demanded a right-to-life constitutional amendment.[1] This amendment would eliminate the civil liberty granted under *Roe v. Wade*, and thus represents a movement contrary to the general spirit of the party platform favoring increased individual liberty and less government intervention in social issues.

Clearly, from the Republican Party point of view, there is a difference between civil liberty to pursue economic relations in the public and private spheres and civil liberty to pursue personal decisions and relations within the private sphere of the family. In other words, it is acceptable to cut taxes and ease government regulations in order to promote capitalism within a free market, but it is another thing to allow the same type of freedom in matters pertaining to the family. Unrestrained civil liberty does not extend to issues of abortion, same-sex marriage, and the like.

Feminist critics of liberalism have often suggested that liberalism depends on certain family arrangements unfavorable to women.[2] In order for the possessive individual of liberalism to function within the free market system, he needs a wife to perform unremunerated labor within the private sphere to ensure social reproduction. Feminists have argued that the autonomous, free, independent individual in the public sphere is, first of all, male and, second, dependent on a female. Feminist critiques have called for a reexamination of liberalism's prohibition against interfering in the private sphere, maintaining that relations within the private sphere are thoroughly politicized.

The 1996 Republican national convention, as I have represented its central concerns, demonstrates a weak point in liberalism's attempt to provide a workable political solution for late twentieth-century society, namely, the difficulty of simultaneously favoring limited government *and* regulating the private sphere. While the classical liberalism of the seventeenth and eighteenth centuries relied upon other social institutions to regulate relations within the private sphere, such as rigid social hierarchies, a family structure with gender-specific roles, the lack of social mobility, and the church, late twentieth-century society, particularly in the United States, no longer relies upon these institutions to regulate private and personal relations. Into the vacuum created by cultural diversity, secularization, the women's movement, and greater civil liberties, the Republican Party seeks to insert wide-ranging regulations, which, I argue, are ultimately implemented by the same types of social controls once prevalent in the ancien regime.

This chapter explores the desire for regulation within the private sphere of personal relations that coexists uneasily with radical libertarian versions of liberalism. Taking the paradoxical case of the Marquis de Sade, I create unlikely bedfellows: the Republican Party, civil libertarians, and the eighteenth-century pornographer.

The State of Nature and Radical Civil Liberties

The Marquis de Sade's political pamphlet, "Français encore un effort si vous voulez être républicains," embedded within *La Philosophie dans le boudoir* (1795), although clearly parodic, nonetheless expresses many views characteristic of classical liberalism.[3] Sade's insistence on the importance of establishing a code of civil law that is consistent with the dictates of natural law echoes the social contract tradition of Hobbes, Locke, and Rousseau insofar as it is designed to protect individual liberties from interference by the state. Where Sade clearly departs from the social contract tradition is in his characterization and interpretation of natural law and his ideas for adapting it for codification in civil society.

In contrast to social contract theorists who most often invoke the need to protect private property (Hobbes, Locke) as justification for limiting the claims of the government against individual citizens, Sade instead invokes the need to protect the right to pleasure of the individual libertine.[4] Hobbes's and Locke's possessive individuals, to use C. B. Macpherson's phrase, are replaced by sensual egoists whose primary interest lies in satisfying their desires. The first principle of Sadean natural law proclaims the right to "natural" pleasures, which in truth encompass all sensual pleasures:

> if nature prohibited sodomite pleasure, incestuous pleasure, emissions, etc., would she allow us to find so much pleasure in them? It is impossible that she could tolerate that which truly outrages her.[5]

This right to pleasure underlies and conditions the conception of what is natural, which in turn determines the character and extension of legitimate civil law according to Sade.

Whereas in the social contract tradition, it is the need to protect private property that limits the degree of government interference in the public and private spheres and in fact limits governmental power and authority, in Sade it is the need to protect the right to unlimited physical and psychological pleasure that severely limits the conception of governmental authority. In both conceptions, the limits placed on the state's legitimate exercise of power relate directly to and are derived from the conception of the state of nature. In other words, the role of the government is restricted in order to preserve and protect the liberties that were present in the state of nature, and which are now to be protected in the form of individual civil liberties in the creation of civil society. Thus, it is only in looking at the conception of the state of nature in Sade, and specifically at the rights and freedoms that he ascribes to the natural state, that one can begin to understand his argument in favor of a minimalist government.[6]

The Sadean state of nature departs radically from the visions of Locke and Rousseau, more closely resembling the Hobbesian egoistic war of all against all.[7] More problematically, the word "nature," as Sade uses it, seems to refer to several things at once: (1) natural laws that govern a natural state of being, in which humans exist outside civil society, similar to the social contractarian notion of the state of nature; but also, (2) a force that determines habits and tastes, closely resembling the conception of environmental determinants in Montesquieu; (3) a primitive state of war and perpetual destruction as in Hobbes; and finally, (4) the "natural" state in which animals live. All of these conceptions come together to form a vision of what is "natural" according to Sade, namely that which is not subject to question or problematization and also those practices that ought to be protected within civil society.

A careful look at the representation of the state of nature in Sade uncovers several key principles that come into play in this conception. First, as I suggested above, the natural state is a state of war and perpetual destruction: "here is the primitive state of perpetual war and destruction for which her hand [Nature] created us."[8] Cruelty, rather than Rousseauan pity, is the first natural feeling in this primitive state of war:[9]

> [C]ruelty, very far from being a vice, is the first sentiment that nature imprints in us. The child breaks his rattle, bites his nurse's breast, strangles his bird, well before the age of reason. Cruelty is imprinted in animals, in whom, as I think I have said to you, the laws of nature are more energetically read than in us.[10]

This natural cruelty aids self-interest and egoism in the individual; these traits are also inspired by Nature herself and clearly entangled in mutual dependence in Sade's conception of the individual.

Further, this state of perpetual war and destruction is ruled by injustice and something that Sade characterizes as equality but in the end amounts to nature's equal indifference toward all individuals. He maintains that "injustices [are] essential to the laws of nature," and that, "all individuals being equal before the eyes of nature, . . . the action that serves one in harming another is perfectly indifferent to nature."[11] Any effort at redistribution of wealth or protection of one individual from another is, thus, reinterpreted by Sade as serving the interests of inequality rather than aiding equality.

Sade's state of nature enacts, much like Hobbes's, a situation in which self-interested individuals are, for the most part, in a competitive relation with one another. Happiness depends on the strong taking advantage of the weak, matching Macpherson's description of the "market society model" in Hobbes and Locke that is "essentially contentious" and in which individuals are "contentious and invasive."[12] Rather than maximizing property and possessions at others' expense, Sade's egoistic individuals maximize pleasure based on an almost utilitarian—albeit totally self-interested—calculus.[13]

Above all, this Sadean state of nature resembles the egoism, competition, and antagonism of an unregulated, capitalist free-market economy in which self-interest and greed are rewarded by economic gains at the expense of the financial ruin of others. But rather than financial ruin, the libertines most often cause pain, disfigurement, and death. Thus, it is not surprising that the arguments in favor of extremely limited government and minimal laws in Sade parallel arguments in favor of similar libertarian policies regarding limited government designed to support an unregulated free market.

In keeping with this competitive view of human nature and shaping Sade's assessment of laws and government as a general principle diametrically opposed to the Rousseauian conception of the general will, Sade maintains that general laws are always in contradiction with personal interest.[14] Laws always restrict and limit the individual's freedom, which was virtually unbounded, except by physical limitations, in the state of nature:

> [L]aws are not made for the individual but for the collectivity, which puts them in perpetual contradiction with personal interest, it being understood that personal interest is always in contradiction with the general interest. But laws, which are good for society, are very bad for the individuals who make up society; because if they at one time protect or shelter the individual, they impede and imprison him for three-quarters of his life.[15]

This natural antagonism between laws and private interest necessitates placing severe limitations on government and calling for minimal legislation in order to preserve the nearly unbounded freedom that existed in the state of nature.

Sade's minimalist vision of government is also designed to protect what he perceives to be natural differences between men concerning their tastes and, therefore, their morals. Extending Montesquieu's insights to their ultimate logical conclusion, and clearly to suit his own purposes, Sade maintains that

> There is no action, however peculiar you might suppose it to be, that
> is truly criminal; none that might really be called virtuous. Everything
> is relative to our manners, to our morals, and to the climate in which
> we live; what is a crime is often a virtue a few hundred leagues hence,
> and the virtues of one hemisphere might reverse themselves and be
> crimes for us.[16]

These natural differences in manners, morals, and taste, determined as
much by social, cultural, and geographical context as by "natural" determinants such as individual character and heredity, place further
limitations on the types of legislation that Sade finds to be legitimate.
Since tastes differ so widely, adherence to strictly codified law, while
easy for some, will be exceedingly difficult for others. Sade, therefore,
argues that in order not to create greater inequality by imposing a uni-
form law on a diverse population, it is necessary to make as few laws as
possible:

> It is a frightful injustice to require that men of unequal characters
> bend to equal laws: that which suits one does not suit another. I agree
> that one cannot make as many laws as there are men, but the laws can
> be so lenient and so few that all men, of whatever character they may
> be, can easily bend to them.[17]

Government, on this account, becomes no more than an abstract
coordinating principle that has abandoned any notion of the public per
se.[18] Ultimately, this radical form of liberalism, which in Sade's case insofar as the state is concerned does not distinguish between the public
and private spheres, sacrifices virtually everything to protect individual
civil liberties. Any normative conception of law either in the service of
the public interest or of morality has disappeared entirely.[19]

Regulating the Private Sphere

Despite the nearly unrestricted liberty championed by Sade's radical
liberalism, a careful examination of the representation of the private
sphere of the boudoir does not reveal the chaos and lack of order that
would seemingly be necessary for the pursuit of unlimited pleasure, at
least according to Sade's proclaimed political views. Given the antagonism, selfishness, competition, and invasiveness of Sade's model of the
state of nature, there is a surprising amount of cooperation among libertines. Granted, their victims are sacrificed to their whims, but among
the libertines themselves there is a high level of mutual aid, in order to
maximize pleasure. Rather than chance encounters and chaotic couplings as one might expect from the account of the state of nature, the

Sadean boudoir presents a realm of orderly, disciplined, and organized "eroticism."[20] In many respects, the erotic realm in Sade resembles the calculations of the capitalist market, here used in the service of bodily pleasure. The libertines plan, strategize, manage, orchestrate, and carry out their schemes designed to augment pleasure, all the while ensuring that they will be able to duplicate and/or even improve on the current scenario in any future erotic encounter.

What am I suggesting concerning the regulation of pleasure in Sade runs counter to a tradition of criticism that highlights the excesses celebrated in Sade. This tradition, associated principally with Bataille, Blanchot, Klossowski, and Paulhan recognizes in Sade the transgression of limits and the *jouissance* of excess.[21] Even Barthes's reading, in spite of its recognition of the importance of order, identifies an economy of excess in Sade.[22] These critics have most often concentrated not only on the depiction of excess within Sade's representation but also the attempt to exceed the limits of narratibility demonstrated by such texts as *The 120 Days of Sodom*. My aim here is not to contradict that particular line of criticism, which operates for the most part within an aesthetic-metaphysical framework. Rather, by considering the relationship between Sade's announced political agenda and his representation of the private sphere, I would like to underscore a rather conservative connection between liberalism, libertarianism, and libertinage.

The Sadean libertines often proclaim the necessity of allowing the imagination to run free, to go beyond the limits of society and to transgress into disorder. Madame de Saint-Ange, in *Philosophy in the Bedroom*, thus maintains that

> The imagination only serves us when our mind is absolutely free of prejudices: just one suffices to cool it down. This capricious part of our mind is of a libertinage that nothing can contain; its greatest triumph, its most eminent delights consist in breaking all the limits imposed on it; the imagination is the enemy of rules and the idolater of disorder and everything that wears the colors of crime.[23]

And yet, without these limits, rules, and order, there would be no crimes to commit. Sade's political philosophy finds itself caught in a catch-22: if it outlaws nothing, then libertines will have no laws to transgress. Yet, if it maintains the current social and political order so that libertines have laws to break, the libertines will be prosecuted and imprisoned for their crimes, as Sade himself was.

Setting aside for a moment the philosophical conundrum of transgression, a closer examination of the libertines' actual practices in the boudoir reveals a carefully established and maintained order underlying all of their orgies. Paradoxically, unbounded pleasure requires planning and adherence to certain rules. As Mme de Saint-Ange says to an over-eager Dolmancé, "Please, let's put a little order into these orgies; some is necessary even in the bosom of delirium and infamy."[24] Order enables the libertines to maximize pleasure in this sexual economy.

In terms of purely physical limitations, the libertines have to control themselves in order to prolong their pleasure. They often practice early withdrawal, against the dictates of their immediate needs and desires, in order to attain a higher pleasure: "I see it, it is necessary, whatever my pleasure may be, that I pull myself out entirely of this divine mouth. . . . I would leave all my cum there!"[25] This self-discipline, even self-denial, is necessary on the physical level in order to prolong the sexual act. By exercising self-control, the libertines willfully frustrate themselves, thereby eventually achieving greater pleasure.

But maximizing pleasure also requires establishing another type of order in addition to the self-discipline designed to frustrate desire. In virtually all of the scenes in *Philosophy in the Bedroom*, Dolmancé acts as a kind of director of the sexual encounters. As the libertine chosen by Mme de Saint-Ange to educate and initiate Eugénie (because of his extreme corruption and lack of morals [3–4:372]), it is his duty to create practical scenarios that will illustrate the lessons he is teaching: "I'm going to direct the scene, it's my right; the object of this one is to show Eugénie the mechanism of ejaculation."[26] In other scenes, he not only establishes the initial set of relations but also dictates when and how the tableau will be readjusted *in medias res.*

Directing the scenes represents another form of pleasure, above and beyond the pleasure afforded by participating in them: "it is a pleasure to command you to execute tableaux."[27] Dolmancé, as principal instructor, along with Mme de Saint-Ange, experiences the added pleasures of corrupting this virgin (3–4:376), forming her (3–4:389), and ordering the others to do his bidding.

But Dolmancé's role is important beyond the added pleasure that the power to command affords him. Dolmancé's position of power enables the self-interested, normally antagonistic libertines to cooperate in acts of mutual satisfaction. In the state of nature, these individuals would compete and perhaps even maim and kill each other. Instead, Dolmancé takes responsibility for the group's pleasure, performs a utilitarian calculus, and arranges the ensuing scenes accordingly. Within the space of the boudoir, the libertines submit to the authority of a distinguished libertine for their mutual benefit.

This type of discipline and regulation is necessary within the boudoir because of Sade's conception of pleasure. The exceeding of limits depends not so much on qualitative acts of transgression that go beyond the bounds of the thinkable but rather on sheer accumulation. To further amplify Barthes's recognition of the use of the combinative in Sade, it is as though Sade wishes to create a form of infinity within the closed system of the combinative. In this respect, ironically, his logic most closely resembles the sense of the *combinatoire* with its calculations of probability developed in Port-Royal during the seventeenth century.[28]

Greater pleasure often depends on an accumulation of "transgressive acts." As Mme de Saint-Ange cries:

> See, my love, see all that I am doing at the same time: scandal, seduction, bad example, incest, adultery, sodomy! . . . Oh Lucifer! One and only god of my soul, inspire in me something more.[29]

This type of accumulation intensifies the experience by adding more to the act. According to this same principle, the text of *Philosophy in the Bedroom* is organized by adding more characters as participants. With each successive dialogue a new participant is added to the orgy, each with a larger member than the one who preceded him. Even the successive versions of the other novel(s), *Les Infortunes de la vertu*,[30] *Justine* (1791), and *La Nouvelle Justine, ou les malheurs de la vertu, suivie de l'histoire de Juliette, sa soeur* (1797), rely on amplification and accumulation to reach beyond what was previously written.

The logic of accumulation also explains the necessity of mirrors to intensify the experience. Mirrors present multiple images to the participants, engaging the eyes in the experience of pleasure. Replying to Eugénie's inquiry concerning all the mirrors in the bedroom, Mme de Saint-Ange explains,

> It's so that, repeating the positions in a thousand different ways, they multiply *to infinity* the same pleasures in the eyes of those who experience them on this ottoman. In this way, not one of the parts of either of the bodies can be hidden: it is necessary that everything be in view.[31] [My emphasis.]

This infinite multiplication of pleasure represents a mathematical accumulation similar to the addition of more and more participants in the orgiastic encounters. Mirrors certainly add another dimension to the pleasure by engaging the gaze, but Sade's highlighting of repetition and multiplication points to an underlying quantifiable understanding of measuring the degree of pleasure: the more participants, the greater the pleasure. The larger the penis/dildo (or contrarily, the smaller the orifice), the more exquisite the pleasure. The more violations of traditional morals, the greater the pleasure. And, likewise, the more times the scene is represented (in mirrors or in narrative), the greater the pleasure. Ultimately, even exponential increases still remain within the closed numerical system that Sade has established.[32]

This quantifiable and controlled form of pleasure reaches its zenith in *Justine*, in the extended episode in which Justine encounters the monks of the convent of Sainte-Marie-des-Bois. In this detailed episode, Justine finds herself the captive of four libertine monks who have raised *libertinage* to a science of imprisonment and continuous debauchery. Both the narrative itself and Justine's life while a prisoner of the monks display a precision, control, and order consistent with a quantifiable form of pleasure and clearly resemble Sade's own experiences in prison.

First, much of the monks' pleasure derives from the systematic desecration of the religious order that they are supposed to represent. Many of their orgies are organized around a central theme of blasphemy and thus borrow their organizational principles from religious ceremony. In other words, in order to profane the religious symbols and practices, the monks are obligated to mimic religious ceremony in their libertine orgies. This organized desecration introduces order and control into what would otherwise be chaotic orgiastic behavior. As Father Clément (like Madame de Saint-Ange and Dolmancé) insists upon Justine's introduction into the convent, "let's put a little order into our proceedings, you know our formulas for reception."[33] Thus, for example, the monks take turns violating a young woman dressed as the Virgin Mary, all the while pushing the bounds of transgression by increasing the blasphemous acts: lighting candles, placing an icon of the Savior on the small of her back, using the Host for acts of sodomy, and so on. (3–4:213). In this way, order and discipline are established and maintained in part through the conscious parody of religious ceremony.

Beyond the religious order imposed by the desecration of religious practices, the monks establish a strict order within the convent, not unlike the austere discipline of religious orders and of institutions such as prisons, schools, and the military.[34] During Omphale's long explanation to Justine of the history and workings of the convent, the attention to detail in descriptions of the architecture and the daily life of the convent reveal an obsession with order. Both the content of the narrative— that is to say, the description of the practices of the convent—and the narrative itself betray a pleasure in maintaining mastery and control through regulation and discipline.

At the level of the content of the narrative, Justine's introduction to convent life requires her familiarity with the daily workings of the institution as well as a knowledge of its past. Not unlike a novice, Justine must be indoctrinated into this antireligious order. She receives from Omphale a detailed description organized around four principal articles: the house, the keeping of the women, the monks' pleasures, and the history of "reforms," that is to say, of women who were expelled from the convent (3–4:177). Under each of these categories, the information conveyed to Justine reveals an obsession with organizational detail and numerical precision. For example, the women within the convent are divided into two groups composed of eight women each. Within each group are two representatives of four classes of women, divided according to their age. These groups are distinguished by the color garment they wear, and so on.

Sade's narrative goes to great lengths in specifying the food, clothing, practices, crimes, and punishments of the convent. In all the accounts there is a numerical precision that seems to become an end in itself: The women receive all their underwear in packets of six (3–4:182), there are four deaf-mute servants (3–4:179), there are six walls surrounding the convent (3–4:178). Even the meals are described according to an almost arithmetical formula:

> [A]t one o'clock dinner is served; each table of eight is served in the same way: a very good soup, four appetizers, one dish of roast meat and four side dishes, some dessert in every season. . . . supper is excellent without a doubt, if it is the monks'; if we don't attend it, since we are only four to a bedroom, we are served at the same time three dishes of roast meat and four side dishes; we have each of us every day one bottle of white wine, one of red, and a half-bottle of liqueur.[35]

The pleasure in order is betrayed in the incredibly specific detail presented throughout Omphale's discourse to Justine.

At the level of the narrative itself, that is to say, Justine's account of her life and in particular her stay in the convent, one finds the same order and detail. Justine describes both the monks and the women of the convent in order of age, following the order established by the monks in dividing the women into four classes. The logic underlying the order of presentation in the descriptions often follows the organizational principles of the convent itself. But beyond this extension of the institutional order into the narrative order, there is further evidence of obsession with order and numbers. At one point, near the beginning of Justine's stay, the narrative is numbered in order to convey the five points on which Dom Severino questioned her. Thus, the narrative form itself takes on the appearance of order and strict regulation as numbers abound and paragraph divisions and order of presentation are determined by the logic of this parodic religious order. This same obsession with tabulations in *The 120 Days of Sodom* and in Sade's own journal prompts Joan DeJean to dub him a "numerologist."[36]

To return to the broader question of order within the Sadean boudoir, the examination of both *Philosophy in the Bedroom* and *Justine* has revealed that order and discipline reign within the confines of the libertine erotic sphere. Rather than revealing chaotic orgies composed of random couplings, these texts demonstrate that erotic behavior is organized and carried out according to principles designed to maximize pleasure. These principles include a well-regulated life in *Justine* and require someone to orchestrate the erotic behavior. Not unlike *metteurs en scène*, Dolmancé and various monks alternately dictate the tableaux that will be performed within the boudoir and the convent. Thus, order and regulation are required to maximize pleasure, making the economy of pleasure resemble the capitalist market in its strategic manipulation aimed at achieving greater and greater profits.

At the head of these economies of pleasure there is a ruler of sorts: Someone distinguished in the art of libertinage who commands. For, as Barthes puts it, "Every combinative needs an operator for continuity."[37] Such a figure signals an important reversal in Sade's understanding of the relation between and among the state of nature, civil society, and the private sphere. Whereas in Hobbes the state of nature ends in the creation of an all-powerful sovereign, who will rule the state and bring order to civil society, in Sade, the conception of the state of nature leads to the creation of a minimal form of government and, seemingly, all-powerful sovereigns in the private sphere. Dolmancé and all the other assorted libertines who play the role of *metteur en scène* coordinate all the particular interests into a utilitarian calculus to maximize the group's pleasure. In effect, the model of the state is displaced into the bedroom where a new form of Leviathan emerges. Not unlike the husband and father with his nearly absolute power over his family in the eighteenth century, the head libertines are absolute masters of the private domain.

Disciplinary Practices and Radical Liberalism

The careful examination of Sade's calls for political reform, alongside his representation of libertine sexual practices, has brought to light a contradiction. On the one hand, the desire to protect individual civil liberties at all costs minimizes government regulation, yet, on the other hand, the desire to maximize pleasure requires the precise regulation of erotic activity. While the public sphere goes virtually unregulated, the private sphere abides by strict procedures and practices. Victims, out of fear, and even the libertines themselves, in order to maximize pleasure, follow the codes and guidelines established for each erotic encounter. In the case of Justine's prolonged confinement in the convent, the practices are codified in such a way as to resemble the institutional regulation of religious orders and prisons.

Insofar as Sade's representations of the libertine boudoir manipulate and regulate the body and its functioning, and especially in the case of Justine's confinement in the convent, they display the type of power that Foucault associates with the rise of disciplines in the eighteenth century. According to Foucault's analysis of the micro-techniques of disciplinary power in *Discipline and Punish*, there are four principal techniques employed in the creation of what he terms "docile bodies."[38] Of these four, three are particularly helpful in understanding the form of power deployed within the Sadean boudoir. Foucault isolates the distribution of individuals in space, the control of activity, and the composition of forces as broad categories describing sets of practices that emerge in order to meticulously control and thereby exercise power over individuals.

Within these three broad categories, Foucault further describes specific practices that enable the disciplining of bodies and individuals. These micro-techniques are easily identifiable within Sade's narrative of libertine activity. To begin with the distribution of bodies in space, Foucault identifies—and we have already seen in Sade—the acts of enclosure, partitioning, the creation of functional or useful sites, and the establishment of rank.[39] Justine's and the other women's confinement in the convent, the division of the women into two groups of eight who eat and sleep together as units, the specification of the boudoir in *Philosophy in the Bedroom* and the use of particular sites in the convent, and finally, the division of the women of the convent into four ranks and the hierarchical power relations between libertines in *Philosophy in the Bedroom* all demonstrate the disciplining of bodies in carefully circumscribed and regulated spaces.[40]

Sade's use of what Foucault describes as techniques for controlling activity are even more pronounced. Foucault outlines five techniques developed primarily in the military, but extended to factories and schools, designed to discipline the body in its various activities. These techniques include the use of the timetable, the temporal elaboration of the act, the correlation of the body and the gesture, the body-object articulation, and the principle of exhaustive use.[41] While use of the first of these techniques by Sade is self-evident (the timetable), the remaining four require some explanation.

The other four disciplinary techniques primarily involve the precise control of the body and its parts in relation to particular acts. Foucault describes the temporal elaboration of the act as the creation of an "anatomo-chronological schema of behaviour." He specifies that

> The act is broken down into its elements; the position of the body, limbs, articulation is defined; to each movement are assigned a direction, an aptitude, a duration; their order of succession is prescribed. Time penetrates the body and with it all the meticulous controls of power.[42]

All of these precise indications are given when one of the numerous directors of the Sadean orgies describes the tableau that the participants are to execute. As Barthes has remarked, the bodies are coordinated together like a machine, precisely synchronized in their movements: "children, Ganymedes, preparers, everyone creates an immense and subtle mechanism, a meticulous clockwork, whose function is to connect the sexual discharges, to produce a continuous tempo, to bring pleasure to the subject on the conveyor belt."[43]

What Foucault terms the "correlation of the body and the gesture" further breaks down the act into the relation of a specific gesture to overall body posture. Thus, an act may be isolated and delineated in relation to overall body positioning. This technique is used repeatedly by Sade, particularly but not exclusively in those texts, such as *Philosophy in the Bedroom* and *The 120 Days of Sodom*, in which the action of the novel is limited to a particular space that is itself defined in relation to a specific piece of furniture: in these texts the ottoman. Thus, the libertines strategically position their bodies and those of their victims in relation to the ottoman or armchair before specifying particular acts to be performed.

Body-object articulation prescribes the use of objects to perform acts in what Foucault calls an "obligatory syntax." "Over the whole surface of contact between the body and the object it handles, power is introduced, fastening them to one another. It constitutes a body-weapon, body-tool, body-machine complex."[44] Whether in relation to the libertine's body or the victim's, or at times, to both their bodies, the use of dildoes, whips, religious paraphernalia, and other devices fuses the bodies to the objects used in such a way as to exercise power over both libertine and victim.

Finally, what Foucault terms "exhaustive use" denominates a new understanding of the body's relation to time and contrasts with a prior understanding that was conceived of negatively. The older understanding of time was predicated on a "principle of non-idleness" and attempted to avoid wasting it. In the new disciplinary economy of exhaustive use,

> it is a question of extracting, from time, ever more available moments and, from each moment, ever more useful forces. This means that one must seek to intensify the use of the slightest moment, as if time, in its very fragmentation, were inexhaustible or as if, at least by an ever more detailed internal arrangement, one could tend towards an ideal point at which one maintained maximum speed and maximum efficiency.[45]

Whether in the convent of Sainte-Marie-des-Bois, whose activities are organized around maximizing pleasure and therefore carefully timing expenditure and recovery, or in Monsieur de Gernande's castle, where his wife can be bled only every four days if she is to survive, every moment is filled, if not by erotic pleasure, by philosophical dissertation, eating, or recovery. The use of time is carefully organized so that every minute of the day may be utilized.

The last of Foucault's general categories, the composition of forces, aims at efficiency. Although the libertines do not directly desire to promote efficiency in any overt sense, they do employ some of the micro-techniques aimed at fostering an efficient distribution of bodies. Particularly with respect to their victims, they treat human beings as part of a machine. Thus, according to Foucault, "The individual body becomes an element that may be placed, moved, articulated on others."[46] Furthermore, this type of efficient coordination requires attention to time as well as a system of command. We have seen these techniques at work both in *Philosophy in the Bedroom* and *Justine* in the service of erotic pleasure.

Ultimately, Foucault's analysis of the micro-techniques of disciplinary power suggests a partial answer to the contradiction I noted earlier between Sade's proposed political program of minimal liberalism and the regulation of the boudoir. Foucault maintains that these micro-techniques represent a "political investment of the body" and that "[d]iscipline is a political anatomy of detail."

> Small acts of cunning endowed with a great power of diffusion, subtle arrangements, apparently innocent, but profoundly suspicious, mechanisms that obeyed economies too shameful to be acknowledged, or pursued petty forms of coercion—it was nevertheless they that brought about the mutation of the punitive system, at the threshold of the contemporary period. . . . They are the acts of cunning, not so much of the greater reason that works even in its sleep and gives meaning to the insignificant, as of the attentive "malevolence" that turns everything to account.[47]

The first question we must ask in relation to Sade is, then, in the service of what or whom are the disciplinary techniques employed to produce docile bodies in the boudoir?[48] In other words, what "shameful economies," to borrow Foucault's phrase, do these practices obey and what do they "turn to account"?

From Sade's conception of both human nature and the state of nature, he derives a minimal theory of government designed not to interfere with the pursuit of pleasure. But as we have seen in the analysis of the boudoir, regulatory principles operate to maximize pleasure according to the dictates of a sovereign of sorts. Society in Sade becomes a well-coordinated, disciplined series of isolated units directed by certain powerful individuals. Taken as a whole, the isolated units present a coordinated machine model of society directed—albeit minimally—by an abstract governing principle, which is government.

What this model combines is an aristocratic ideology of privilege that does not question the roles assigned to and by particular libertines: Dolmancé directs because he has distinguished himself. Such power and authority go unquestioned in Sade because they reflect an older, aristocratic worldview. What is new in Sade is the way in which this aristocratic ideology combines with the market model of society to enable the accumulation of pleasure in the hands of the privileged few. The libertines are immune from the perils of a real market because their power and privilege are protected by the deregulation of the public sphere. Their wealth and privilege are safeguarded because, in this system, the rich will get richer. The only competition in this version of the market society is for pleasure.

In this respect, Sade represents a transitional figure. Poised astride the revolution, Sade's texts nonetheless correspond, at least to some extent, to a historical reality that predates their writing.[49] He describes a reality known to the nobility of the midcentury, which he witnessed during his youth. This reality is one of privilege predicated on membership in the aristocracy, before the upheavals of the later years of the century. The wealth and privilege of the monks and aristocrats who make up the bulk of the libertines was challenged, threatened, and even to some extent destroyed by the social and economic changes brought about during Sade's lifetime. Yet Sade's work represents an aristocratic world closed off to invasion or intrusion, cloistered and sequestered from the harsh realities of the outside world.

This cloistering enables libertine practices to flourish. The victims cannot escape, the libertines cannot be arrested and incarcerated, but more importantly, the world in which the libertines live can be a recreation of an earlier time. This vision of the well-regulated space closed off from the chaos of the outside world serves the interests of the privileged few who benefit from libertine practices. They are the wealthy and powerful who are in a position to create a world unto itself for their own pleasure and amusement. Within this space they are free to practice the disciplinary techniques that will continually increase their pleasure.

The radical form of political liberalism that does not regulate the outside world ultimately serves their ends as well. The lack of regulation in the public sphere enables the profoundly political regulation and order of the private sphere. It is precisely the negatively defined freedom of Sadean liberalism that allows for the hierarchy of privilege and the regulated pleasure of the libertine boudoir. Libertinage depends upon an absence of organized social controls in the form of government regulation in order that well-regulated pleasure may flourish in the closed world of the boudoir.

Contractual Minimalism

If, in the eighteenth-century context, the radical liberalism of the Marquis de Sade serves to maintain and even increase the privileges of the aristocracy, what is gained in the twentieth century when government regulations are minimized? Likewise, if the libertines regulate the private sphere in order to maximize pleasure for their own egoistic benefit, who regulates the private sphere under contemporary radical forms of liberalism and to what end?

My invocation at the beginning of this chapter of the Republican Party convention in 1996 suggests the beginning of an answer to these questions. If Sade's representations further the privileges of his own class, then it seems likely that the interests served at the present day are those of the people calling for minimal government. Just as in Sade, as we all know by now, the very wealthiest get even wealthier under the trickle-down theory. Very little actually trickles down, leaving a moneyed elite free to pursue a life of privilege.

But as we have also seen, hand in hand with economic policies designed to protect the wealthy and ensure that they remain wealthy go cries for a constitutional amendment outlawing abortion and same-sex marriage. These broad measures designed to regulate the private sphere sketch the outlines of practices that will be enforced by other social institutions. Just as in the work of Sade, government is reduced to a minimum in order to preserve and protect wealth and privilege, while individual disciplinary practices are determined within the confines of each enclosed libertine space liberated from government (outside) interference. The private sphere is "depoliticized," thereby allowing it to become thoroughly infused with political techniques of discipline and control.[50]

This radical form of liberalism depends on a minimalist conception of contract. In effect, Sade asks only that the government not interfere in the egoistic and antagonistic pursuit of personal gain. Libertinage means protecting a sphere of "private" forms of exploitation in the interests of a privileged few. The older aristocratic model of hierarchy and privilege remains, but without the imperative to protect the less fortunate: no more noblesse oblige. The new model reinscribes privilege within the competitive market model. Ultimately, the contract between government and citizen amounts to nothing more than a negative version of "you scratch my back, I'll scratch yours." In radical liberalism the contract between state and citizen amounts to "I won't bother you, if you won't bother me."[51] Or even "I'll turn a blind eye if you do the same."

Corresponding to Kohlberg's preconventional stages of moral development, this contract cannot provide anything more than a limited and negative form of freedom.[52] Being both amoral and apolitical, it cannot provide a foundation for human community because it is devoid of positively defined value. Citizens of the state are reduced to competing interests without any common goals or bonds. This sort of "contract," so often favored by political conservatives, mimics contracts in the economic sphere. It cannot provide a basis for government or morality, because it assumes antagonism, egoism, and greed. If Hobbes managed to turn this conception of the state of nature into an absolute political obligation to the sovereign, Sade instead creates a more nihilistic vision in which multiple sovereigns rule over the private domain. These smaller Leviathans rule by force and create a community of self-interested elites coordinated to exploit the weak and poor. One can only shudder to imagine what the model would become if these elites turned against one another: at the very least *la Fronde*, at worst, civil war. What Sade provides is a framework for the selfish pursuit of personal interest free from reprisal by the government in the name of an almost contentless "common good."

Notes

[1]To quote from a Republican analysis of Wilson's proposed compromise, "The Personal Responsibility Plank focused on parental (as opposed to governmental) responsibility, stressing sexual abstinence, contraception, prosecu-

tion of statutory rape, enforcement of child support payments, and welfare reform that would create strong disincentives for irresponsible sexual behavior. The plank also called for tolerance of different views." Fred Davis, "Dole, Wilson, Abortion in San Diego," *Grass Roots* 6, no. 5 (summer 1996).

[2]See Susan Moller Okin, *Women in Western Political Thought* (Princeton, N. J.: Princeton University Press, 1979); Carole Pateman, *The Sexual Contract* (Stanford, Calif.: Stanford University Press, 1988); Zillah R. Eisenstein, *The Radical Future of Liberal Feminism* (Boston: Northeastern University Press, 1993); Jean Bethke Elshtain, *Public Man, Private Woman: Women in Social and Political Thought*, 2d ed. (Princeton, N. J.: Princeton University Press, 1981).

[3]Philippe Roger cautions against taking any of Sade's political declarations seriously. He argues that "Sade 'fictionalizes' ideology to stir, displace, shock. Ambiguity prevails in all of his political declarations." See Philippe Roger, "A Political Minimalist," in *Sade and the Narrative of Transgression*, ed. David B. Allison, Mark S. Roberts, and Allen S. Weiss, (Cambridge: Cambridge University Press, 1995), p. 80. For my purposes here, it is unimportant whether Sade believed in the version of liberalism he sets forth in the embedded pamphlet; it matters more that as parodic discourse it represents a clear articulation of an extremist position.

[4]See Simone de Beauvoir, *Faut-il brûler Sade?* (Paris: Gallimard, 1955), pp. 58–68; "Must We Burn Sade?" in Marquis de Sade, *The 120 Days and Other Writings*, comp. and trans. Austryn Wainhouse and Richard Seaver (New York: Grove Press, 1966), pp. 3–64.

[5]"[S]i la nature défendait les jouissances sodomites, les jouissances incestueuses, les pollutions, etc., permettrait-elle que nous y trouvassions autant de plaisir? Il est impossible qu'elle puisse tolérer ce qui l'outrage véritablement" (421). Donatien-Alphonse-François, Marquis de Sade, *Oeuvres complètes du Marquis de Sade*. 16 vols. (Paris: Cercle du livre précieux, 1966), vols. 3–4, *Justine ou les malheurs de la vertu* and *La Philosophie dans le boudoir*. All parenthetical references in chapter 6 (text and notes) are to this edition and cite the volume followed by the page number. Translations are my own.

[6]The conceptions of the state of nature differ widely between Hobbes, Locke, and Rousseau, but all use the conception as a type of regulative ideal or hypothetical construct on which to build a just conception of civil society and government. For this reason John Rawls recasts the state of nature into the original position. See John Rawls, *A Theory of Justice* (Cambridge: Harvard University Press, 1971), pp. 11–12.

[7]Roger identifies a post-Hobbesian anthropology in Sade, in which all men are monsters. According to Roger, a materialist metaphysics combines with what he dubs historical negativism and results in a fundamental denial of the social link. See Roger, "A Political Minimalist," pp. 87–88.

[8] "[V]oilà l'état primitif de guerre et de destruction perpetuelles pour lequel sa main [la nature] nous créa" (3–4:129).

[9]There are several points in the text at which it is clear that Sade is parodying Rousseau. See, most notably, his critique of the motivations behind the social contract. See *La Philosophie dans le boudoir*, vols. 3–4, pp. 213–14. Compare Joan DeJean's discussion of Sade's parody of Rousseau in *Literary Fortifications: Rousseau, Laclos, Sade* (Princeton, N. J.: Princeton University Press, 1984), pp. 289–90.

[10] "[L]a cruauté, bien loin d'être un vice, est le premier sentiment qu'imprime en nous la nature. L'enfant brise son hochet, mord le téton de sa nourrice, étrangle son oiseau, bien avant que d'avoir l'âge de la raison. La cruauté est empreinte dans les animaux, chez lesquels, ainsi que je crois vous l'avoir dit, les lois de la nature se lisent bien plus énergiquement que chez nous" (3–4:437).

[11] "[L]es injustices [sont] essentielles aux lois de la nature" (394) and that "tous les individus étant égaux aux yeux de la nature, . . . l'action qui sert à l'un en nuisant à l'autre est d'une indifférence parfaite à la nature" (3–4:466).

[12]C. B. Macpherson, "Natural Rights in Hobbes and Locke," in *Political Theory and the Rights of Man*, ed. D. D. Raphael (Bloomington: Indiana University Press, 1967) pp. 4, 10.

[13]John W. Chapman levels the charge against Macpherson that he has reduced liberal ethics to utilitarianism by reading the market society into Hobbes and Locke. See John W. Chapman, "Natural Rights and Justice in Liberalism," in *Political Theory and the Rights of Man*, ed. D. D. Raphael, pp. 27–42.

[14]This particular issue does present some difficulty for Rousseau insofar as it is difficult to conceive of an individual whose interest would legitimately be in conflict with the general will not being banished from or executed by the collectivity. See my "Militarisme et vertu chez Rousseau," in *Actes du IIe Colloque International de Montmorency. J.-J. Rousseau: Politique et Nation*, ed. Robert Thiéry (Oxford: Voltaire Foundation, forthcoming).

[15] "[L]es lois ne sont pas faites pour le particulier, mais pour le général, ce qui les met dans une perpétuelle contradiction avec l'intérêt, attendu que l'intérêt personnel l'est toujours avec l'intérêt général. Mais les lois, bonnes pour la société, sont très mauvaises pour l'individu qui la compose; car pour une fois qu'elles le protègent ou le garantissent, elles le gênent et le captivent les trois quarts de sa vie" (3–4:470).

[16] "Il n'y a aucune action, quelque singulière que vous puissiez la supposer, qui soit vraiment criminelle; aucune qui puisse réellement s'appeler vertueuse. Tout est en raison de nos moeurs et du climat que nous habitons; ce qui est crime est souvent vertu quelque cent lieues plus bas, et les vertus d'un autre

hémisphère pourraient bien réversiblement être des crimes pour nous" (3–4:401).

[17] "C'est une injustice effrayante que d'exiger que des hommes de caractères inégaux se plient à des lois égales: ce qui va à l'un ne va point à l'autre. Je conviens que l'on ne peut faire autant de lois qu'il y a d'hommes; mais les lois peuvent être si douces, en si petit nombre, que tous les hommes, de quelque caractère qu'ils soient, puissent facilement s'y plier" (3–4:492–93).

[18]Compare Philippe Roger's assessment that "when Sade deals with more than two, he plays with numbers, not human beings; he computes figures and does not let himself be concerned with empirical, historical humanity." "A Political Minimalist," p. 95. This "more algebraico," as Roger calls it, is as well reflected in Sade's conception of "excess," as I shall argue in the next section.

[19]Thomas A. Spragens, Jr., in a communitarian critique of libertarianism, highlights the oversimplification of the concept of freedom to the detriment of other social goods and obligations. See Spragens, "The Limitations of Libertarianism," in *The Essential Communitarian Reader*, ed. Amitai Etzioni (Lanham, Md.: Rowan and Littlefield, 1998). I will return to the questions of community and justice in the conclusion.

[20]See Joan DeJean's discussion of two voices in Sade, "a voice of liberation and a voice of control," that she locates specifically in *The 120 Days of Sodom*. DeJean, *Literary Fortifications*, p. 271.

[21]This tradition asserts that the Sadean text operates a continual building up of energy that explodes in a continual dialectic with the social norms. As Pierre Klossowski maintains, "Transgression presupposes the existing order, the apparent maintenance of norms, under which energy accumulates, thereby making the transgression necessary. . . . Transgression is then something other than the pure explosion of an energy accumulated by means of an obstacle. It is an incessant recuperation of the possible itself—inasmuch as the existing state of things has eliminated the possibility of another form of existence." Klossowski, "Sade, or the philosopher-vilain," in *Sade and the Narrative of Transgression*, pp. 39–41.

[22] According to Barthes, "Order is necessary for vice, i. e., transgression; order is precisely that which separates transgression from contention. This is because vice is an area of exchange: one practice for one pleasure; 'excesses' must be profitable; thus they must be subject to an economy, and this economy must be planned." See Roland Barthes, *Sade/Fourier/Loyola*, trans. Richard Miller (Berkeley: University of California Press, 1976), p. 161.

[23] "[L]'imagination ne nous sert que quand notre esprit est absolument dégagé de préjugés: un seul suffit à la refroidir. Cette capricieuse portion de notre esprit est d'un libertinage que rien ne peut contenir; son plus grand triomphe, ses délices les plus éminentes consistent à briser tous les freins qu'on

lui oppose; elle est ennemie de la règle, idolâtre du désordre et de tout ce qui porte les couleurs du crime" (3–4:417).

[24] "Mettons, s'il vous plaît, un peu d'ordre à ces orgies, il en faut même au sein du délire et de l'infamie" (3–4:424).

[25] "[J]e le vois, il faut, quel que soit mon plaisir, que je me retire absolument de cette bouche divine. . . . j'y laisserais mon foutre!" (3–4:425).

[26] "Je vais diriger la scène, c'est mon droit; l'objet de celle-ci est de faire voir à Eugénie le mécanisme de l'éjaculation" (3–4:444).

[27] "[C]'est un plaisir que de vous commander des tableaux" (3–4:531).

[28]Marcel Henaff recognizes one form of infinity in Sade which he defines as "$n + 1$, repeated indefinitely." He also recognizes another type of excess in Sade, related to the efforts of exhaustiveness, which attains the type of transgression that I am intentionally downplaying here. See Henaff, "The Encyclopedia of Excess," in *Sade and the Narrative of Transgression*, p. 163. The other form of infinity, which achieves transcendence, is similar to Kant's formulations for the mathematical sublime. And in Kant, there is the same tension between two different forms of infinity. See Immanuel Kant, *Critique of Judgement*, trans. J. H. Bernard (New York: Hafner, 1951), pp. 86–89. Compare also Max Horkheimer and Theodor W. Adorno, "Juliette or Enlightenment and Morality," in *Dialectic of Enlightenment*, trans. John Cumming (New York: Continuum, 1988), pp. 81–119.

[29] "Vois, mon amour, vois tout ce que je fais à la fois: scandale, séduction, mauvais exemple, inceste, adultère, sodomie! . . . O Lucifer! seul et unique dieu de mon âme, inspire-moi quelque chose de plus" (3–4:455).

[30] *Les Infortunes de la vertu* was published posthumously in 1930.

[31] "C'est pour que, répétant les attitudes en mille sens divers, elles multiplient *à l'infini* les mêmes jouissances aux yeux de ceux qui les goûtent sur cette ottomane. Aucune des parties de l'un ou de l'autre corps ne peut être cachée par ce moyen: il faut que tout soit en vue " (3–4:387). [My emphasis.]

[32] Interestingly, in defense of his own novel, *Lolita*, Vladimir Nabokov criticizes traditional pornography writing: "the sexual scenes in the book must follow a crescendo line, with new variations, combinations, new sexes, and a steady increase in the number of participants (*in a Sade play they call the gardener in*), and therefore the end of the book must be more replete with lewd lore than the first chapters." Nabokov, "On a Book Entitled *Lolita*," *Lolita* (New York: Vintage, 1997), p. 313.

[33] "[M]ettons de l'ordre à nos procédés; vous connaissez nos formules de réception" (3–4:168).

[34]I discuss the rise of disciplinary practices in reference to Michel Foucault's analysis in *Discipline and Punish: The Birth of the Prison*, trans. Alan Sheridan (New York: Vintage, 1979) in the next section.

[35] "[A] une heure on sert le dîner; chaque table de huit est servie de même: un très bon potage, quatre entrées, un plat de rôti et quatre entremets; du dessert en toute saison. . . . le souper est excellent sans doute, si c'est celui des moines; si nous n'y assistons pas, comme nous ne sommes alors que quatre par chambre, on nous sert à la fois trois plats de rôti, et quatre entremets; nous avons chacune par jour une bouteille de vin blanc, une de rouge, et une demi-bouteille de liqueur." (3–4:183).

[36] See De Jean, *Literary Fortifications*, p. 307.

[37] See Barthes, *Sade/Fourier/Loyola*, p. 126.

[38] Foucault, *Discipline and Punish*, pp. 135–69.

[39] Ibid., pp. 141–49. These phenomena are noted by other critics as well, yet not within the matrix of an understanding of the deployment of disciplinary power. For example, see Barthes, *Sade/Fourier/Loyola*, pp. 125–26, 140–53.

[40] Of course these practices are also apparent in *Juliette* and in *The 120 Days of Sodom*.

[41] Foucault, *Discipline and Punish*, pp. 149–56.

[42] Ibid., p. 152.

[43] Barthes, *Sade/Fourier/Loyola*, p. 125.

[44] Foucault, *Discipline and Punish*, p. 153.

[45] Ibid., p. 154.

[46] Ibid., p. 164.

[47] Ibid., p. 139.

[48] Carole Pateman draws a connection between Foucault's "automatic docility" and what she terms the "fraternal social contract." See Pateman, *The Disorder of Women: Democracy, Feminism, and Political Theory* (Stanford: Stanford University Press, 1989), p. 51.

[49] Whether or not one can speak of verisimilitude or realism in Sade is clearly highly debatable. Yet, the social reality described resembles the France of his youth. See Barthes, *Sade/Fourier/Loyola*, p. 130; and DeJean, *Literary Fortifications*, p. 271.

[50] Recent Federalist decisions by the Supreme Court have also increased states' rights, thereby giving individual states tremendous latitude to determine behaviors in the private sphere as well. I am grateful to Henry Piper for pointing this out.

[51] See my discussion of various other versions of the Golden Rule in chapter 5.

[52] See Lawrence Kohlberg, *Child Psychology and Childhood Education: A Cognitive-Developmental View* (New York: Longman, 1987). The moral attitude I am describing falls somewhere between stages and 1 and 2 on Kohlberg's scale.

7: The Marriage Contract: Obligation and Commitment in the Bourgeois Marriage

Enfin, mon cher Aza, il semble qu'en France les liens du mariage ne soient réciproques qu'au moment de la célébration, et que dans la suite les femmes seules y doivent être assujetties.

—Françoise de Graffigny, *Lettres d'une Péruvienne*

[O]ur Marriages are made, just like other common Bargains and Sales, by the meer Consideration of Interest and Gain, without any Love or Esteem, of Birth or of Beauty itself, which ought to be the true Ingredients of all Happy Compositions of this kind, and of all generous Productions. Yet this Custom is of no ancient Date in *England*, and I think I remember, within less than fifty years, the first Noble Families that married into the City for downright Money, and thereby introduced by degrees this Publick Grievance. . . .

—Sir William Temple, *An Essay on Popular Discontent*

IN THE AFTERMATH of the sudden death of Diana, Princess of Wales, there was a great emotional outpouring, not only because of the senseless circumstances surrounding the fatal car accident—the pursuit by the paparazzi, the blood-alcohol level of the driver, and evidence that he had taken antidepressants and medication for alcoholism—but also because of the enormous amount of sympathy American women in particular felt for her. The demise of her storybook romance with Prince Charles, their admissions of marital infidelity, her admissions of difficulties with eating disorders and depression, and finally her divorce all endeared her in the hearts and minds of middle-class American women.

I want to rehearse the story of Princess Diana, not because the narrative is unfamiliar, but to underscore the elements of a fairy-tale love story that continue to exert an emotional force over bourgeois women. Closely resembling the stories of Cinderella, Snow White, and Sleeping Beauty, Diana's story testifies not only to the enduring power of narratives of princely rescues but also to our deep-seated suspicions concerning these narratives' ability to actually produce the promised result. We all want to believe that we will be rescued from a life of toil by a handsome prince, yet we all know, or think we know, that such a rescue is impossible. In recollecting Diana's marriage story, I would like to invoke the enduring class relations that determine and enable the tale. Both this love story and its subtext of class are central for examining the status of the marriage contract in eighteenth-century France as an emerging group of bourgeois wives redefined love, commitment, and despair.

Aristocratic Marriage

In an article in the *New York Times* on September 7, 1997, the day after Diana's funeral, Alessandra Stanley makes a very astute observation. Reminding readers of the process by which Diana was chosen to become Charles's wife, she writes:

> Diana didn't just become a princess; she was carefully chosen for the role. The royal selection process was as cold and prosaic as any thoroughbred auction. At 20, she had the lineage, the upbringing and the docility to appear to meet the requirements for a future queen of England. But the battery of tests and double-checks missed something. She turned out to be an aristocrat with an unabashedly bourgeois heart. [1]

According to Stanley, this "bourgeois heart" believed that marriage entailed love and passion. Like the heroines of fairy tales rescued through marriage to the prince, and like many young women of today still influenced by those tales and their avatars in mass culture, Diana "craved pleasure, passion, true love and all the other common yearnings that royalty is supposed to forgo or overcome." However, the end of Stanley's sentence jolts us back to another version of reality. Aristocratic marriages—and even more so royal alliances—have had very little to do with love and much to do with the consolidation of wealth and power. Diana's marriage to Charles was arranged to suit the needs of the royal family. If Diana got swept up in the hype and forgot that it was an aristocratic arranged marriage, it was perhaps because, as Stanley asserts, she had a "bourgeois heart."

Diana's story and the way that it has been (over)represented in the media signal some very important ways in which our collective modern Western European culture has come to understand the marriage contract. Most importantly for my purposes here, Diana's narrative of marriage, infidelity, depression, and divorce foregrounds the axes on which the story is centered: the axis of class, running from royalty to the bourgeoisie with the nobility in the middle, and the axis of sex represented by Diana and Charles. In other words, although it was a marriage between a man from the royal family to a woman of the nobility, it came to represent and to be represented as a marriage between a prince and a woman of the people. And because of this confusion concerning Diana's class origins—a confusion perhaps shared by Diana herself, as Stanley suggests—the narrative of the marriage contract itself was interpreted and misinterpreted to be at the same time an arranged marriage of convenience and a marriage of love.

Throughout my discussions of liberalism in the preceding chapters of this study, I have emphasized the extension of the contractual model into the field of morality that has accompanied this brand of political theory. I have emphasized the ways in which contractual models borrowed from political science and the economic realm have shaped conceptions of obligation in such a way as to make moral obligations reducible to mere formulas, often with deficient results. In the case of the marriage contract, historical development presents an interesting and paradoxical case of an area of moral and private life, codified by the public realm and already understood in terms of the contract model well before the appearance of liberalism. As Diana's narrative has reminded us, arranged marriages between noble families have always implied a contract between the two parties, or between the two families.[2] In its crudest versions, the marriage contract involves the exchange of a body, along with property or money or both, for a title.[3] The woman's body is traded between families for the progeny that it will produce, and along with it comes a dowry in exchange for political and economic ties to another aristocratic family. Most often the future bride's family pays to rid itself of the burden of the female body, which for the future groom represents the continuation of his family line as his title and lands will be passed on to his eldest son.[4]

This "contract" is analogous to an exchange of goods (and services) and no doubt was first conceived in this manner.[5] It establishes the parameters for the subsequent marital relationship insofar as the services required of the woman's body necessitate her fidelity; however, no reciprocal fidelity is required on the husband's part.[6] In this way, the "public" marriage contract stipulates the grounds of the contractual exchange by requiring sexual fidelity. The contract does not determine relations in the private sphere—in this it is entirely consistent with the liberal views explored in the previous chapter—for this behavior is "private" in the sense that it is not subject to regulation by contract. Furthermore, because there is no love relationship implied in such a pragmatic union, there are virtually no grounds save infidelity (on the part of the wife) for dissolving the contract, from the point of view of the patriarchal culture that established its conditions in the first place.

What I seek to examine in this chapter are the mutations in the understanding of the marriage contract brought about by the introduction of the bourgeois conception of the marriage of love.[7] At first glance, one would expect that the notion of a marriage for love would entail the disappearance of the contractual understanding of marriage and perhaps a shift in emphasis, away from pragmatic considerations of property, duty, and obligation toward considerations of passion or, at the very least, minimal notions of care. But a careful look at the fictional representations of bourgeois marriages and marriage contracts indicates precisely the reverse. Against the backdrop of the historical transition to increasing secular control over laws concerning marriage and the family, there is an increased emphasis on contracts, which seems to overshadow considerations of love and passion.[8] Rather than dreamy depictions of passionate, carefree, romantic, happy marriages, the novels represent pragmatic women freely choosing reasonable, respectable, mature, and often, boring husbands.

Perfect and Imperfect Duties: The Marriage Contract

Before turning to two different eighteenth-century French representations of bourgeois marriage, I would like first to sketch some of the moral implications of the use of the notion of the contract to understand the marital relationship. I have already invoked the relationship between Diana and Charles as a reminder of the aristocratic version of arranged marriages. I now turn to a brief discussion of Abelard and Heloise's correspondence and, specifically, Peggy Kamuf's reading of it, to uncover the reductionism from the standpoint of the moral obligations involved in the use of contracts to delineate the nature and scope of obligations in private, interpersonal relations.

Peggy Kamuf's *Fictions of Feminine Desire* uses Abelard and Heloise's correspondence as a point of departure for examining the inscription of the excess of women's desire in various fictional reincarnations of the lovers' relationship during the seventeenth and eighteenth centuries.[9] Her deconstructionist-inspired readings of these texts highlight ways in which female desire exceeds the bounds of the representations that inevitably seek to contain it. In her discussion of the complex series of negotiations in Abelard and Heloise's letters, she highlights Heloise's efforts to thwart Abelard's attempts to rewrite their passion in a narrative framework consistent with his renewed Christian faith.

In the course of her reading, Kamuf pinpoints the moments of excess that for her signal the inscription of Heloise's feminine desire. I, however, would like to shift the focus of the discussion slightly and turn my attention to the tension between a discourse of containment borrowed from the legal sphere and Heloise's invocation of absolute moral duties. Rather than concentrating on the representation of gendered desire, focusing on debt, obligation, duty, and the marriage contract in the correspondence highlights the difficulties of limiting an understanding of the marital bond to its contractual aspects. In particular, Kamuf's reading of Heloise's characterization of her love as "beyond all bounds" emphasizes the contradictions inhering in such efforts to characterize and circumscribe love relationships in terms of contracts. Of special interest to Kamuf, and to my purposes here as well, is a passage in which Heloise characterizes the relationship in terms of obligation:

> Yet you must know that you are bound to me by an obligation which is all the greater for the further close tie of marriage sacrament uniting us, and are the deeper in debt because of the love I have always borne you, as everyone knows, a love which is beyond all bounds.[10]

Kamuf's attentive analysis of this passage underscores Heloise's use of the concept of boundless love to thwart Abelard's efforts at containment:

> This passage first evokes Abelard's relationship to Heloise in the bound and binding terms of marriage, which inaugurates contractual debt as the form of exchange between the partners. It is thus comparable to any other exchange . . . where debt is also the binding force. Here, however, the similarity ends, or rather is surpassed by Heloise's final formulation: a debt owed for a love which is "beyond all bounds." This formulation upsets the contractual model, for a contract is necessarily and by definition an institution of limits. . . . The formulation of an *unbounded* obligation . . . by destroying the limit which alone gives meaning to the concept, undermines not only the terms of the comparison, but the very notion that Abelard is indebted to Heloise.[11]

While Kamuf's reading seeks to highlight the struggle between Abelard and Heloise to inscribe (feminine) desire, my purpose in quoting this passage is to signal the ethical arguments entangled within the discourse of the marriage contract. Contractual obligations, as we have seen throughout this book, always entail establishing specific limits to debts. Through the model of exchange conceived in many different ways, the notion of contract defines and sets up the parameters for equitable exchange. In Kantian terms, it takes all relationships of obligation—whether perfect or imperfect—and reworks them into perfect duties.[12] Kamuf underscores Heloise's resistance to the setting of such a limit. In the face of contractual obligation and perfect duty, Heloise opposes the imperfect duty of her boundless love. In other words, her love for Abelard cannot be contained within a traditional understanding of contractual obligation—it will always go beyond those limits.

Returning to the context of aristocratic marriages, we see that the concept of perfect duty is entirely consistent with the obligations obtaining in the marriage relationship. The partners are joined together in an exchange of goods and services that clearly defines their obligations to one another. Marital infidelity on the part of the wife violates the terms of the contract, for it endangers her ability to produce legitimate heirs. Since no love relationship is involved in the contract, no other behavior between the parties is subject to definition or limit by the contract.

However, Heloise's efforts to undermine Abelard's invocation of the discourse of debt and obligation introduce a new wrinkle in the understanding of the marriage contract. Making the love relationship itself subject to the terms of the contract implies establishing the parameters of a perfect duty. It is precisely these efforts that Heloise rejects in her talk of "a love which is beyond all bounds." Similarly, in the context of the marriage of love, bourgeois wives will be faced with the same paradox: how does one make the love relationship—which fits the criteria of Kant's conception of an imperfect duty—consistent with the limits and constraints imposed by the notion of contractual obligation? When both parties promise "to love, honor, and cherish," how can such promises be enforced within the confines of a negatively defined set of behaviors consistent with perfect duties?

Bourgeois Marriage: Rousseau's *Julie*

The bourgeois marriage turns out to be a very curious phenomenon indeed. As I have suggested, aristocratic marriages represented pragmatic, contractual unions that were independent of "love." By contrast, bourgeois marriages were often marriages based on "love." Bourgeois fathers more often sought the consent of their daughters, even if the daughters did not exactly freely choose their future husbands.[13] As Elisabeth Badinter has argued, the shift toward concerns with happiness, particularly among the rising bourgeoisie, made arranged marriages less and less popular.[14] Marriages based on love, or at the very least affection, and friendship helped to foster greater equality between the marriage partners. Badinter asserts that

> If the status of women as women did not change significantly during the eighteenth century, even during the Revolution, the status of the wife-mother did. At the end of the century the husband's behavior toward his wife seems to have changed not only in the well-to-do classes but also among the more modest middle class. The two main reasons for this change were the new vogue of marriages based on love, which transformed the wife into a cherished companion, and the desire of men in positions of responsibility to see their wives play a more significant role in the family and particularly with their children.[15]

This change in manners, which helped to produce greater equality between the marriage partners, indicates an ideological shift in the conception of both marriage and the family. The family home becomes the locus of happiness and fulfillment.

Yet, coupled with this tendency toward marriages based on "love" was the bourgeois attachment to contracts and to relationships based on agreements, with which they were familiar from the sphere of trade and commerce. Thus, on the one hand, the bourgeoisie believed in "romantic love" and marriage based on sentimental attachment—more than the aristocracy did—and on the other hand, the bourgeoisie was enamored of the drawing up of contracts. In fact, the two seemingly opposed tendencies reinforced one another, as I shall argue, to produce a more binding conception of the marriage contract. The new perception of the marriage partners as being on a more or less even footing, entering the contractual arrangement of marriage as "free" individuals, highlights the points of overlap between the bourgeois conceptions of marriage and of contract. The "new" marriage contract represented a relationship of obligation between more or less "equal" partners who freely entered into the arrangement.

In the realm of fiction, the influence of Richardson's *Pamela* (1740) cannot be overstated.[16] As Nancy Armstrong has argued, *Pamela* established a new paradigm for depicting the marriage contract, even between members of different classes, by underscoring the importance of the love relation between Mr. B and Pamela and, more importantly, the heroine's insistence that she be loved for "herself"—not her body.[17] Although Pamela is a servant and Mr. B is a member of the older landed gentry, according to Armstrong their union embodies all the qualities of a middle-class marriage of love. As Armstrong suggests, "The gentry was permeable, a class one could enter through marriage, and its features as a group . . . could be remodeled to the specifications of the middle-class family."[18] Thus, Pamela and Mr. B's marriage and subsequent life together in a well-organized household represent an eighteenth-century ideal incorporating a morally decent love between "metaphysical" selves and a clearly articulated marriage contract.

Rousseau's *Julie ou la nouvelle Héloïse* (1761) does not fit as neatly into the new bourgeois paradigm established by Richardson.[19] Underlying Julie's decision to marry Wolmar is an ethical dimension that allows both the legal and moral aspects of contractual obligation to surface in Rousseau's representation of the marriage. Julie's marriage entails a contractual obligation that transcends the context of the families involved, invoking a personal ethic of private conscience within the contractual model. This personal ethic has its corollary in the legal sphere, as Rousseau blends social contract theory and a representation of the space of liberal private conscience.

Further complicating Rousseau's portrayal is what Nancy Miller has called the "double trial" of Julie.[20] While Richardson's Pamela only endures an assault on her virtue as an unmarried woman and, having passed the test, accedes to a happily married life with Mr. B, Julie must endure a double test of her virtue both as an unmarried and later as a married woman. This "double test" again foregrounds the way Rousseau blends the personal and private ethic with his discussion of a more general social tendency toward contracts.

The idea of marrying Julie d'Etange to M. de Wolmar first appears in the novel as part of M. d'Etange's aristocratic value system based on concepts of duty related to honor. Opposing the more bourgeois and clearly more modern view that Julie should marry the untitled tutor whom she loves is her father's view that the promise of his daughter to an old friend outweighs his daughter's romantic attachment to a non-noble.[21] His discourse with his daughter, repeated by Julie in the long letter recapitulating her love for Saint-Preux and her subsequent decision to marry Wolmar, is marked by the aristocratic code of shame and honor. M. d'Etange's understanding of his obligation to Wolmar is based on loyalty between old friends. To renege on the agreement would be to disgrace himself within the community of his peers, especially because of Wolmar's loss of his fortune since the arrangement was first made. Furthermore, in his efforts to persuade his daughter to go along willingly with his wishes, M. d'Etange contrasts the honor of upholding such an obligation with the dishonor involved in Julie's relationship with Saint-Preux:

> M. de Wolmar is a man of high birth, distinguished by all those qualities that accompany it, who enjoys public esteem, and who merits it. I

owe him my life; you know the engagements that I made with him. . . . Will I say to him: Sir, I promised you my daughter when you were rich, but now that you no longer have anything, I retract my agreement and my daughter wants nothing to do with you? . . . we will be taken, you for a ruined girl and me for a dishonest man who sacrifices his duty and his faith to vile interest, someone who joins ingratitude to infidelity. My daughter, it is too late to finish in shame a life without stains, and sixty years of honor are not abandoned in fifteen minutes.[22]

M. d'Etange's invocation of Wolmar's birth and his well-deserved reputation within the aristocratic public sphere set up the possibility that d'Etange himself will be disgraced within the same sphere that respects Wolmar. More important than the personal obligation he feels toward Wolmar for saving his life and for promising him his daughter's hand are the public consequences of backing out of such an agreement.

Characterizing Julie's love for Saint-Preux as a "vile interest" suggests not only the illicit nature of their romantic involvement from her father's point of view but, more importantly, the private and individual character of their love. Julie's aristocratic father sees her attachment to her tutor as inappropriate on two levels: first, he does not believe that considerations of "love" (read sexual attraction) should interfere in marriage relations; and second, he sees Julie and Saint-Preux as two individuals inappropriately joined together. To their "individualist" love he contrasts love relationships set within the context of aristocratic peer relations. In other words, the romantic love between Julie and Saint-Preux cannot lead to marriage because marriage for d'Etange exists within a community of nobles already bound together by strong ties of loyalty. Julie and Saint-Preux's love is based on self-interest, which must be viewed as vile against the backdrop of a communal understanding of marriage ties.

M. d'Etange's view of marriage is perfectly consistent with the aristocratic marriage contract as I have represented it in the arranged marriage between Diana and Prince Charles. D'Etange sees the marriage contract as an even exchange between himself and Wolmar. His future son-in-law receives his daughter and, with her, a dowry and the family home in exchange for Wolmar's title, his respectability in the noble community, and his having saved d'Etange's life. The question of romantic attachment between the two future partners is never raised; it is not an issue. What matters most to d'Etange is honor: "honor has spoken, and in our bloodline, it is always honor that decides."[23]

If Julie capitulates to her father's pleas, it is not because she accepts his value system. In fact, she explicitly rejects his reasoning, but she fears the knowledge he has of her relation with Saint-Preux. She also attributes her reaction to shame, claiming that although she believes that her love for Saint-Preux was and always will be virtuous, she cannot get over guilt at having been an indirect cause of her mother's death.[24]

Agreeing to marry Wolmar initially represents for Julie merely a secondary commitment that will not interfere with her primary commitment to Saint-Preux. As she describes the moments leading up to her marriage, she describes her intention of going through with the ceremony, all the while harboring a deep commitment to her first love:

> In the very instant that I was ready to swear eternal fidelity to another, my heart was still swearing eternal love to you, and I was taken to the temple like an impure victim that defiles the sacrifice at which it is to be immolated.[25]

Rousseau's language here is unequivocal. He already suggests—in his metaphoric characterization of the act Julie intended to commit (as a sacrifice that would dirty the sacred space)—the ethical basis of the marriage contract. In the depiction of Julie's epiphanic conversion in the moments leading to her taking the marriage vow, Rousseau develops a profoundly moral understanding of the marriage contract that departs radically from M. d'Etange's value system based on aristocratic honor.

Julie's first *prise de conscience* involves an awareness of a legal violation she had intended to commit. In characterizing the act of marrying Wolmar, while maintaining her internal pledge of eternal love to Saint-Preux, as one of perjury, Julie invokes the legal realm of oath-swearing and commisive speech acts:

> The somber light of the edifice, the profound silence of the audience, their modest and contemplative demeanor, the procession of all my relatives, the imposing look of my venerated father, all of this gave to what was about to happen an air of solemnity that roused me to attention and to respect and that would have made me shudder at the mere idea of *perjury*.[26] [My emphasis.]

Clearly the context plays an important role in Julie's self-examination that ultimately leads to her dramatic change of heart. In typically Rousseauean fashion, she explores the depths of her private conscience in the moments before taking her marriage vows and discovers that she cannot utter a speech act promising eternal fidelity to Wolmar if she still loves Saint-Preux. In a very private act of conscience, she refuses to commit perjury and, in effect, wipes the slate of her conscience clean in order to swear an oath of fidelity to Wolmar that she will be able to keep.

This act of private conscience bears a striking resemblance to the clearly Protestant-inspired strands of Rousseau's religious/ethical philosophy so apparent in the "Profession de foi du vicaire savoyard."[27] Here, in a language that combines religion and ethics, Julie is cleansed of her yet-to-be-committed sin of perjury by the hand of Providence; at the same time, Rousseau's ambiguous language also suggests that she both redirects herself and is redirected toward a path of virtue:

> The purity, the dignity, the sanctity of marriage, so clearly laid out in the words of the Scriptures, its chaste and sublime duties so crucial to happiness, to order, to peace, to the continuation of the human species, so sweet to fulfill in themselves; all of this made such an impression on me that *I believed that I felt a sudden interior revolution. An unknown power seemed all at once to correct the disorder of my affections and to reestablish them according to the law of duty and of nature.*[28] [My emphasis.]

As an individual, Julie refuses to commit an act of perjury before God and the community. She now understands the marriage vow and the ensuing obligation as an absolute promise of fidelity that cannot be violated even within the private realm of conscience. Her oath of fidelity to Wolmar cannot be contradicted in any way by her feelings for Saint-Preux, for such a contradiction in her heart represents a moral violation of the oath.

Rousseau, by insisting on Julie's moral conscience in the act of swearing her allegiance in the marriage ceremony, has refocused the marriage contract as Richardson's portrayal in *Pamela* had before him, but in a new way. While Richardson insisted on the moral nature of the love between Mr. B and Pamela, founded on their "metaphysical" rather than physical/sexual love for one another, Rousseau shifts the love relation to the moral realm. To marry someone in this blend of aristocratic and bourgeois values is to individually pledge an allegiance that must be absolutely pure. It is two souls and two moral consciences that are joined together in this reworking of the marriage contract. To legitimately bind them together requires that the promises they undertake to keep in the course of the marriage be made with the purest of intentions.

But Rousseau does not end his discussion of the marriage vow at the level of the individual. In the passage quoted above, describing Julie's epiphany in the church, she/Rousseau alludes to the backdrop for the marriage contract supplied by the community ("the continuation of the human species"). It is not enough for the two individuals involved to pledge themselves to one another; they must live in a community and their marriage must represent the very foundation and possibility of the continuation of the community in which they live.

Julie's love for Saint-Preux at the thematic level enables Rousseau to pivot at the theoretical level between the individual act of promise-making with the obligations it entails, and the broader problem of the community. Representing both an impurity within her own heart that prevents her from making a true oath *and* the general threat of infidelity, Julie's attachment to Saint-Preux allows Rousseau to move the discussion of the marriage contract into the context of the community. In this context, Saint-Preux represents more than simply a particular individual to whom Julie is attached; he is, more generally, the threat of marital infidelity.

At the same time that Julie pledges herself until death to Wolmar and, in so doing, at the level of her private conscience, wipes Saint-Preux from her heart, she also makes her pledge in front of a community. For Julie/Rousseau, this community both mirrors and sets up the conditions for the marriage contract:

> It is not only in the interest of the spouses, but also the common cause of all men, that the purity of marriage not be adulterated/corrupted. Every time that two spouses unite by a solemn knot, a tacit engagement of all humankind intervenes to respect this sacred tie, to honor in them the conjugal union; . . . The public is in some sense the guarantor of an agreement made in its presence, and one can say that the honor of a chaste woman is under the protection of all people of good will.[29]

The marriage vow is taken before a community that itself was formed through the same type of solemn contract. To violate any contract—be it a marriage contract, a business contract, or the social contract—is to undermine the stability of human society. While it is clear that the future of humanity depends on reproduction achieved through marriage, it seems that human society conceived in moral/contractual terms also depends on the sanctity of the marriage contract.

Rousseau's language in this formulation compacts many issues by invoking the community as horizon and guarantor of the marriage contract. As I have already suggested, the community stands as a guarantor of the marriage contract, in that its own survival depends on respecting contractual engagements. For legitimate progeny to be produced, thereby ensuring social reproduction, the partners must remain faithful to one another. But clearly there is more at stake. When the two individuals bind themselves together, Rousseau claims, there is also a tacit engagement of the community. This engagement involves respecting the terms of the contract. In relation to the problem of Saint-Preux (or any other man) as a possible interloper in the marriage contract, making a marriage vow before the community engages the community to uphold and protect the marriage contract. To interfere with the marriage contract by having an affair with one of the parties (especially the wife) destroys not only the marriage but also the foundation of trust that binds individuals to the community. In other words, the marriage contract must be respected like all other contractual obligations, because to interfere would be not only to break the engagement between the two contracted parties but, more generally, to disrupt the underlying social contract that enables men to live peaceably in society. That is, it would violate the implicit contract that underwrites all others.

Thus, Rousseau's reworking of the marriage contract in *Julie* uses the pivot of Julie's attachment to Saint-Preux to move between an understanding of the marriage contract as a private, individual ethical engagement and an understanding of it as an act of public, communal trust. This representation manages to walk a thin line between the moral and legal spheres. While Julie does not want to commit an act of perjury—and her avoidance steers her back to the path of virtue—the act of perjury is understood at the same time as both an illegal and an immoral act. To promise oneself in marriage at the level of individual conscience thus entails both a legal and, more strongly, a moral commitment. At the social level, the oath of marriage represents a promise made before a community that both enforces and protects the marriage contract. Again, this act is understood in both moral and legal terms. The community enforces the marriage as the legal horizon for settling any disputes that may arise, but also the community represents a moral underpinning of the marriage contract that binds not only the two individuals together but also the entire society, both as miniature incarnations of the social contract.

But has this representation moved beyond the aristocratic conception of obligation? Recalling M. d'Etange's reasons for wanting to marry his daughter to his close friend, we see that the community of peers played an important role in his desire for the union. Julie's understanding of her marriage vows reiterates these same concerns for a community of peers, but the focus has shifted from honor and standing within that community (the father's aristocratic values) to the value of the community itself, as it is instantiated in the marriage contract. In other words, Rousseau has preserved certain aspects of the aristocratic conception of marriage, including the horizon of the broader community, but he has recast these values in legal and moral terms, rather than in terms of an honor code. This recasting is very important, because it allows for the expression of individual conscience—here the individual conscience of the female—while preserving ties to the community.

But while Rousseau makes significant advances in reconceiving the marriage contract in *Julie* as simultaneously an ethical and a legal form of engagement, he never articulates what Julie's duties and obligations are—save sexual fidelity—within the institution of marriage. Although Nancy Miller and other critics have quite rightly described the novel as structured around the competing conceptions of Julie as daughter, as mother, and as lover of Saint-Preux, few characterize her duties in the role of wife to Wolmar.

The major difficulty in interpreting her role as Mme de Wolmar is also the central problem that the novel has long posed for critics: determining the relation between her death and her feelings for Saint-Preux. If one interprets her death as symptomatic of her failure to repress her passion for Saint-Preux and as a sacrifice of her own feelings of romantic passion to her role as mother, one is left without a satisfactory articulation of her role as a wife to Wolmar and, perhaps more pointedly, without a sense of whether or not love exists in this consensual and utopian marriage of "beautiful souls." In fact, her death read as self-sacrifice underscores the ways in which her marriage is unsatisfying at a personal level. In this respect, the novel has been conventionally read as rejoining the tradition that equates passionate love with obstacles, making it incompatible with marriage.[30] For if Julie throws herself in the lake to save her son, she dies as a good mother and faithful wife in this life, adhering strictly to the letter of the promise that she made to Wolmar, "'til death do us part."[31] Her final letter to Saint-Preux supports her fear of infidelity: "One more day and perhaps I would have been guilty!"[32] If marriage requires that she sacrifice the deep feelings she has for Saint-Preux, feelings that can only be successfully overcome through death, then this view of marriage can hardly be said to represent a state of bliss for a wife.

Since Rousseau allows Julie's passion for Saint-Preux and her efforts to overcome it within her marriage to overshadow his depiction of her duties as wife to Wolmar, we are left without a representation of marital obligation once the contract is concluded, save a strict adherence to the letter of the contract.[33] Reminiscent of problems discussed in chapter 3 in conjunction with Diderot's *Entretien d'un père avec ses enfants*, strict adherence to the letter of the law is hardly consistent with Rousseau's insistence on the purity of Julie's heart in the scene in the church. If she commits an act of perjury by swearing an act of fidelity to one man while still loving another, how can we interpret her continued struggle to erase her passion for Saint-Preux from her heart after she is married? And what about her death? If she sacrifices herself in order to preserve the marriage promise of fidelity, then clearly her marriage vows were violated in her heart, if not in actual physical practice. This again goes against the grain of the moral reinterpretation of the marriage contract that Rousseau provided earlier in the novel.

Although some would point to Julie's self-deception ("I deluded myself for a long time")[34] as a way of resolving the difficulty I am emphasizing here, I do not think that such an explanation squares with the reconceived marriage relation as Rousseau first presents it. Self-deception as an excuse for an enduring passion for another stands in sharp contrast to the soul-searching and conscience-cleansing language of Julie's description of her marriage in Part 3 of the novel. Her death-bed admission of an unextinguished passion in her heart—and the circumstances surrounding her death, which enable it to be interpreted as a suicide—only reinforce the sense in which the "consensual, reasonable" marriage to Wolmar really meant adhering to the strict provisions of a contract.

While Rousseau's reworking of the marriage vow is commendable at the level of personal conscience and in its implications for relations to the broader community, it nonetheless fails to represent what the marriage contract entails in terms of positive duties, once the vows are taken. As we have seen, the "double trial" structure of the novel shifts the focus away from the more ethical interpretation of the marriage bond, back toward an insistence on sexual fidelity. I turn now to Isabelle de Charrière's *Lettres de Mistriss Henley* to explore another representation of "bourgeois" marriage, which foregrounds relations between husband and wife after the vows are taken.

A Marriage of Despair: Charrière's Mistriss Henley

As Nadine Bérenguier has convincingly argued, there are good textual reasons to pair a reading of Rousseau's *Julie* with Charrière's *Lettres de Mistriss Henley* (1784).[35] Although the latter was written as a direct response to Samuel de Constant's misogynist *Le Mari sentimental*,[36] as Bérenguier points out, in addition to several direct references to Rousseau in the *Lettres*, there is also a striking resemblance between Wolmar and Mr. Henley: "Mr. Henley is a younger more seductive version of M. de Wolmar. Describing their husbands, both wives mention reason and moderation as the men's fundamental traits."[37] And, like Julie, Mrs. Henley (we never learn her first name) agrees to marry a man whom she respects, even if she doesn't feel real passion for him. "I was, if not passionate, at least quite touched."[38] But unlike Julie, what prevents Mrs. Henley from loving her husband and finding happiness in her married life in the country is not an undying, repressed passion for her first love. Charrière's more devastating critique of marriage does not rely on the "test of virtue" structure but instead locates all of the difficulty in the relation between the married partners.

Charrière's description of the process by which Mrs. Henley chooses a suitable husband for herself marks a significant departure from the arranged marriage scenario that was present even in *Julie*. Being an orphan raised by an aunt who cannot pass on a means of support to her niece, the future Mrs. Henley finds herself in financial need of a husband, after the cousin whom she had intended to marry dies. The necessity of finding a husband is made more urgent by her advancing years and her growing reputation as "picky."[39] Faced with two competing suitors, she makes a "reasonable" choice. While one suitor promises a comfortable life of riches and the pleasures of socializing, thanks to a fortune made in India, the other offers a quiet family life in the country. Forced to choose for herself, Mrs. Henley is torn between what she characterizes as a conflict between base and noble motives:

> It was, so to speak, the base part of my heart that preferred the riches of the Orient, London, total freedom, a more brilliant opulence; the noble part disdained all that and was penetrated by the sweetness of a completely reasonable and sublime happiness such that angels would applaud.[40]

There is no coercion involved in Mrs. Henley's choice of a husband, save the exigencies of financial need. But, certainly, this plays no role in her choice of a thirty-five-year-old widower who lives in the country, as opposed to a forty-year-old nabob who lives in London. What motivates the decision is rather her self-perception as a virtuous person who values certain things over others. Those things she believes that she values and that will bring her a life of happiness can only be characterized as bourgeois, already clearly inscribed by 1784 in the novels of the period.

In this same passage, Charrière carefully juxtaposes the character's situation of choosing for herself with the more common fictional (and perhaps real) scenario of being forced by a tyrannical father to marry the nabob. What Charrière reveals in the juxtaposition represents a very astute commentary on the female subject position with respect to marriage:

> If a tyrannical father had made me marry the nabob, perhaps I would have made it my duty to obey. . . . In a word, forced to become happy

in a vulgar way, I would have become happy without shame and maybe with pleasure; *but to give myself of my own choosing, in exchange for diamonds, pearls, rugs, perfumes, chiffons embroidered with gold, suppers, parties—to this I could not bring myself, and I promised my hand to Mr. Henley.*[41] [My emphasis.]

Mrs. Henley cannot choose riches for herself for several reasons. First, clearly, her sense of shame derives from identifying herself publicly as someone who prefers riches and glamour to a peaceful life in the country. She would not feel shame if she were forced into such a match by someone else, but to choose this type of life for herself would indicate greed and base desires. Second, and by extension, she would have to admit to herself that she is not as moral a person as she believes herself to be, if she were to choose the nabob as a husband. Or, at the very least, she would self-consciously have to shift her own value system. Third, she seems to indicate that choosing the nabob would be less noble and even possibly humiliating to her because it might appear as though she were selling herself in exchange for such a life of luxury, "to give myself of my own choosing, in exchange for . . ." In fact, such an exchange resembles an aristocratic arranged marriage more than it does a "modern" marriage of consent. Rather than appear immoral to herself and others, she chooses the "reasonable," and clearly more bourgeois, Mr. Henley.

What Charrière's text suggests is a difficulty that other fiction of the period seems to have passed over silently: how were women supposed to make marriage choices that would ultimately make them happy in this new social arrangement, if their subject position precluded them from wanting things for themselves? Echoing Julie's capitulation to her father's wishes and efforts to find happiness in a "reasonable" marriage, Mrs. Henley's inability to choose the nabob for herself indicates a fundamental conflict between two different bourgeois values: on the one hand, the bourgeois premium set on a consensual relation being established between husband and wife, and on the other hand, the competing interest of a bourgeois conception of virtue that makes it exceedingly difficult for men, but even more especially women, to choose what they desire for themselves. Faced with the choice between husbands, Mrs. Henley weighs the perceptions of herself—both her own and others'—against her values and her future happiness. In this tangle of competing interests, she is unable to thread a path toward her own happiness and instead makes a choice based on incomplete self-understanding fostered by social expectations and class values. In other words, she chooses to marry Mr. Henley because she thinks she values the things that her society and class say she is supposed to value.

Nor is Mrs. Henley alone in making a choice based on these types of motivation. As Charrière plainly asserts through her character with reference to her own unhappy marriage, "I believe that many women are in my position."[42] Faced with such an important decision, it is doubtful that many eighteenth-century women were in a position to choose appropriate husbands for themselves because few, if any, had been able to develop the requisite sense of self and attendant self-awareness that such a decision requires.[43] Furthermore, men, due to various social constraints, no doubt found themselves at a loss as well. In other words, the new ideology of an equal partnership entered into freely by both partners and its dissemination in various discourses clearly developed more rapidly than the actual social change.

Leaving aside the question of the development of female subject identity, which is beyond the scope of the present study, I return to the question of the marriage contract posed by the terms in which it is represented by Charrière. The lack of a female subject position requisite for making informed choices based on self-knowledge interferes at the level of the marriage contract as well. If the bourgeois ideal is a marriage based on a consensual relation between more or less equal partners—although this is clearly problematic from many perspectives, not the least of which is the legal perspective—then Mrs. Henley or any future wife needs to enter into the contract as an individual. That is to say, the consensual marriage posits the albeit idealized notion of two individuals freely choosing for themselves to be joined together legally, socially, and personally through a contract. For Mrs. Henley, who clearly does not know her own needs and desires, and even if she did, still might not be able to act on them, this means that her gendered subject identity precludes her from behaving as an individual. She cannot freely enter into the contract as an individual on an equal footing with her future partner.

The lack of equality and reciprocity at the outset plays itself out in the marriage as a game of domination and submission between Mr. and Mrs. Henley. They cannot negotiate a relationship based on equality and reciprocity for several reasons. One obvious reason is the difference in their social backgrounds, reflected in their different sensibilities. But, perhaps more importantly, the terms of the marriage contract effectively if not explicitly stipulate that Mrs. Henley be assimilated to Mr. Henley's way of life—she is to move to Hollow Park and become the second Mrs. Henley. This assimilation of Mrs. Henley is perfectly consistent with eighteenth-century French marriage law, which, to all intents and purposes, considered married partners as becoming one person, namely, the husband.[44] This results in Mr. Henley's domination of Mrs. Henley insofar as matters in their daily life are concerned. Thus, most often when a disagreement arises from their different sensibilities, Mrs. Henley acquiesces to Mr. Henley's wishes and adjusts her behavior accordingly. They do not negotiate a compromise, for she is expected by her husband and by herself to adapt to the constraints of the lifestyle she has "freely" chosen for herself, which include Mr. Henley's attitudes.

Such problems never arise between Julie and Wolmar because Julie, consistent with the pedagogical model of the entire novel, becomes Wolmar's student and disciple. But Mrs. Henley is not, explicitly at least, in the same type of subordinate position with respect to her husband. And yet her behavior demonstrates that even when she stands up for her own differing opinions, she feels guilty for having done so and vows to change her ways. In the most poignant and psychologically insightful passage, Charrière represents her character vacillating between standing up for her own beliefs and blaming herself for decisions she has made:

> Could he be right, my dear friend? Could I be wrong again, always wrong, wrong in everything? No, I cannot believe that: . . . I think nonetheless that I have been too hasty. I could have waited a day or two, consulted Mr. Henley. . . . I have too much obeyed my impetuosity of temperament.[45]

Mrs. Henley repeatedly chastises herself for acting on her own beliefs when these actions cause conflict with her husband. This self-recrimination is emblematic of the lack of a well-defined subject position, which prohibits her from being on an equal footing with her husband in the marriage. Ultimately, it signals the inability of most women to function as independent, free, equal individuals in a reciprocal partnership, even if they have "freely" entered into that "partnership" by choosing their spouse.

So what becomes of the marriage contract under these conditions? The open ending of *Lettres de Mistriss Henley* does not leave much room for hope. Mrs. Henley flatly states that either she will force herself to become "reasonable" and happy like her husband or else she will die: "In a year, in two years, you will learn, I trust, that I am reasonable and contented, or that I am no more."[46] In other words, she will either assimilate to the life she has chosen for herself or die because she cannot assimilate.

In contractual terms, she clearly does not see the possibility of breaking her contract through divorce (although this was not prohibited by religious belief in the novel's English setting), nor does she imagine negotiating a compromise living situation in which she and Mr. Henley jointly participate in making decisions concerning their life and their children's lives.[47] Charrière's pointed use of the word "reasonable" in her character's final letter signals the degree to which Mrs. Henley must see things the way her husband sees them in order to be "contented." Happiness in marriage thus depends upon lack of conflict enabled by the wife's acquiescence, adaptation, and ultimate assimilation to her husband's life and values. The marriage contract, then, while theoretically representing the possibility of an equal, reciprocal partnership between free individuals, in practice amounts to the obligation of the wife to adapt herself to the needs and desires of the husband. The new ideology of bourgeois happiness in marriage reveals itself under Charriere's critique to be ideological—it masks the reality lying beneath the belief system. The marriage partners are not equal, nor are they free. Therefore, happiness in marriage still remains out of reach.

As I have already suggested, this is in part due to Mrs. Henley's lack of a clearly defined subject identity. She does not have the self-knowledge requisite for making the type of decision that choosing a marriage partner requires. But, beyond this lack of self-knowledge, she is unable to make demands for herself. Given the social context of women's subject identities in the eighteenth century, it seems highly unlikely that many women were in a position to make informed and well-motivated choices about marriage partners. Even assuming that some were able to make "better" choices than Mrs. Henley, that is, choices better suited to their needs and temperaments, it still remains unlikely that they would have been able to act as equal partners making decisions that would shape the course of their life together.

More often, according to Charrière, the new bourgeois marriage becomes a life sentence in which the wife adapts herself to the needs, desires, values, and temperament of her husband. Since divorce was most often out of the question both for religious and social reasons, and since the women were not coerced into marriage by tyrannical fathers but instead chose their husbands presumably out of considerations of "love" and "affection," it seems ironic that they found themselves even more bound by the marriage contract than were their aristocratic predecessors. While aristocratic women were not usually expected to love their husbands, and they often had extramarital relationships and retained a personal circle of friends after marriage, bourgeois women were, by contrast, expected to love their husbands and to remain faithful to them. Most devastatingly, bourgeois wives were isolated in the "home" by the new class ideal of the nuclear family and the happiness it was supposed to provide. In reality, the move to the husband's house often removed them from friends and relatives and required them, as with Mrs. Henley, to become contented with their life or die. All the intertexts within Charrière's novel suggest that she is responding not only to fellow writers like Rousseau and Constant but to a social reality as well. Her critique of fictional depictions of domestic bliss—positioned in relation to these texts—suggests a pointed critique of a reality that the other fictions ignore. In other words, Charrière's depiction of bourgeois marriage functions as a kind of ideology critique of other fictions of the period. While Pamela and Julie live happily ever after in an isolated world of bourgeois tranquility because there is no conflict between them and their spouses, Mrs. Henley suffers from severe depression in a marriage that does not allow for her self-actualization or the satisfaction of her needs and desires.

Class, Marriage, and Contract

Returning to where I began, Mrs. Henley's situation bears a striking resemblance to Princess Diana's. Both suffered from depression in a marriage that did not bring them what they expected. Where they both expected to live happily ever after, like Cinderella, Snow White, Pamela, and Julie, instead they found themselves in loveless, affectionless marriages to which they were bound by modern conceptions of the contract. Mrs. Henley felt obligated to remain in her unhappy marriage and, to a certain extent, so Diana did before the divorce, because she felt bound not to break a contract she had willfully and freely entered into. If anything, the bourgeois contract between the Henleys was even more binding than the usual aristocratic contract, or even the modified royal contract between Diana and Charles, because there was no means of escape through extramarital affairs or a social circle of family and friends. Instead, Mrs. Henley had to suffer in isolation as she struggled to align herself with the terms established by her husband for their life together.

Following Rousseau's lead, Charrière also depicts the obligation entailed in the marriage contract as a profoundly personal and moral form of engagement. As we have already seen, Julie's conscience-cleansing episode in the church before making her vows clearly establishes the moral foundation for the marriage contract within the context of a social bond. In other words, for Rousseau, marriage is both a deeply personal moral obligation *and* a publicly executed contract guaranteed by and guaranteeing the community that witnesses it. Although Charrière never directly invokes Mrs. Henley's relation to her own marriage vow, her decision at the end of the novel either to find happiness in the marriage or die trying signals the importance she attaches to the vow she has made. The milieu of the English landed gentry (and their clear relation to the values of the bourgeoisie as Armstrong has maintained) further reinforces the moral overtones of her commitment to the marriage with Mr. Henley. Even more than the gentry, the emerging bourgeoisie holds to ethical standards on an individual level rather than to the socially based honor code (exemplified by M. d'Etange) of the nobility. In spite of the fact that Charrière's character realizes her mistake in choosing Mr. Henley over the nabob as a husband, she nonetheless remains committed to the consequences of that decision, that is, marriage. It seems as though, because she has chosen this man as a husband of her own free will, she is all the more committed to him and to making the marriage work. For Charrière, as for Rousseau, marriage is a deeply felt personal moral commitment that cannot be broken except under the most extreme conditions.

The bourgeois reinterpretation of the marriage contract infuses it with ever greater binding power, due both to the degree of personal moral commitment entailed and to the conception, borrowed from the realm of economic transactions, of the individuals entering into the contract. In the realm of trade and commerce, free, reciprocal, and equal partners bind themselves in clearly stated obligations negotiated by the parties of the contract. But this model cannot be easily shifted to the private realm. As we have seen, the parties to the marriage contract are not equal at the outset, nor do they negotiate the terms of the obligations—even though various discourses of the period make such assertions. While the wife "freely" chooses to enter into a permanent relationship with the husband, she does not participate in an equal way in the establishment of the terms of the ensuing partnership—at least not in the representative novels I have examined. Nor are the obligations clearly spelled out. Recalling my earlier discussion of Abelard and Heloise's letters, the imperfect duties entailed in the marriage bond are ill suited to the perfect duties normally stipulated by contracts. Thus, the wife finds herself contractually bound to adapt herself to imperfect duties that include remolding herself to fit the needs and desires of her husband. In the eighteenth-century context, conduct-book fiction like Richardson's and Rousseau's attempted to show women how to behave in order to achieve happiness in the new style marriage. Charrière's critique of these fictions and of the social reality that they did not accurately reflect demonstrates the degree to which the new conception of marriage only worsened bourgeois women's fates.

Both on the personal level of moral commitment and on the public level of legal engagement, the bourgeois marriage contract bound wives even more intimately to the marriage relation than the earlier aristocratic model did. Held in check both by social norms and expectations and by their own feelings of commitment, bourgeois wives like Mrs. Henley did not have the avenue of divorce open to them. Instead, they no doubt languished in marriages of despair that were neither physically abusive nor visibly unhappy to the outside world. Much like Diana before her divorce from Charles, bourgeois wives felt trapped by the new conceptions of the free individual that ironically bound them even more tightly to their partners. Against the historical backdrop of the steady evolution in the understanding of the marriage bond as a contract rather than as a sacrament, the level of personal moral engagement increased simultaneously with the appearance of the ideal of married love and familial happiness. Unfortunately, the notions of marriage as civil contract and married love would take many years to become reconciled—and perhaps are still not completely reconciled in modern practice—before wives could contract with husbands as equal partners to produce a happy marriage.[48]

Notes

[1]Alessandra Stanley, "A Fairy-Tale Hamlet with a Diamond Tiara," *New York Times* (September 7, 1997, Week in Review, section 4), p. 1.

[2]Traditional marriage contracts were often signed by the two families. See Jean A. Perkins, "Love, Marriage and Sex in Eighteenth-Century France," *Studies on Voltaire and the Eighteenth Century* 256 (1988), p. 292.

[3] Among the lower classes, the dowry was also an essential element of the exchange, for it provided "starting capital" for the new family. For a discussion of the importance of marriage in the policing of the lower classes, see Jacques Donzelot, *The Policing of Families*, trans. Robert Hurley (Baltimore: Johns Hopkins University Press, 1979), pp. 31–45.

[4]The right of primogeniture (*droit d'aînesse*) existed throughout the eighteenth century in France. According to this law, the eldest male stood to inherit "the castle or principal manor and between one-half and four-fifths of his parents' immovable family property (*propres*)." James Traer, *Marriage and the Family in Eighteenth-Century France* (Ithaca, N. Y.: Cornell University Press, 1980), p. 42.

[5]Compare Claude Lévi-Strauss, *Les Structures élémentaires de la parenté* (Paris: Mouton, 1967): "c'est toujours un système d'échange que nous trouvons à l'origine des règles de mariage, . . . que ce soit sous une forme directe

ou indirecte, globale ou spéciale, immédiate ou différée, explicite ou implicite, fermée ou ouverte, concrète ou symbolique, c'est l'échange, toujours l'échange, qui ressort comme la base fondamentale et commune de toutes les modalités de l'institution matrimoniale." [it is always a system of exchange that we find at the origin of the rules of marriage, . . . whether it be a direct or indirect form, global or special, immediate or differed, explicit or implicit, closed or open, concrete or symbolic, it is exchange, always exchange, that comes out again and again as the fundamental and common base of all modalities of the institution of marriage.] Lévi-Strauss, *Structures*, pp. 548–49.

[6]This is borne out in eighteenth-century civil law, in which adultery was a female offense. See Nadine Bérenguier, "Victorious Victims: Women and Publicity in *Mémoires Judiciaires*," in Elizabeth C. Goldsmith and Dena Goodman eds, *Going Public: Women and Publishing in Early Modern France* (Ithaca, N. Y.: Cornell University Press, 1995), p. 67. See also, James Traer, *Marriage and the Family in Eighteenth-Century France*, p. 40; and, for a review of feminist critiques of the marriage contract, Carole Pateman, *The Sexual Contract* (Stanford, Calif.: Stanford University Press, 1988), pp. 154–88.

[7] For an overview of the historical changes in the conceptions of marriage and the family in France, see William F. Edmiston, *Diderot and the Family: A Conflict of Nature and Law, Stanford French and Italian Studies 39* (Saratoga, Calif.: Anma Libri, 1985), pp. 1–19.

[8]James Traer asserts that "By the end of the eighteenth century, the French monarchy had assumed substantial control over legislation and litigation involving marriage and had fostered the development of doctrinal change to justify that control" (32). For a study of the transition from ecclesiastical control to civil code, see Traer, *Marriage and the Family in Eighteenth Century France*. See also Nicole Fermon, *Domesticating Passions: Rousseau, Woman, and Nation* (Hanover, N. H.: Wesleyan University Press, 1997), pp. 49–96.

[9]While Kamuf's analysis centers on problems of representation and the gendering of erotic discourse, it is nonetheless helpful for my purposes here in stressing the tension between Heloise's efforts to characterize her love and Aberlard's efforts to contain it, in their use of the terminology of contracts.

[10]See Peggy Kamuf, *Fictions of Feminine Desire: Disclosures of Heloise* (Lincoln: University of Nebraska Press, 1982), chapter 1, for the discussion of Abelard and Heloise's correspondence. The passage from Heloise's letter is quoted in Kamuf and is taken from *The Letters of Abelard and Heloise*, trans. and ed. Betty Radice (Baltimore: Penguin, 1974), p. 113.

[11] Kamuf, *Fictions of Feminine Desire*, pp. 11–12.

[12] See Immanuel Kant, *The Metaphysical Elements of Justice*, trans. John Ladd (Indianapolis: Bobbs-Merrill, 1965). Compare my discussion of negative duties in Rousseau in chapter 2.

[13]See Philippe Ariès, *L'Enfant et la vie familiale sous l'ancien régime* (Paris: Seuil, 1973).

[14] See Elisabeth Badinter, *Mother Love: Myth and Reality: Motherhood in Modern History* (New York: Macmillan, 1981), pp. 117–67.

[15] Ibid., p. 143.

[16]Jean-Louis Flandrin has suggested that "the notion that anglo-mania had made fashionable among the French élites in the eighteenth century was married love." See Jean-Louis Flandrin, *Families in Former Times: Kinship, Household and Sexuality*, trans. Richard Southern (Cambridge: Cambridge University Press, 1979), p. 169.

[17]See Nancy Armstrong, *Desire and Domestic Fiction: A Political History of the Novel* (Oxford: Oxford University Press, 1987).

[18] Ibid., p. 112.

[19] For a reading of *Julie* as a continuation of Richardson's *Clarissa* and as a critique of bourgeois practices in arranged marriages, see Fermon, *Domesticating Passions*, pp. 49–96.

[20]Nancy Miller, *The Heroine's Text: Readings in the French and English Novel 1722–1782* (New York: Columbia University Press, 1980), pp. 106–9.

[21]In contrast to the plot of *Julie*, Sophie is told by her parents that she is to choose her husband and that they will simply approve or disapprove her decision: "Dans les mariages qui se font par l'autorité des péres, on se régle uniquement sur les convenances d'institution et d'opinion; ce ne sont pas les personnes qu'on marie, ce sont les conditions et les biens; . . . Je vous propose un accord qui vous marque nôtre estime et rétablisse entre nous l'ordre naturel. Les parens choisissent l'époux de leur fille, et ne la consultent que pour la forme; tel est l'usage. Nous ferons entre nous tout le contraire; vous choisirez, et nous serons consultés" (Rousseau, *Emile, Oeuvres complètes*, vol. 4, pp. 755–57). [In marriages made by the authority of fathers, the dictates of institution and opinion are the only rule: it is not people who are married, but conditions and goods; . . . I propose to you an agreement that demonstrates our regard for you and reestablishes between us the natural order. Parents choose the husband of their daughter and only consult her as a matter of form: that is current practice. We will do the opposite amongst ourselves: you will choose and we will be consulted.] In spite of the apparent difference between Julie's and Sophie's situations with respect to their authority in the matter of choosing a husband, as Joan Landes points out, in the end, Sophie was chosen for Emile by his tutor. The whole match was a set-up from the beginning. Landes goes further to suggest that, "it is Sophie who is being exchanged, circulated between the men, the two fathers" (83). See Joan B. Landes, *Women and the Public Sphere in the Age of the French Revolution* (Ithaca, N. Y.: Cornell University Press, 1988), pp. 83–85. See also Susan Moller Okin's comparative discussion of Julie and Sophie in *Women in West-*

ern Political Thought (Princeton, N. J.: Princeton University Press, 1979), pp. 167–194.

[22] "M. de Wolmar est un homme d'une grande naissance, distingué par toutes les qualités qui peuvent la soutenir, qui jouit de la considération publique et qui la mérite. Je lui dois la vie; vous savez les engagements que j'ai pris avec lui. . . . Lui dirai-je: Monsieur, je vous ai promis ma fille tandis que vous étiez riche, mais à présent vous n'avez plus rien, je me rétracte, et ma fille ne veut point de vous? . . . [N]ous passerons, vous pour une fille perdue, moi pour un malhonnête homme qui sacrifie son devoir et sa foi à un vil intérêt, et joint l'ingratitude à l'infidelité. Ma fille, il est trop tard pour finir dans l'opprobre une vie sans tache, et soixante ans d'honneur ne s'abandonnent pas en un quart d'heure." Jean-Jacques Rousseau, *Julie ou la nouvelle Héloïse* in *Oeuvres complètes*, ed. Bernard Gagnebin and Marcel Raymond, 5 vols. (Paris: Gallimard, 1959–), vol. 2, pp. 349. All parenthetical reference to this work in the notes to chapter 7 are to this edition and include the page number only. Translations are my own.

[23] "[L]'honneur a parlé, et, dans le sang dont tu sors, c'est toujours lui qui décide" (257).

[24] For psychoanalytically inspired readings of Julie's family triangle, see Nancy Miller, *The Heroine's Text*, pp. 96–115; and Tony Tanner, *Adultery in the Novel, Contract and Transgression* (Baltimore: Johns Hopkins University Press, 1979).

[25] "Dans l'instant même où j'étais prête à jurer à un autre une éternelle fidélité, mon coeur vous jurait encore un amour éternel, et je fus menée au temple comme une victime impure qui souille le sacrifice où l'on va l'immoler" (260).

[26] "Le jour sombre de l'édifice, le profond silence des spectateurs, leur maintien modeste et recueilli, le cortège de tous mes parents, l'imposant aspect de mon vénéré père, tout donnait à ce qui s'allait passer un air de solennité qui m'excitait à l'attention et au respect, et qui m'eût fair frémir à la seule idée d'un *parjure*" (260). [My emphasis.]

[27] See *Emile*, Book 4, in *Oeuvres complètes*, vol. 4, pp. 565–635, and my discussion in chapter 2.

[28] "La pureté, la dignité, la sainteté du mariage, si vivement exposées dans les paroles de l'Ecriture, ses chastes et sublimes devoirs si importants au bonheur, à l'ordre, à la paix, à la durée du genre humain, si doux à remplir pour eux-mêmes; tout cela me fit une telle impression, que *je crus sentir intérieurement une révolution subite. Une puissance inconnue sembla corriger tout à coup le désordre de mes affections et les rétablir selon la loi du devoir et de la nature*" (260). [My emphasis.]

[29] "Ce n'est pas seulement l'intérêt des époux, mais la cause commune de tous les hommes, que la pureté du mariage ne soit point altérée. Chaque fois que deux époux s'unissent par un noeud solennel, il intervient un engage-

ment tacite de tout le genre humain de respecter ce lien sacré, d'honorer en eux l'union conjugale; . . . Le public est en quelque sorte garant d'une convention passée en sa présence, et l'on peut dire que l'honneur d'une femme pudique est sous la protection spéciale de tous les gens de bien" (265).

[30]See Denis de Rougemont's well-known reading of the novel as a bourgeois reinterpretation of the traditional medieval opposition between passionate love and marriage, *L'Amour et l'Occident* (Paris: Plon, 1939), pp. 205–9. Many critics, including Jean Starobinski, read Julie's death as a sacrifice in this way; however, Starobinski underscores her duty as a mother, which gives it a new twist: "Julie, il est vrai, ne meurt pas d'une mort d'amour, mais pour avoir accompli son *devoir* de mère: Rousseau a transposé sur le plan de la vertu un acte qui, selon le mythe de l'amour-passion, aurait dû être motivé par la volonté de destruction inhérente à la passion elle-même." [Julie, it is true, does not die for love, but for having fulfilled her *duty* as mother: Rousseau transposed onto the level of virtue an act that, according to the myth of passionate love, should have been motivated by the desire for destruction inherent in passion itself.] See Starobinski, *Jean-Jacques Rousseau: La transparence et l'obstacle* (Paris: Plon, 1957), p. 141.

[31]Carole Pateman suggests such a reading when she writes, "If the good order of Clarens is not to be fatally disrupted, Julie must take the one course left to her; the only solution to the problem of the disorder of women is her 'accidental' death." Pateman, *The Disorder of Women: Democracy, Feminism, and Political Theory* (Stanford, Calif.: Stanford University Press, 1989), p. 22.

[32] "Un jour de plus, peut-être, et j'étois coupable!" (741)

[33] One might assert, consistent with the change in ideology documented by Elisabeth Badinter, that the importance of Julie's role as mother overshadows her role as wife. This reading would made *Julie* consistent with discourses of the period that emphasize the value of children, analyzed by Badinter. See *Mother Love*, pp. 120–67.

[34] "Je me suis longtemps fait illusion" (740).

[35]Nadine Bérenguier, "From Clarens to Hollow Park, Isabelle de Charrière's Quiet Revolution," *Studies in Eighteenth-Century Culture* 21 (1991), pp. 219–43.

[36]See Joan Hinde Stewart and Philip Stewart, "Introduction" to Charrière, *Lettres de Mistriss Henley* (New York: Modern Language Association, 1993), pp. xi–xxii. All parenthetical references to this work in the notes to chapter 7 are to this edition and include the page number only. Translations are my own.

[37] Bérenguier, "From Clarens to Hollow Park," p. 229.

[38] "J'étais, sinon passionnée, du moins fort touchée" (8).

[39]Many critics have pointed out the autobiographical elements in Charrière's depiction in *Mistriss Henley*. See Joan Hinde Stewart and Philip Stewart, "Introduction," pp. xvi–xviii.

[40] "C'était, pour ainsi dire, la partie vile de mon coeur qui préférait les richesses de l'Orient, Londres, une liberté entière, une opulence plus brillante; la partie noble dédaignait tout cela, et se pénétrait des douceurs d'une félicité toute raisonnable, toute sublime et telle que les anges devaient y applaudir" (9).

[41] "Si un père tyrannique m'eût obligée à épouser le Nabab, je me serais fait peut-être un devoir d'obéir. . . . En un mot, forcée de devenir heureuse d'une manière vulgaire, je le serais devenue sans honte et peut-être avec plaisir; *mais me donner moi-même de mon choix, contre des diamants, des perles, des tapis, des mousselines brodées d'or, des soupers, des fêtes, je ne pouvais m'y résoudre, et je promis ma main à M. Henley*" (9). [My emphasis.]

[42] "Je crois que beaucoup de femmes sont dans le même cas que moi" (5).

[43]If Isabelle de Charrière's case is any indication, even intelligent, educated women who were allowed to choose for themselves found themselves in Mrs. Henley's predicament.

[44]See Adrienne Rogers, "Women and the Law," in *French Women and the Age of Enlightenment*, ed. Samia I. Spencer (Bloomington: University of Indiana Press, 1984). Rogers maintains that, "If, in this partnership of the couple called *communauté* two individuals were molded as one, it would nonetheless be erroneous to suppose that the two individuals were equal. A more accurate description would be the assimilation of one by the other. Theologically, it was determined that the union need have only one head, and that head, naturally, had to be the husband." "Women and the Law," p. 35.

[45] "Aurait-il raison? ma chère amie. Aurais-je eu tort, toujours tort, tort en tout? Non, je ne veux pas le croire; . . . Je crois pourtant bien m'être trop précipitée. J'aurais pu attendre un jour ou deux, consulter M. Henley, . . . J'ai trop suivi l'impétuosité de mon humeur" (26–27).

[46] "Dans un an, dans deux ans, vous apprendrez, je l'espère, que je suis raisonnable et heureuse, ou que je ne suis plus" (45).

[47]Divorce was not a viable option unless physical abuse or squandering of the dowry money was involved, and even then, women usually obtained a legal separation rather than a divorce. As Nadine Bérenguier has argued, women were reluctant to make their private business public by appearing in court, thereby destroying their reputations. Thus, divorce and separation were a last resort. See Bérenguier, "Victorious Victims: Women and Publicity in *Mémoires Judiciaires*," in *Going Public*, pp. 64–65. See also James Traer's discussion of arguments in favor of divorce in *Marriage and the Family in Eighteenth-Century France*, pp. 48–78, 105–36.

[48]Jean-Louis Flandrin has argued that there was a time lag between the ideal of love in marriage and its actual appearance, due to the need for economic changes to enable the ideal to become a reality: "The love-match was to cease to be a fantasy, in that social milieu [among the elites], only when the essence of inherited capital became cultural—that is, in the twentieth century. The new aspirations were expressed for a long time before economic changes made possible their realization. However, the revolution of the conjugal system did not take place until after that of the economic system, for only then could the marriage founded on love be instituted without challenging the hierarchical structures of society." *Families in Former Times*, p. 173.

Conclusion: Some Closing Thoughts on Rights, Justice, and Community

I am not disembodied reason. Nor am I Robinson Crusoe, alone upon his island. It is not only that my material life depends upon interaction with other men, or that I am what I am as a result of social forces, but that some, perhaps all, of my ideas about myself, in particular my sense of my own moral and social identity, are intelligible only in terms of the social network in which I am (the metaphor must not be pressed too far) an element.

—Isaiah Berlin, "Two Concepts of Liberty"

Everyone has duties to the community in which alone the free and full development of his personality is possible.

–*Universal Declaration of Human Rights*, Article 29.1

THE CONTRACTUAL MODEL OF OBLIGATION established within the liberal political paradigm creates an atomistic society predicated on the need to protect individual freedom and autonomy, particularly in the private realm.[1] This atomistic view of society, with its concomitant divide between the public and private spheres, fosters a very limited notion of obligation between the individuals who make up the liberal community. Whether in the realm of education (chapters 1 and 2), in which either the state or the family assumes the role, authority, and responsibility of educating children, or in the realm of public relations between citizens (chapters 3, 4, and 5), where private moral conscience is held in check by formalizable rules of obligation established in negative terms, or finally in the realm of the family and private relations (chapter 6 and 7), where the freedom allowed in the public sphere is counterbalanced by careful controls on private behavior, in all of these areas the model carried over from political liberalism fails to provide an adequate means for understanding and defining moral relations.

Most disturbing in the liberal arrangement is the divide between the public and private spheres. The purpose of the divide was initially to protect "private relations between citizens," understood as their right to conclude economic contracts. However, the divide was extended to protect not only the economic sphere but also the realm of personal and family life from government interference. While in the American context this divide had certain very important positive consequences for individual liberties—in particular with regard to matters of personal conscience and religious tolerance—it had, and continues to have, its negative effects as well. As we have seen most pointedly in chapters 2, 5, and 7 (concerning education and the questions of tolerance and marriage) the protection of the private sphere from government interference has created many paradoxes for both private conscience and family life.

First, the family is supposed to provide the sense of community and belonging that is absent from the atomistic political model of society created by Hobbes's and Locke's versions of the social contract. Independent, free, equal, and autonomous individuals conclude contracts based on self-interest in the economic sphere. In much the same way, they also participate in political public life through elections, debates, and so on.[2] And yet, these same individuals are supposed to return to the private sphere of hearth and home for a sense of connectedness and belonging that relations in the other spheres do not and cannot provide. As we have seen in chapters 6 and 7, the sphere of the family can hardly provide the sense of belonging required of the model. If relations in the private sphere of the family are either modeled on the public sphere—as they seem to be in the deficient conceptions of the marriage relation analyzed in chapter 7—or are subject to other kinds of regulation and control—as in the case of Sade's representations—then they cannot provide the sense of membership in a group that is lacking in public, economic, and/or political life. Alienated relations in the private sphere can hardly compensate for alienated relations in the public sphere.

Second, as is evident in the chapters on education (1 and 2), educating children to lead a double existence—divided between the alienation of the public sphere and of economic relations and the supposed wholeness of family life—ends in two very different models of education: the first being thoroughly public and driven by the needs of republicanism, and the second being thoroughly privatized and overly attentive to the development of individual autonomy. Neither model provides the kind of balance one would hope for in such a divided model of society. Thus, the individual ends up like Emile, unable to function in the political realm and equally incapable of functioning as a parent to his own children.

Third, the realm of private conscience finds itself at odds with the realm of public obligations. Because the model of the divided society relies so heavily on the private sphere to compensate for deficient conceptions of personal relations in the public sphere, it creates a situation in which the individual constantly faces contradictions between the private life of moral obligation consistent (or nearly consistent) with the realm of private moral conscience and the realm of contractual obligations that falls short of embodying true moral relations. As was most evident in chapters 3 and 5 concerning the relationship between private morality and public legality and between tolerance and sympathy (and evident in other ways in other chapters as well), there is a significant gap between what is required of the "moral" person in the public and economic spheres and what the private moral person feels is the right thing to do. In Diderot's versions of the dilemma in his dialogue, as well as in Charrière's depictions of sympathy in her novel, the distinction between what is required legally and what is right morally does not help the individual decide what to do in difficult cases. It is my contention that the liberal model of society contributes to the difficulties in these gray areas.

All of these difficulties point to a lack of a notion of community that would help ease the tension between the types of relations that obtain in the public and economic spheres and the kinds of relations that exist in the private sphere. More pointedly, the liberal model creates a situation in which private interests are pitted against the public or collective good. Ironically, this problem is best exemplified in Rousseau's version of the social contract, in which the individual is subsumed by the general will. Any type of resistance to the majority—either individual or collective—although explicitly sanctioned by Rousseau, is nonetheless difficult to imagine. For the general will as expression of the common good effectively eliminates the tension between the individual and the collectivity.

In our contemporary liberal, American, society, modeled more closely on Locke's version of the social contract than on Hobbes's or Rousseau's, this antagonism between individual interest and collective good in effect erases any sense of common purpose. Individuals become suspicious of projects undertaken in the name of the public good on the grounds that such efforts will deprive them as individuals of rights, freedom, and/or wealth. Without a sense of community to provide a backdrop for moral relations by creating a sense of connection that exceeds the limited bounds of the private sphere, the atomistic individuals fail to coalesce into a true community. This is not, however, to say, that communitarian conceptions of the social bond would remedy liberalism's atomism, although my criticisms echo theirs. Rather than invoke communitarian remedies, I would like to conclude by again exploring the problems associated with positive and negative definitions of obligation within the moral and political context in view of developing a revised liberal position.

As we have already seen, in the social contract tradition, particularly in Hobbes and Locke, the general emphasis is on protecting individual freedom rather than on fostering a sense of community. It is only in Rousseau's reworking of the social contract that one finds an articulation of an ideal of community—the *volonté générale*—that begins to respond to the problem of community. But, as I have argued elsewhere, the notion of community that emerges from Rousseau's version of the social contract does little to foster the type of bond or connection, and particularly the moral connection, that I am problematizing here.[3] In spite of his "collectivist" or "republican" conception of the general will, my analyses of *Emile* and *Julie* have demonstrated that Rousseau's representations of relations within the private sphere fail to provide the kind of moral obligation that the general will would seem to imply. Instead, relations within the private sphere return to minimal standards of obligation based on contracts. Emile's relation to the gardener, and Julie's obligation to remain faithful to Wolmar until her death both amount to contractual obligations defined in negative terms. Neither of these scenarios enacts the type of moral connectedness that would seem to underlie the *volonté générale* or that even Charrière's version of sympathy requires.

The difficulty resides in the functioning of the general will in Rousseau, and in the conceptions of the state of nature and of the compact itself in the social contract tradition generally. All three function as regulative ideals. In this respect, the general will, the state of nature, and the original contract provide limits that establish minimal standards of decency. Whereas regulative ideals can function to provide positive models toward which societies and individuals strive,[4] the regulative ideals associated with liberalism function as negative limits to political and moral behavior. Whether it be Hobbes's assumption of an original contract to establish absolute sovereignty, or Locke's empowering of a third-party judge to protect private property, or even Rousseau's use of the general will to curb private interests, all of these ideal authorities draw limits around private interest, power, and authority but fall short of articulating positive, collective ideals for a common interest or public good. Even John Rawls's reinterpretation of the social contract as the original position makes its negative function clear:

In justice as fairness the original position of equality corresponds to the state of nature in the traditional theory of the social contract. This original position is not, of course, thought of as an actual historical state of affairs, much less as a primitive condition of culture. It is understood as a purely hypothetical situation characterized so as to lead to a certain conception of justice. Among the essential features of this situation is that no one knows his place in society, his class position or social status, nor does any one know his fortune in the distribution of natural assets and abilitites, his intelligence, strength and the like. *I shall even assume that the parties do not know their conceptions of the good* or their special psychological propensities. The principles of justice are chosen behind a veil of ignorance.[5]

Rawls's specific rejection of a notion of the good from the original position posits conditions under which only minimal standards of equality can be established. In other words, the original position ensures that minimal requirements of fairness be met by a minimal standard of equality. The veil of ignorance further ensures a kind of blind equity at the most basic level. Yet, without a shared substantive or even procedural conception of the good, there can be no basis for community in the ensuing society.

While it is clear that political liberalism protects individual freedom and autonomy by ensuring fairness and equality through the imposition of negative limits derived from the situation of the original contract, it is also clear that no positive relations between citizens are defined. It is my contention that extending the negative relations between citizens into the realm of private life leads to the deficient conceptions of moral relations that are represented in the various texts I have analyzed. The emphasis on negative liberty and rights has fostered weak, problematic visions of education, tolerance, sympathy, familial relations, and marriage.

But the social contract tradition is not doomed to accept this version of moral relations. I do not wish to maintain that the liberal tradition cannot be reconciled with a more positive and substantive notion of community and consequently of the good. On the contrary, conceptions of the original contract and of the state of nature can be made consistent with a vision of the public good that enforces a notion of community that does not necessarily tip toward a totalitarian version of republicanism. The state of nature and the original contract can be made consistent with positive regulative ideals toward which a community can strive.

Such a vision of the tradition is offered in Diderot's article, "Droit naturel" (1755), in the *Encyclopédie*.[6] Arguing in favor of a conception of natural law/right that provides a basis for justice understood as moral obligation, Diderot appeals to a conception of the general will that anticipates Kant's categorical imperative.[7] Insisting that natural law/rights depend on the human capacity to reason and communicate, he maintains that consulting the general will provides the foundation for all duties. The following lengthy citation contains all of the essential points of Diderot's understanding of natural law/right:

> It is to the general will that the individual must address himself in order to know how far he must go to be a man, a citizen, a subject, a father, a child, and when it is appropriate to live or to die. It is up to the general will to fix the limits of all duties. You have the most sacred *natural right* to everything that is not contested by the entire species. It is the general will that enlightens you on the nature of your thoughts and your desires. All that you conceive, all that you meditate, will be good, great, elevated, sublime, if it partakes of the general and common interest. There is no essential quality of your species, except that which you require in your fellow-creatures, for your happiness and theirs. It is this conformity of you to all of them, and of all of them to you, that will mark you when you depart from your species, and when you stay with it. Never lose sight of it, for without it you will see the notions of goodness, justice, humanity, and virtue stumble in your understanding. Tell yourself often: I am a man, and I have no other truly inalienable *natural rights* than those of humanity.[8]

Echoing the language of the seventeenth- and eighteenth-century natural law theorists—including Rousseau to whom he makes reference elsewhere in the article—Diderot nonetheless offers a fascinating twist on the tradition. Diderot's reading of the concept of natural rights ties it directly to a conception of the general will that serves as a regulative ideal for both moral and political obligation. Rather than use the concept of natural right in a negative way to limit the claims of the community against the individual, he instead links the exercise of rights to the common interest. Appealing to a notion that approaches a more contemporary conception of human rights, he argues for a dialectical interdependence between natural individual rights and the general will.

On Diderot's reading, individuals only exercise their rights as part of a collective. Rather than repeating the usual liberal insistence on individual freedom and autonomy, Diderot underscores the ways in which membership in a group that shares interests (all of humanity) enables the exercise of individual rights insofar as the individual defines himself in various roles (citizen, subject, father, child) that relate back to the group. These individual roles in fact have no meaning without reference back to the group. Diderot's sexist language notwithstanding, sidestepping what has been identified by feminists and communitarians as the difficulty of liberalism's conception of the individual, Diderot requires each individual to consider his/her various relationships to the group in assessing his/her moral and political responsibilities. The notion of all of humanity is always present as a limit, both positive and negative, on the individual's rights and freedom.

The linking of the individual with a community in Diderot's presentation of *droit naturel* also highlights a procedural aspect. Like the categorical imperative, Diderot's version of natural law/right requires that individuals think of the group when considering their obligations. In other words, questions of right and wrong must be tried before the hypothetical tribunal of a common humanity embodied in individual rationality. Echoing the dialogue analyzed in chapter 3, in which the Diderot character advocated questioning all laws, the *Encyclopédie* article resists strict adherence to law in favor of rational questioning. The general will determines the limits of individual obligations, within each individual conscience, with reference to a common humanity.

The procedural element in Diderot's conception of the general will does not preclude actual dialogic consultation with others. On the contrary, given the overall tenor of what I would loosely call Diderot's philosophical system, it seems likely that actual dialogue—either in person or through texts—will aid the process of rationally questioning the limits of moral and political obligations.[9] Consulting the tribunal of a common humanity might and perhaps should involve actively discussing questions of obligation with persons whose opinions one respects, as is clearly modeled on several levels in *Entretien d'un père avec ses enfants.*

Diderot's dialectical account of natural law/right eases many of the tensions associated with liberalism that I have underscored. First, the problematic notions of individual identity, rights, and freedom are balanced by the notion of a collective humanity that sets limits to the duties of individuals in the various roles they assume in life. Second, the proceduralist consultation of the general will provides a limit that can be both positive and negative in establishing limits on individual rights and freedom. Finally, private interests are balanced by the common good reflected in the interconnection between personal happiness and group happiness that Diderot asserts: "There is no essential quality of your species, except that which you require in your fellow-creatures, for your happiness and theirs." Overall, the dialectical account reworks natural law and rights into both moral and political obligation to rationally question all obligations against the backdrop of a common humanity.

The insistence on the common and general interests of humanity foregrounds what was already implicit in liberal formulations of natural law and rights, yet in a way that seems to leap forward into the future to anticipate more contemporary conceptions of human rights.[10] While the liberal tradition that I have examined always implies that natural rights and freedoms extend to all members of the species, the theorists never quite put the concept in those terms. Rather, the formulations tend toward identifying rights and freedoms with abstract individuals and tend away from talk of the collectivity. Even Rawls's reconceptualization of the original compact as the original position isolates individuals and then abstracts from the individual case toward the collectivity. Diderot's repeated reference to the whole of humanity reinscribes the implied dialectic of liberal thought. Diderot's individuals never escape their membership in the community of humanity because each moral and political act, on whatever scale, requires a private act of conscience that in Kantian fashion always refers back to a collective humanity.

I believe that such an abstraction is helpful in providing the positive regulative ideal that I have found lacking in other eighteenth-century formulations of obligation. Diderot's appeal to the general community to set the limits of obligations in roles such as citizen and subject, parent and child, leaves behind the minimal standard of decency that underlies many liberal defenses of tolerance (as we saw in chapters 4 and 5) and begins to answer the more difficult questions concerning the limits of obligations that arise in conjunction with the notion of sympathy. Consulting the general and common interests and remembering that one belongs to a collective species reinforces striving toward a more positively conceived goal than the negative, contractual obligations that I have examined in the various texts. Fully consistent with his problematization of morality and legality that we saw in chapter 3, Diderot's account of natural law/rights reinscribes the dialectic of individual and community within each moral and political act.

But I believe that Diderot's account of natural law/right does more than simply offer a dialectical interpretation of the liberal tradition from an eighteenth-century perspective. I believe that his repeated references to a common humanity anticipate present-day concerns with human rights.[11] If the social contract tradition has any relevance today, and I believe strongly that it does, it is because it contains powerful formulations concerning individual rights and freedoms that we still want to defend. In the context of international relations, the concept of human rights plays a crucial role in justifying, for example, pressure exerted by the United States to end what are perceived to be human rights violations in other countries. Whether it is a question of apartheid, imprisonment of political dissidents, ethnic cleansing, or genital mutilation, the concept of human rights overrides cultural relativism to establish minimal standards of decency for the treatment of human beings. At once minimalist and idealist, individualist and collectivist, the dialectic of human rights as it is practiced in the international context appeals to the general notion of humanity articulated by Diderot. I believe that it is the appeal to a general humanity within the context of a conception of individual rights that makes Diderot's formulation so attractive: it both protects individual freedom and rights with a negative limit, but it also provides a positive regulative ideal in its conception of a common humanity.

If the liberal model is to provide a workable conception of justice for a multicultural future, I maintain that it is within such a dialectical working of the relation between individual and community.

Notes

[1] For a defense of liberalism against charges by communitarians along these lines, see Will Kymlicka, *Liberalism, Community, and Culture* (Oxford: Clarendon Press, 1989). Although I agree with many of Kymlicka's defenses of particular aspects of liberalism against specific charges by contemporary critics, I do not believe that he is entirely successful in responding to the problem of liberalism's atomistic society.

[2] Alienated participation in political life is more true of the twentieth century than it was of the eighteenth and nineteenth centuries. Ironically, increased democratization has led to more alienated and individual forms of political participation.

[3] See my *Mass Enlightenment: Critical Studies in Rousseau and Diderot* (Albany: State University of New York Press, 1995), chapters 1 and 2.

[4] Habermas's ideal speech situation and its adaptations to moral and political life provide an example of a positive regulative ideal. See Jürgen Habermas, *The Theory of Communicative Action*, trans. Thomas McCarthy, 2 vols. (Boston: Beacon Press, 1984–); and *Between Facts and Norms: Contributions to a Discourse Theory of Law and Democracy*, trans. William Rehg (Cambridge: MIT Press, 1996).

[5] John Rawls, *A Theory of Justice* (Cambridge: Harvard University Press, 1971), p. 12. [My emphasis.]

[6] Denis Diderot, "Droit naturel," in his *Oeuvres complètes*, ed. Herbert Dieckmann, Jacques Proust, Jean Varloot, et al. (Paris: Hermann, 1990–), vol. 7, pp. 24–29.

[7]For a discussion of similarities between Diderot and Kant in the area of aesthetics see Suzanne Gearhart, "The Dialectic and Its Aesthetic Other: The Problem of Identification in Diderot and Hegel," in Gearhart, *The Interrupted Dialectic: Philosophy, Psychoanalysis, and Their Tragic Other* (Baltimore: Johns Hopkins University Press, 1992), pp. 157–81; Philippe Lacoue-Labarthe, "L'Imprésentable," *Poétique* 21 (1975); and my *Mass Enlightenment*, pp. 147–68.

[8] "C'est à la volonté générale que l'individu doit s'adresser pour savoir jusqu'où il doit être homme, citoyen, sujet, père, enfant, & quand il lui convient de vivre ou de mourir. C'est à elle de fixer les limites de tous les devoirs. Vous avez le *droit naturel* le plus sacré à tout ce qui ne vous est point contesté par l'espèce entière. C'est elle qui vous éclairera sur la nature de vos pensées & de vos désirs. Tout ce que vous concevrez, tout ce que vous méditerez, sera bon, grand, élevé, sublime, s'il est de l'intérêt général & commun. Il n'y a de qualité essentielle à votre espèce, que celle que vous exigez dans tous vos semblables pour votre bonheur & pour le leur. C'est cette conformité de vous à eux tous & d'eux tous à vous, qui vous marquera quand vous sortirez de votre espèce, & quand vous y resterez. Ne la perdez donc jamais de vue, sans quoi vous verrez les notions de la bonté, de la justice, de l'humanité, de la vertu, chanceler dans votre entendement. Dites-vous souvent: Je suis homme, & je n'ai d'autres *droits naturels* véritablement inaliénables que ceux de l'humanité." Diderot, "Droit naturel," in *Oeuvres complètes*, vol. 7, p. 28.

[9]Rational, critical thought, for Diderot, entails movement, relations, and dialogue. Although Diderot is subtle and elusive, his clearest formulation of this appears in his article "Encyclopédie" within the *Encyclopédie*. On the necessity of "movement" within the *Encyclopédie*, and within any system of knowledge, see Jacques Proust, "Diderot et le système des connaissances humaines," *Studies on Voltaire and the Eighteenth Century* 256 (1988: 117–27); Proust, "De l'*Encyclopédie* au *Neveu de Rameau*: L'objet et le texte," *Recherches nouvelles sur quelques écrivains des Lumières*, ed. Jacques Proust (Geneva: Droz, 1972: 273–340); and Georges Benrekassa, "La Pratique philosophique de Diderot dans l'article 'Encyclopédie' de l'*Encyclopédie*," *Stanford French Review* 8, nos. 2–3 (fall 1984), pp. 189–212.

[10]I am grateful to Dick Terdiman for suggesting the "timelessness" of Diderot's thought, the ways in which he always seems to leap into the future—both his own and ours.

[11]Maurice Cranston explains the revival of the concept of natural rights from the eighteenth century as a response to historical events of the twentieth century with the name change to human rights, designed to avoid "committing one too ostentatiously to any traditional doctrine of Natural Law." "Human Rights, Real and Supposed," *Political Theory and the Rights of Man*, ed. D. D. Raphael (Bloomington: Indiana University Press, 1967), pp. 44–5. In the same volume, see also D. D. Raphael, "Human Rights, Old and New," pp. 54–67.

Bibliography

Ackerman, Bruce A. *Social Justice in the Liberal State*. New Haven, Conn.: Yale University Press, 1980.

Allison, David B., Mark S. Roberts, and Allen S. Weiss, eds. *Sade and the Narrative of Transgression*. Cambridge: Cambridge University Press, 1995.

Allison, Jenene J. *Revealing Difference: The Fiction of Isabelle de Charrière*. Newark: University of Delaware Press, 1995.

Althusser, Louis. *Montesquieu, Rousseau, Marx: Politics and History*. Trans. Ben Brewster. London: Verso, 1982.

Altman, Janet Gurkin. *Epistolarity: Approaches to a Form*. Columbus: Ohio State University Press, 1982.

Anderson, Wilda. *Diderot's Dream*. Baltimore: Johns Hopkins University Press, 1990.

Andrews, Richard Mowery. *Law, Magistracy, and Crime in Old Regime Paris, 1735–1789*. 1 vol. to date. Vol. 1, *The System of Criminal Justice*. Cambridge: Cambridge University Press, 1992.

Archard, David. *Children: Rights and Childhood*. New York: Routledge, 1993.

Ariès, Philippe. *L'Enfant et la vie familiale sous l'ancien régime*. Paris: Seuil, 1973.

Ariès, Philippe, and André Béjin, eds. *Western Sexuality: Practice and Precept in Past and Present Times*. Trans. Anthony Forster. New York: Barnes and Noble, 1997.

Ariès, Philippe, and Georges Duby, eds. *Histoire de la vie privée*. 5 vols. Vol. 3, *De la Renaissance aux Lumières*. Paris: Editions du Seuil, 1986.

Armstrong, Nancy. *Desire and Domestic Fiction: A Political History of the Novel*. Oxford: Oxford University Press, 1987.

Auroux, Sylvain, Dominique Bourel, and Charles Porset. *L'Encyclopédie, Diderot, l'esthétique: Mélanges en hommage à Jacques Chouillet, 1915–1990*. Paris: Presses Universitaires de France, 1991.

Avineri, Shlomo, and Avner De-Shalit, eds. *Communitarianism and Individualism*. Oxford: Oxford University Press, 1992.

Badinter, Elisabeth. *Mother Love: Myth and Reality: Motherhood in Modern History*. New York: Macmillan, 1981.

Barber, Benjamin R. "Mandate for Liberty: Requiring Education-Based Community Service." In *The Essential Communitarian Reader*, ed. Amitai Etzioni. Lanham, Md.: Rowman and Littlefield, 1998: 237–45.

Barrière, P. "L'Humanisme de l'*Esprit des lois*" In *La Pensée politique et constitutionnelle de Montesquieu. Bicentenaire de l'Esprit des lois 1748–1948.* Paris: Faculté de Droit de Paris. Recueil Sirey, 1952: 97–115.

Barthes, Roland. *Sade, Fourier, Loyola.* Trans. Richard Miller. Berkeley: University of California Press, 1976.

Beauvoir, Simone de. *Faut-il brûler Sade?* Paris: Gallimard, 1955.

———. "Must We Burn Sade?" In *The 120 Days and Other Writings.* Comp. and trans. Austryn Wainhouse and Richard Seaver. New York: Grove, 1966: 3–64.

Bell, Daniel. *Communitarianism and Its Critics.* Oxford: Clarendon Press, 1993.

Bellah, Robert N. "Community Properly Understood: A Defense of 'Democratic Communitarianism.'" In *The Essential Communitarian Reader.* Ed. Amitai Etzioni. Lanham, Md.: Rowman and Littlefield, 1998: 15–19.

Bellamy, Richard. *Liberalism and Modern Society: A Historical Argument.* University Park: Pennsylvania State University Press, 1992.

Benhabib, Seyla. "The Generalized and the Concrete Other: The Kohlberg-Gilligan Controversy and Feminist Theory." In *Feminism as Critique*, ed. Seyla Benhabib and Drucilla Cornell. Minneapolis: University of Minnesota Press, 1987: 77–95.

Benrekassa, Georges. "La Pratique philosophique de Diderot dans l'article 'Encyclopédie' de l'Encyclopédie." *Stanford French Review* 8, nos. 2–3 (fall 1984): 189–212.

Bentham, Jeremy. *The Utilitarians: An Introduction to the Principles of Morals and Legislation.* New York: Anchor, 1973.

Bérenguier, Nadine. "From Clarens to Hollow Park, Isabelle de Charrière's Quiet Revolution." *Studies in Eighteenth-Century Culture* 21 (1991): 219–43.

———. "Victorious Victims: Women and Publicity in *Mémoires Judiciaires.*" In Elizabeth C. Goldsmith and Dena Goodman eds, *Going Public: Women and Publishing in Early Modern France.* Ithaca, N. Y.: Cornell University Press, 1995: 62–78.

Berlin, Isaiah. *Against the Current: Essays in the History of Ideas.* New York: Viking, 1955.

———. "Two Concepts of Liberty." In Isaiah Berlin, *Four Essays on Liberty.* Oxford: Oxford University Press, 1969.

Bien, David D. *The Calas Affair: Persecution, Toleration, and Heresy in Eighteenth-Century Toulouse.* Princeton, N. J.: Princeton University Press, 1960.

Blakeney, Edward Henry, ed. *Horace on the Art of Poetry.* Freeport, N. Y.: Books for Libraries Press, 1970.

Bloom, Allan. "The Education of Democratic Man: *Emile.*" In *Jean-Jacques Rousseau,* ed. Harold Bloom. New York: Chelsea House, 1988: 149–71.

———. "Rousseau's Critique of Liberal Constitutionalism." In *The Legacy of Rousseau,* ed. Clifford Orwin and Nathan Tarcov. Chicago: University of Chicago Press, 1997.

Blum, Carol. *Diderot: The Virtue of a Philosopher.* New York: Viking, 1974.

Caplan, Jay. *Framed Narratives: Diderot's Genealogy of the Beholder.* Minneapolis: University of Minnesota Press, 1985.

Carey, John A. *Judicial Reform in France before the Revolution of 1789.* Cambridge: Harvard University Press, 1981.

Cassirer, Ernst. *The Question of Jean-Jacques Rousseau.* Ed. and trans. Peter Gay. 2d ed. New Haven, Conn.: Yale University Press, 1989.

Cauvière, Henry. *L'Idée de codification en France avant la rédaction du Code Civil.* Paris: Arthur Rousseau, 1910.

Certeau, Michel de. *Heterologies: Discourse on the Other.* Trans. Brian Massumi. Minneapolis: University of Minnesota Press, 1986.

Chapman, John W. "Natural Rights and Justice in Liberalism." In *Political Theory and the Rights of Man.* Ed. D. D. Raphael. Bloomington: Indiana University Press, 1967: 27–42.

Chapman, John W., and Ian Shapiro, eds. *Democratic Community.* New York: New York University Press, 1993.

Chapman, John W., and William A. Galston, eds. *Virtue.* New York: New York University Press, 1992.

Charrière, Isabelle de. *Caliste ou lettres écrites de Lausanne.* Paris: Editions des Femmes, 1979.

———. *Letters of Mistress Henley Published by Her Friend.* Trans. Philip Stewart and Jean Vache. New York: Modern Language Association, 1993.

———. *Lettres de Mistriss Henley publiées par son amie.* Ed. Joan Hinde Stewart and Philip Stewart. New York: Modern Language Association, 1993.

Clifford, James. *The Predicament of Culture: Twentieth-Century Ethnography, Literature, and Art.* Cambridge: Harvard University Press, 1988.

Cobban, Alfred. *Rousseau and the Modern State.* London: George Allen & Unwin, 1964.

Cook, Malcolm. *Fictional France: Social Reality in the French Novel, 1775–1800.* Oxford: Berg Publishers, 1993.

Cranston, Maurice. "Human Rights, Real and Supposed." In *Political Theory and the Rights of Man*, ed. D. D. Raphael. Bloomington: Indiana University Press, 1967: 43–53.

Crocker, Lester. *Jean-Jacques Rousseau*. 2 vols. New York: Macmillan, 1968.

Dallmayr, Fred R., ed. *From Contract to Community: Political Theory at the Crossroads*. New York: Marcel Dekker, 1978.

Darnton, Robert. *The Great Cat Massacre and Other Episodes in French Cultural History*. New York: Vintage Books, 1985.

Davis, Fred. "Dole, Wilson, Abortion in San Diego." *Grass Roots* 6, no. 5 (summer 1996).

Deguise, Alix. *Trois femmes: Le monde de Madame de Charrière*. Geneva: Slatkine, 1981.

DeJean, Joan. *Literary Fortifications: Rousseau, Laclos, Sade*. Princeton, N. J.: Princeton University Press, 1984.

de Marneffe, Peter. "Contractualism, Liberty, and Democracy." *Ethics* 104 (July 1994): 764–83.

Descartes, René. *Discours de la méthode*. Paris: Garnier-Flammarion, 1966.

Dewey, John. *Democracy and Education*. New York: Free Press, 1916, 1944.

Diderot, Denis. *This Is Not a Story and Other Stories*. Trans. P. N. Furbank. Columbia: University of Missouri Press, 1991.

———. *Oeuvres complètes*. Ed. Herbert Dieckmann, Jacques Proust, Jean Varloot, et al. 25 vols. Paris: Hermann, 1975–.

———. DiPiero, Thomas. *Dangerous Truths and Criminal Passions: The Evolution of the French Novel, 1569–1791*. Stanford, Calif.: Stanford University Press, 1992.

Donzelot, Jacques. *The Policing of Families*. Trans. Robert Hurley. Baltimore: Johns Hopkins University Press, 1979.

Durkheim, Emile. *Montesquieu et Rousseau: Précurseurs de la sociologie*. Paris: Marcel Rivière, 1953.

Dworkin, Ronald. *A Matter of Principles*. Cambridge: Harvard University Press, 1977.

———. *Taking Rights Seriously*. Cambridge: Harvard University Press, 1977.

Edmiston, William F. *Diderot and the Family: A Conflict of Nature and Law*. Stanford French and Italian Studies 39. Saratoga, Calif.: Anma Libri, 1985.

Eisenstein, Zillah R. *The Radical Future of Liberal Feminism*. Boston: Northeastern University Press, 1993.

Elshtain, Jean Bethke. "Democracy and the Politics of Difference." In *The Essential Communitarian Reader*. Ed. Amitai Etzioni. Lanham, Md.: Rowman and Littlefield, 1998: 259–68.

———. *Public Man, Private Woman: Women in Social and Political Thought*. 2d ed. Princeton, N. J.: Princeton University Press, 1981.

Etzioni, Amitai, ed. *The Essential Communitarian Reader*. Lanham, Md.: Rowman and Littlefield, 1998.

Ferguson, Frances. "Reading Morals: Locke and Rousseau on Education and Inequality." *Representations* 6 (spring 1984): 66–84.

Fermon, Nicole. *Domesticating Passions: Rousseau, Woman, and Nation*. Hanover, N. H.: Wesleyan University Press, 1997.

Ferrara, Alessandro. *Modernity and Authenticity: A Study of the Social and Ethical Thought of Jean-Jacques Rousseau*. Albany: State University of New York Press, 1993.

Fishkin, James S. *The Dialogue of Justice: Toward a Self-Reflective Society*. New Haven, Conn.: Yale University Press, 1992.

Flanagan, Owen J., and Amelie Oksenberg Rorty, eds. *Identity, Character, and Morality: Essays in Moral Psychology*. Cambridge: MIT Press, 1990.

Flandrin, Jean-Louis. *Families in Former Times: Kinship, Household, and Sexuality*. Trans. Richard Southern. Cambridge: Cambridge University Press, 1979.

Forbes, H. D. "Rousseau, Ethnicity, and Difference." In *The Legacy of Rousseau*, ed. Clifford Orwin and Nathan Tarcov. Chicago: University of Chicago Press, 1997: 220–45.

Foucault, Michel. *Discipline and Punish: The Birth of the Prison*. Trans. Alan Sheridan. New York: Vintage, 1979.

Fried, Michael. *Absorption and Theatricality: Painting and Beholder in the Age of Diderot*. Berkeley: University of California Press, 1980.

Freud, Sigmund. *An Outline of Psycho-Analysis*. Trans. James Strachey. New York: W. W. Norton, 1969.

Gaus, Gerald F. *Value and Justification: The Foundations of Liberal Theory*. Cambridge: Cambridge University Press, 1990.

Gay, Peter. "Introduction." In Ernst Cassirer. *The Question of Jean-Jacques Rousseau*. Ed. and trans. Peter Gay. 2d ed. New Haven, Conn.: Yale University Press, 1989.

Gearhart, Suzanne. *The Interrupted Dialectic: Philosophy, Psychoanalysis, and Their Tragic Other*. Baltimore: Johns Hopkins University Press, 1992.

———. *The Open Boundary of History and Fiction: A Critical Approach to the French Enlightenment*. Princeton, N. J.: Princeton University Press, 1984.

Gilligan, Carol. *In a Different Voice: Psychological Theory and Women's Development*. Cambridge: Harvard University Press, 1993.

Giroux, Henry. *Border Crossings: Cultural Workers and the Politics of Education*. New York: Routledge, 1992.

Goldsmith, Elizabeth C., and Dena Goodman, eds. *Going Public: Women and Publishing in Early Modern France*. Ithaca, N. Y.: Cornell University Press, 1995.

Gordon, Deborah. "The Politics of Ethnographic Authority: Race and Writing in the Ethnography of Margaret Mead and Zora Neale Hurston." In *Modernist Anthropology: From Fieldwork to Text*. Ed. Marc Manganaro (Princeton, N. J.: Princeton University Press, 1990): 146–62

Goyard-Fabre, Simone. *Montesquieu: la nature, les lois, la liberté*. Paris: Presses Universitaires de France, 1993.

Gray, John. *Enlightenment's Wake: Politics and Culture at the Close of the Modern Age*. New York: Routledge, 1995.

Gutmann, Amy. "Undemocratic Education." in *Liberalism and the Moral Life*. Ed. Nancy L. Rosenbloom. Cambridge, Mass.: Harvard University Press, 1989: 71–88.

Habermas, Jürgen. *Between Facts and Norms: Contributions to a Discourse Theory of Law and Democracy*. Trans. William Rehg. Cambridge: MIT Press, 1996.

———. "Modernity: An Unfinished Project." In *Critical Theory: The Essential Readings*, ed. David Ingram and Julia Simon-Ingram. New York: Paragon House, 1991: 342–56.

———. *The Theory of Communicative Action*. Trans. Thomas McCarthy. 2 vols. Boston: Beacon Press, 1984–.

———. *The Structural Transformation of the Public Sphere: An Inquiry into a Category of Bourgeois Society*. Trans. Thomas Burger with the assistance of Frederick Lawrence. Cambridge: MIT Press, 1992.

Henaff, Marcel. "The Encyclopedia of Excess." In *Sade and the Narrative of Transgression*. Ed. David B. Allison, Mark S. Roberts, and Allen S. Weiss. Cambridge: Cambridge University Press, 1995: 142–70.

Hobbes, Thomas. *De Cive: Philosophical Rudiments Concerning Government and Society*. Ed. Howard Warrender. Oxford: Clarendon Press, 1983.

———. *Leviathan*. Ed. Richard Tuck. Cambridge: Cambridge University Press, 1991.

Hobhouse, L. T. *Liberalism and Other Writings*. Ed. James Meadowcroft. Cambridge: Cambridge University Press, 1994.

Hollinger, Robert. *The Dark Side of Liberalism: Elitism vs. Democracy*. Westport, Conn.: Praeger, 1996.

Horkheimer, Max., and Theordor W. Adorno. *Dialectic of Enlightenment*. Trans. John Cumming. New York: Continuum, 1988.

Hufton, Olwen H. "Women, Work and Marriage in Eighteenth-Century France." In *Marriage and Society: Studies in the Social History of Marriage*, ed. R. B. Outhwaite. New York: St. Martin's Press, 1981: 186–203.

Hume, David. *Enquiry Concerning the Principles of Morals*. Indianapolis: Hackett, 1983.

Hunt, Lynn. *The French Revolution and Human Rights: A Brief Documentary History*. Boston: Bedford Books, 1996.

Ingram, David. *Reason, History, and Politics: The Communitarian Grounds of Legitimation in the Modern Age*. Albany: State University of New York Press, 1995.

Kamuf, Peggy. *Fictions of Feminine Desire: Disclosures of Heloise*. Lincoln: University of Nebraska Press, 1982.

Kant, Immanuel. *Critique of Judgement*. Trans. J. H. Bernard. New York: Hafner, 1951.

———. *Critique of Practical Reason*. Trans. Lewis White Beck, New York: Macmillan, 1985.

———. *The Metaphysical Elements of Justice*. Trans. John Ladd, Indianapolis: Bobbs-Merrill, 1965.

Kennedy, Duncan. *Sexy Dressing Etc.: Essays on the Power and Politics of Cultural Identity*. Cambridge: Harvard University Press, 1993.

King, Martin Luther, Jr. *Letter from Birmingham City Jail*. Philadelphia: American Friends Service Committee, 1963.

King, Preston. *Toleration*. London: George Allen & Unwin, 1976.

Klossowski, Pierre. "Sade, or the philosopher-vilain." In *Sade and the Narrative of Transgression*, ed. David B. Allison, Mark S. Roberts, and Allen S. Weiss. Cambridge: Cambridge University Press, 1995: 33–61.

Kohlberg, Lawrence. *Child Psychology and Childhood Education: A Cognitive-Developmental View*. New York: Longman, 1987.

Kymlicka, Will. *Contemporary Political Philosophy: An Introduction*. Oxford: Clarendon Press, 1990.

———. *Liberalism, Community, and Culture*. Oxford: Clarendon Press, 1989.

Lacan, Jacques. "Kant avec Sade." In Sade, Donatien-Alphonse-François, Marquis de, *Oeuvres complètes du Marquis de Sade*. 16 vols. Paris: Cercle du livre précieux, 1962–. Vol. 3: 551–77.

Lacoue-Labarthe, Philippe. "L'Imprésentable." *Poétique* 21 (1975): 53–95.

Landes, Joan B. *Women and the Public Sphere in the Age of the French Revolution*. Ithaca, N. Y.: Cornell University Press, 1988.

Lebigre, Arlette. *La Justice du roi: La vie judiciaire dans l'ancienne France*. Paris: Albin Michel, 1988.

Lemmings, David. "Marriage and the Law in the Eighteenth Century: Hardwicke's Marriage Act of 1753." *Historical Journal* 39, no. 2 (June 1996): 339–60.

Lévi-Strauss, Claude. *Les Structures élémentaires de la parenté*. Paris: Mouton, 1967.

Lévy-Bruhl, Henri. *Sociologie du droit*. Paris: Presses Universitaires de France, 1961.

Locke, John. *The Educational Writings of John Locke*. Ed. John William Adamson. Cambridge: Cambridge University Press, 1922.

———. *Epistola de Tolerantia: A Letter on Toleration*. Latin text ed. Raymond Klibansky. Trans. J. W. Gough. Oxford: Clarendon Press, 1968.

———. *A Letter Concerning Toleration in Focus*. Ed. John Horton and Susan Mendus. New York: Routledge, 1991.

———. *The Second Treatise of Government*. Ed. Thomas P. Peardon. Indianapolis: Bobbs-Merrill, 1952.

———. *Two Treatises of Government*. Ed. Peter Laslett. Cambridge: Cambridge University Press, 1963.

Lomasky, Loren E. *Persons, Rights, and the Moral Community*. Oxford: Oxford University Press, 1987.

Mackenzie, Catriona. "Reason and Sensibility: The Ideal of Women's Self-Governance in the Writings of Mary Wollstonecraft." *Hypatia* 84 (fall 1993): 180–201.

Macpherson, C. B. "Natural Rights in Hobbes and Locke." In *Political Theory and the Rights of Man*. Ed. D. D. Raphael. Bloomington: Indiana University Press, 1967: 1–15.

———. *The Political Theory of Possessive Individualism: Hobbes to Locke*. Oxford: Oxford University Press, 1962.

Manganaro, Marc, ed. *Modernist Anthropology: From Fieldwork to Text*. Princeton, N. J.: Princeton University Press, 1990.

Marejko, Jan. *Jean-Jacques Rousseau et la dérive totalitaire*. Lausanne: Editions l'Age d'Homme, 1984.

Marsh, P. D. V. *Comparative Contract Law: England, France, Germany*. Aldershot, England: Gower, 1994.

Marshall, David. *The Surprising Effects of Sympathy: Marivaux, Diderot, Rousseau, and Mary Shelley*. Chicago: University of Chicago Press, 1988.

Martin, Kingsley. *French Liberal Thought in the Eighteenth Century: A Study of Political Ideas from Bayle to Condorcet.* Ed. J. P. Mayer. New York: Harper and Row, 1962.

Masters, Roger D. *The Political Philosophy of Rousseau.* Princeton, N. J.: Princeton University Press, 1968.

May, Georges. *Le Dilemme du roman au XVIIIe siècle: Etude sur les rapports du roman et de la critique (1715–1761).* New Haven, Conn.: Yale University Press, 1963.

Mead, Margaret. *Coming of Age in Samoa.* New York: William Morrow, 1928.

Mendus, Susan. *Toleration and the Limits of Liberalism.* London: Macmillan, 1989.

Mill, John Stuart. *On Liberty.* In *The Utilitarians: An Introduction to the Principles of Morals and Legislation.* New York: Anchor, 1973.

Miller, David, and Michael Walzer, eds. *Pluralism, Justice, and Equality.* Oxford: Oxford University Press, 1995.

Miller, Nancy. *French Dressing: Women, Men and Ancien Régime Fiction.* New York: Routledge, 1995.

———. *The Heroine's Text: Readings in the French and English Novel 1722–1782.* New York: Columbia University Press, 1980.

Montesquieu, Charles-Louis de Secondat. *Oeuvres complètes.* Bibliothèque de la Pléiade. 2 vols. Paris: Gallimard, 1949–51.

———. *The Spirit of the Laws.* Trans. Thomas Nugent. New York: Hafner Publishing Company, 1949.

Mulhall, Stephen, and Adam Swift. *Liberals and Communitarians.* Cambridge: Blackwell, 1992.

Mylne, Vivienne. *The Eighteenth-Century French Novel: Techniques of Illusion.* 2d edition. Cambridge: Cambridge University Press, 1981.

Nabokov, Vladimir. *Lolita.* New York: Vintage, 1997.

Newberg, Paula R., ed. *The Politics of Human Rights.* New York: New York University Press, 1980.

Okin, Susan Moller. "Humanist Liberalism." In *Liberalism and the Moral Life*, ed. Nancy L. Rosenblum. Cambridge: Harvard University Press, 1989: 39–53.

———. *Women in Western Political Thought.* Princeton, N. J.: Princeton University Press, 1979.

Orwin, Clifford, and Nathan Tarcov, eds. *The Legacy of Rousseau.* Chicago: University of Chicago Press, 1997.

Pateman, Carole. *The Disorder of Women: Democracy, Feminism, and Political Theory.* Stanford, Calif.: Stanford University Press, 1989.

———. *The Sexual Contract.* Stanford, Calif.: Stanford University Press, 1988.

La Pensée politique et constitutionnelle de Montesquieu: Bicentenaire de "l'Esprit des lois," 1748–1948. Paris: Faculté de droit de Paris, Receuil Sirey, 1952.

Perkins, Jean A. "Love, Marriage and Sex in Eighteenth-Century France." *Studies on Voltaire and the Eighteenth Century* 256 (1988): 283–96.

Pinkard, Terry. *Democratic Liberalism and Social Union.* Philadelphia: Temple University Press, 1987.

Plattner, Marc F. "Rousseau and the Origins of Nationalism." In *The Legacy of Rousseau,* ed. Clifford Orwin and Nathan Tarcov. Chicago: University of Chicago Press, 1997: 183–99.

Pollis, Adamantia, and Peter Schwab, eds. *Human Rights: Cultural Ideologies and Perspectives.* New York: Praeger, 1979.

Poole, Ross. *Morality and Modernity.* New York: Routledge, 1991.

Proust, Jacques. "De l'*Encyclopédie* au *Neveu de Rameau*: L'objet et le texte." In *Recherches nouvelles sur quelques écrivains des Lumières.* Ed. Jacques Proust, Geneva: Droz, 1972: 273–340.

———. "Diderot et le système des connaissances humaines." *Studies on Voltaire and the Eighteenth Century* 256 (1988): 117–27.

Puget, Henry. "L'Apport de *L'Esprit des lois* à la Science Politique et au Droit Public." In *La pensée politique et constitutionnelle de Montesquieu, Bicentenaire de "l'Esprit des lois," 1748–1948.* Paris: Faculté de Droit de Paris. Recueil Sirey, 1952: 25–38.

Raphael, D. D. "Human Rights, Old and New." In *Political Theory and the Rights of Man.* Ed. D. D. Raphael. Bloomington: Indiana University Press, 1967: 54–67.

———, ed. *Political Theory and the Rights of Man.* Bloomington: Indiana University Press, 1967.

Ravitch, Diane. "Pluralism vs. Particularism in American Education." In *The Essential Communitarian Reader,* ed. Amitai Etzioni. Lanham. Md.: Rowman and Littlefield, 1998: 269–81.

Rawls, John. *Political Liberalism.* New York: Columbia University Press, 1996.

———. *A Theory of Justice.* Cambridge: Harvard University Press, 1971.

Ray, William, Jr. *Story and History: Narrative Authority and Social Identity in the Eighteenth-Century French and English Novel.* Cambridge: Basil Blackwell, 1990.

"Responsive Communitarian Platform: Rights and Responsibilities, The." In *The Essential Communitarian Reader.* Ed. Amitai Etzioni. Lanham, Md.: Rowman and Littlefield, 1998: xxv–xxxix.

Roger, Philippe. "A Political Minimalist." In *Sade and the Narrative of Transgression.* Ed. David B. Allison, Mark S. Roberts, and Allen S. Weiss, Cambridge: Cambridge University Press, 1995: 76–99.

Rogers, Adrienne. "Women and the Law." In *French Women and the Age of Enlightenment.* Ed. Samia I. Spencer. Bloomington: Indiana University Press, 1984: 33–48.

Rosenblatt, Helena. *Rousseau and Geneva: From the "First Discourse" to the "Social Contract," 1749–1762.* Cambridge: Cambridge University Press, 1997.

Rosenblum, Nancy L., ed. *Liberalism and the Moral Life.* Cambridge: Harvard University Press, 1989.

Rougemont, Denis de. *L'Amour et l'occident.* Paris: Plon, 1939.

Rousseau, Jean-Jacques. *Essai sur l'origine des langues où il est parlé de la mélodie et de l'imitation musicale.* Paris: Gallimard, 1990.

——. *The Government of Poland.* Trans. Willmoore Kendall. Indianapolis: Bobbs-Merrill, 1972.

——. *Oeuvres complètes.* Ed. Bernard Gagnebin and Marcel Raymond. 5 vols. Paris: Gallimard, 1959–.

——. *The Social Contract and the Discourse on the Origin of Inequality.* Trans. Lester G. Crocker. New York: Simon and Schuster, 1967.

Rudden, Bernard. *A Source-Book on French Law: Public Law—Constitutional and Administrative Law: Private Law—Structure, Contract.* Ed. Otto Kahn-Freund, Claudine Lévy, and Bernard Rudden. 3d revised edition. Oxford: Oxford University Press, 1991.

Ruggiero, Guido de. *The History of European Liberalism.* Trans. R. G. Collingwood. London: Oxford University Press, 1927.

Sade, Donatien-Alphonse-François, Marquis de. *Oeuvres complètes du Marquis de Sade.* 16 vols. Paris: Cercle du livre précieux, 1966–.

——. *The 120 Days and Others Writings.* Comp. and Trans. Austryn Wainhouse and Richard Seaver. 2 vols. New York: Grove Press, 1966.

Saint-Amand, Pierre. *Diderot, le labyrinthe de la relation.* Paris: Vrin, 1984.

Sandel, Michael J. *Liberalism and the Limits of Justice.* Cambridge: Cambridge University Press, 1982.

Selznick, Philip. "Foundations of Communitarian Liberalism." In *The Essential Communitarian Reader*, ed. Amitai Etzioni. Lanham, Md.: Rowman and Littlefield, 1998: 3–13.

Shklar, Judith N. "The Liberalism of Fear." In *Liberalism and the Moral Life*, ed. Nancy L. Rosenblum. Cambridge: Harvard University Press, 1989: 21–38.

———. *Men and Citizens: A Study of Rousseau's Social Theory.* Cambridge: Cambridge University Press, 1969.

———. *Montesquieu.* Oxford: Oxford University Press, 1987.

Showalter, English, Jr. *The Evolution of the French Novel, 1641–1782.* Princeton, N. J.: Princeton University Press, 1972.

Shute, Stephen, and Susan Hurley, eds. *On Human Rights: The Oxford Amnesty Lectures, 1993.* New York: Harper Collins, 1993.

Sigmund, Paul E. *Natural Law in Political Thought.* Cambridge: Winthrop, 1971.

Simon, Julia. *Mass Enlightenment: Critical Studies in Rousseau and Diderot.* Albany: State University of New York Press, 1995.

———. "Militarisme et vertu chez Rousseau." In *Actes du IIe Colloque International de Montmorency, J.-J. Rousseau: Politique et nation,* ed. Robert Thiéry. Oxford: Voltaire Foundation, forthcoming.

Simon, William. *French Liberalism: 1789–1848.* New York: John Wiley and Sons, 1972.

Simon-Ingram, Julia. "Expanding the Social Contract: Rousseau, Gender, and the Problem of Judgment." *Comparative Literature* 43, no. 2 (spring 1991): 134–49.

Snyders, Georges, Roger Chartier, Marie-Madeleine Compère, and Dominique Julia. *La Pédagogie en France aux XVIIe et XVIIIe siècles.* Paris: Presses Universitaires de France, 1965.

Sonenscher, Michael. *The Hatters of Eighteenth-Century France.* Berkeley: University of California Press, 1987.

Spragens, Thomas A. "The Limitations of Libertarianism." In *The Essential Communitarian Reader,* ed. Amitai Etzioni. Lanham, Md.: Rowan and Littlefield, 1998: 21–40.

Starobinski, Jean. *Jean-Jacques Rousseau: La transparence et l'obstacle.* Paris: Plon, 1957.

Steinbrügge, Lieselotte. *The Moral Sex: Woman's Nature in the French Enlightenment.* Trans. Pamela E. Selwyn. Oxford: Oxford University Press, 1995.

Stewart, Joan Hinde, and Philip Stewart. "Introduction." In Isabelle de Charrière, *Lettres de Mistriss Henley.* New York: Modern Language Association, 1993: xi–xxiii.

Tanner, Tony. *Adultery in the Novel, Contract and Transgression.* Baltimore: Johns Hopkins University Press, 1979.

Taylor, Barbara. "For the Love of God: Religion and the Erotic Imagination in Wollstonecraft's Feminism." In *Mary Wollstonecraft and 200 Years of Feminisms*, ed. Eileen Janes Yeo. London: Rivers Oram Press, 1997: 15–35.

Taylor, Charles. "The Dangers of Soft Despotism." In *The Essential Communitarian Reader*, ed. Amitai Etzioni. Lanham, Md.: Rowman and Littlefield, 1998: 47–54.

———. *Multiculturalism: Examining the Politics of Recognition*. Ed. Amy Gutmann. Princeton, N. J.: Princeton University Press, 1994.

———. *Sources of the Self: The Making of the Modern Identity*. Cambridge: Harvard University Press, 1989.

Terdiman, Richard. "Body and Story: Diderot Discovers Postmodernism." Work in progress.

Todorov, Tzvetan. *Frêle bonheur: Essai sur Rousseau*. Paris: Hachette, 1985.

———. *Nous et les autres: La réflexion française sur la diversité humaine*. Paris: Editions du Seuil, 1989.

———. *On Human Diversity: Nationalism, Racism, and Exoticism in French Thought*. Trans. Catherine Porter. Cambridge: Harvard University Press, 1993.

Trachtenberg, Zev M. *Making Citizens: Rousseau's Political Theory of Culture*. London: Routledge, 1993.

Traer, James F. *Marriage and the Family in Eighteenth-Century France*. Ithaca, N. Y.: Cornell University Press, 1980.

van Caenegem, R. C. *An Historical Introduction to Private Law*. Trans. D. E. L. Johnston. Cambridge: Cambridge University Press, 1992.

Voltaire. *Lettres philosophiques*. Paris: Garnier-Flammarion, 1964.

———. *Traité sur la tolérance*. Geneva: Editions du cheval ailé, 1948.

Walzer, Michael. "Justice across the Spheres." In *Pluralism, Justice, and Equality*. Ed. David Miller and Michael Walzer. Oxford: Oxford University Press, 1995: 99–119.

———. *On Toleration*. New Haven, Conn.: Yale University Press, 1997.

———. *Spheres of Justice: A Defense of Pluralism and Equality*. New York: Basic, 1983.

Weber, Max. *From Max Weber: Essays in Sociology*. Trans. and ed. H. H. Gerth and C. Wright Mills. New York: Oxford University Press, 1958.

Weiss, Penny A. "Rousseau, Antifeminism, and Woman's Nature." *Political Theory* 15, no. 1 (February 1987): 81–98.

Wolfe, Christopher, and John Hittinger, eds. *Liberalism at the Crossroads: An Introduction to Contemporary Liberal Political Theory and its Critics.* Lanham, Md.: Rowman and Littlefield, 1994.

Wolff, Robert Paul. *The Poverty of Liberalism.* Boston: Beacon Press, 1968.

Wollstonecraft, Mary. *A Vindication of the Rights of Woman.* London: Penguin, 1992.

Young, Iris Marion. "Impartiality and the Civic Public: Some Implications of Feminist Critiques of Moral and Political Theory." In *Feminism as Critique,* ed. Seyla Benhabib and Drucilla Cornell. Minneapolis: University of Minnesota Press, 1987: 57–76.

Index